S. HRG. 113–654

PRIVACY IN THE DIGITAL AGE: PREVENTING DATA BREACHES AND COMBATING CYBER CRIME

HEARING

BEFORE THE

COMMITTEE ON THE JUDICIARY
UNITED STATES SENATE

ONE HUNDRED THIRTEENTH CONGRESS

SECOND SESSION

TUESDAY, FEBRUARY 4, 2014

Serial No. J–113–48

Printed for the use of the Committee on the Judiciary

U.S. GOVERNMENT PUBLISHING OFFICE

94–640 PDF   WASHINGTON : 2015

For sale by the Superintendent of Documents, U.S. Government Publishing Office
Internet: bookstore.gpo.gov   Phone: toll free (866) 512–1800; DC area (202) 512–1800
Fax: (202) 512–2104   Mail: Stop IDCC, Washington, DC 20402–0001

COMMITTEE ON THE JUDICIARY

CONTENTS

STATEMENTS OF COMMITTEE MEMBERS

WITNESSES

QUESTIONS

ANSWERS

IV

PRIVACY IN THE DIGITAL AGE: PREVENTING DATA BREACHES AND COMBATING CYBER CRIME

TUESDAY, FEBRUARY 4, 2014

U.S. SENATE,
COMMITTEE ON THE JUDICIARY,
Washington, DC.

The Committee met, pursuant to notice, at 10:23 a.m., in Room SD–226, Dirksen Senate Office Building, Hon. Patrick J. Leahy, Chairman of the Committee, presiding.

Present: Senators Leahy, Feinstein, Durbin, Whitehouse, Klobuchar, Franken, Coons, Blumenthal, Hirono, Grassley, Hatch, and Lee.

OPENING STATEMENT OF HON. PATRICK J. LEAHY, A U.S. SENATOR FROM THE STATE OF VERMONT

Chairman LEAHY. Good morning. Because of the time of the opening of the Senate, we are starting a little bit late, and I apologize for that, but I appreciate everybody who is here today from all over, including now snowy Colorado. I see Mr. Bronstein here.

We are going to meet to examine how we can protect Americans from the growing dangers of data breaches and cyber crime in the digital age. Safeguarding American consumers and businesses from data breaches and cyber crime has been a priority of this Committee since 2005. For years, we tried to make sure that everybody understands this is not a Democratic or Republican issue. I have worked closely with Members on both sides of the aisle to advance meaningful data privacy legislation. In fact, I want to thank Senator Grassley for working with me very closely on this hearing, and I hope we can continue working together to advance the Personal Data Privacy and Security Act that I recently reintroduced to protect American consumers.

Now, you watch the news, you pick up the papers, you listen to the news. Most Americans, myself included, have been alarmed by the recent data breaches at Target, Neiman Marcus, and Michaels stores. The investigations into those cyber attacks are ongoing. But they have compromised the privacy and security of millions of American consumers—potentially putting one in three Americans at risk of identity theft and other cyber crimes. I have never had a time when my wife and I have been so assiduous at checking our credit card bills, but that is the same with everybody.

But public confidence is crucial to our economy. I mentioned those three stores. Those are all excellent stores. They are a major part of our economy. But we have to have faith in them. If we do not have faith in businesses' ability to protect their personal information, then our economic recovery is going to falter. And in the digital age, major data breaches involving our private information are not uncommon. There have been significant data breaches involving Sony, Epsilon, and Coca-Cola, but also in Federal Government agencies—the Departments of Veterans Affairs and Energy. In the past few days, we have also learned of data breaches at Yahoo! and White Lodging, which is the hotel management company for national hotel chains such as Marriott and Starwood. In fact, so it will not seem like we are singling out just a few businesses, according to the Privacy Rights Clearinghouse, more than 662 million records have been involved in data breaches since 2005.

Now, we all agree that businesses need to thoroughly assess the damage when a cyber attack is discovered. But time is of the essence for law enforcement seeking to catch the perpetrators and also for consumers who want to protect themselves against further exposure. It is not like when somebody comes in and robs a store. You know where it happened, and you have some general idea of where the perpetrator is. Here the perpetrator could be thousands upon thousands of miles away in another country. American consumers deserve to know when their private information has been compromised and what a business is doing in response to a cyber attack, because most of us rely on being able to do a lot of our business electronically.

We should also remember that the businesses that suffer cyber attacks are also often the victims of a cyber crime. A recent study sponsored by Symantec found that data breaches involving malicious cyber attacks are the most costly data breaches around the globe. The per capita cost of such cyber attacks in the United States was $277 per compromised record in 2013. Times that by millions upon millions upon millions. It is the highest cost for any nation that has been surveyed. And, of course, if you are in a fragile economic recovery, this is a significant hindrance.

So before the Judiciary Committee today are representatives of Target and Neiman Marcus, as well as Consumers Union and Symantec. Later we will hear from the U.S. Secret Service, the Department of Justice, and the Federal Trade Commission.

We are facing threats to our privacy and security unlike any time before in our Nation's history. We have also had hearings about questions of the threats to our privacy by our own government agencies. So I hope in this particular one we can get some good bipartisan support responding to it and get some data privacy legislation out here. I think we will all be better for it.

[The prepared statement of Senator Leahy appears as a submission for the record.]

Senator Grassley.

OPENING STATEMENT OF HON. CHUCK GRASSLEY, A U.S. SENATOR FROM THE STATE OF IOWA

Senator GRASSLEY. It is very important that we have this hearing. We have had well-publicized commercial data breaches. We are still learning about the details. This hearing will help bring more details out, I hope. But it is clear that these and other breaches have potentially impacted tens of millions of consumers nationwide.

Today is an opportunity to learn about the challenges that both industry and law enforcement face in combating cyber attacks from well-organized criminals. The witnesses have a unique ability to provide us various important perspectives as we consider the government's role in securing sensitive data and crafting a breach notification standard.

I hope to learn where the Committee's expertise could be helpful in combating future attacks. Furthermore, I would like to use this hearing to explore areas of common ground so that we can determine what might be accomplished quickly.

It has been a couple of years since our Committee has considered data security legislation. In that time, we have learned a lot about this subject, thanks to broader cybersecurity conversation. The proposals offered by the administration and discussed in Congress, along with other government initiatives, can be helpful for us to proceed as we consider what to do with this legislation.

When considering data security requirements, our approach should provide flexibility and also account for businesses of different sizes and different resources. In a world of crafty criminals, it seems to me that a one-size-fits-all approach will not work, or at least will not work for everybody. Instead, let us see how the government can partner with private business to strengthen data security.

An example may be the National Institute of Standards and Technology's cybersecurity framework, which has received bipartisan support. And as far as the Senate is concerned, unless it is bipartisan, it is not going to go anywhere. That is not because there is something wrong with Democrats or Republicans. That is the institution itself.

As we discuss the creation of a federal breach notification standard, we must avoid the risk of consumer overnotification. Just as there is a potential for harm when a victim is not notified of a breach, overnotification can lead to harm and apathy.

As time permits, I want to explore these and other issues today and will be available to discuss things beyond the Committee process, either with colleagues or with other people. If everyone works together, it seems to me we can tackle these problems and hopefully limit future attacks.

Thanks again, Mr. Chairman, and I would ask unanimous consent to include my full statement in the record along with statements that we received from these groups: the National Business Coalition on E-Commerce and Privacy, the Payment Card Industry, the National Association of Federal Credit Unions, the American Bankers Association, the National Retail Federation, and the Retail Industry Leaders Association.

Chairman LEAHY. Without objection, they will be included in the record.

[The prepared statement of Senator Grassley appears as a submission for the record.]

Chairman LEAHY. Could I ask the four witnesses to please stand and raise your right hand? Do you swear that the testimony you will give in this matter will be the truth, the whole truth, and nothing but the truth, so help you God?

Mr. MULLIGAN. I do.

Mr. KINGSTON. I do.

Ms. DERAKHSHANI. I do.

Mr. ROSCH. I do.

Chairman LEAHY. Let the record show that the four witnesses—
Mr. Mulligan, Mr. Kingston, Ms. Derakhshani—I hope I came
close—and Mr. Rosch—all took the oath. I thought what we would
do is hear from each of the witnesses first, and then we will ask
questions.

John Mulligan is chief financial officer and executive vice president for Target, the second largest general merchandise retailer in
the U.S. Mr. Mulligan joined Target in 1996. His responsibilities
include treasury and internal and external financial reporting, financial planning and analysis, financial operations, tax assurance,
investor relations, flight services. He graduated from the University of Wisconsin in 1988. In 1996, he earned a Master's of Business Administration degree from the University of Minnesota, I
would mention to Senator Klobuchar and Senator Franken.

Mr. Mulligan, please go ahead.

STATEMENT OF JOHN MULLIGAN, EXECUTIVE VICE PRESI-
DENT AND CHIEF FINANCIAL OFFICER, TARGET CORPORA-
TION, MINNEAPOLIS, MINNESOTA

Mr. MULLIGAN. Good morning, Chairman Leahy, Ranking Member Grassley, and Members of the Committee. My name is John
Mulligan. I am the executive vice president and chief financial officer of Target. I appreciate the opportunity to be here today to discuss important issues surrounding data breaches and cyber crime.

As you know, Target recently experienced a data breach resulting from a criminal attack on our systems. To begin, I want to say
how deeply sorry we are for the impact this incident has had on
our guests—your constituents. We know this breach has shaken
their confidence in Target, and we are determined to work very
hard to earn it back.

At Target, we take our responsibility to our guests very seriously,
and this attack has only strengthened our resolve. We will learn
from this incident, and as a result, we hope to make Target and
our industry more secure for consumers in the future.

I would now like to explain the events of the breach as I currently understand them. Please recognize that I may not be able
to provide specifics on certain matters because the criminal and forensic investigations remain active and ongoing. We are working
closely with the Secret Service and the Department of Justice on
the investigation—to help them bring to justice the criminals who
committed this widespread attack on Target, American business,
and consumers.

On the evening of December 12th, we were notified by the Justice Department of suspicious activity involving payment cards
used at Target. We immediately started our internal investigation.

On December 13th, we met with the Justice Department and the
Secret Service. On December 14th, we hired an independent team
of experts to lead a thorough forensics investigation.

On December 15th, we confirmed that criminals had infiltrated
our system, had installed malware on our point-of-sale network,
and had potentially stolen guest payment card data. That same

day, we removed the malware from virtually all registers in our U.S. stores.

Over the next two days, we began notifying the payment processors and card networks, preparing to notify our guests and equipping our call centers and stores with the necessary information and resources to address the concerns of our guests.

Our actions leading up to our public announcement on December 19th—and since—have been guided by the principle of serving our guests, and we have been moving as quickly as possible to share accurate and actionable information with the public.

What we note today is that the breach affected two types of data: payment card data, which affected approximately 40 million guests, and certain personal data, which affected up to 70 million guests. We believe the payment card data was accessed through malware placed on our point-of-sale registers. The malware was designed to capture payment card data that resided on the magnetic strip prior to its encryption within our systems.

From the outset, our response to the breach has been focused on supporting our guests and strengthening our security. In addition to the immediate actions I already described, we are taking the following concrete actions: first, we are undertaking an end-to-end forensic review of our entire network and will make security enhancements, as appropriate. Second, we increased fraud detection for our Target REDcard guests. To date, we have not seen any fraud on our proprietary credit and debit cards due to this breach. And we have seen only a very low amount of additional fraud on our Target Visa card. Third, we are reissuing new Target credit and debit cards immediately to any guest who requests one. Fourth, we are offering one year of free credit monitoring and identity theft protection to anyone who has ever shopped in our U.S. Target stores. Fifth, we informed guests that they have zero liability for any fraudulent charges on the cards arising from this incident. And, sixth, Target is accelerating our investment in chip technology for our Target REDcards and stores' point-of-sale terminals.

For many years, Target has invested significant capital and resources in security technology, personnel, and processes. We had in place multiple layers of protection, including firewalls, malware detection, intrusion detection and prevention capabilities, and data loss prevention tools.

But the unfortunate reality is that we suffered a breach. All businesses—and their customers—are facing increasingly sophisticated threats from cyber criminals. In fact, news reports have indicated that several other companies have been subjected to similar attacks.

To prevent this from happening again, none of us can go it alone. We need to work together.

Updating payment card technology and strengthening protections for American consumers is a shared responsibility and requires a collective and coordinated response. On behalf of Target, I am committing that we will be an active part of the solution.

Senators, to each of you and all of your constituents and our guests, I want to once again reiterate how sorry we are this happened and our ongoing commitment to making this right.

Thank you for your time today.

[The prepared statement of Mr. Mulligan appears as a submission for the record.]

Chairman LEAHY. Well, thank you very much, Mr. Mulligan.

Michael Kingston is senior vice president and chief information officer for Neiman Marcus. In his role as chief information officer, he oversees approximately 500 professionals responsible for all aspects of information technology and security, including technology strategies, system development, information technology service delivery for all Neiman Marcus brands, both in stores and its Web site, and has over 20 years of experience in the field.

Mr. Kingston, thank you for being here. Please go ahead, sir.

STATEMENT OF MICHAEL R. KINGSTON, SENIOR VICE PRESIDENT AND CHIEF INFORMATION OFFICER, THE NEIMAN MARCUS GROUP, DALLAS, TEXAS

Mr. KINGSTON. Mr. Chairman, Senator Grassley, Members of the Committee, good morning. My name is Michael Kingston, and I am chief information officer at Neiman Marcus Group. I want to thank you for your invitation to appear today to share with you our experiences regarding the recent criminal cybersecurity incident at our company. I have submitted a longer written statement and appreciate the opportunity to make some brief opening remarks.

We are in the midst of an ongoing forensic investigation that has revealed a cyber attack using very sophisticated malware. From the moment I learned that there might be a compromise of payment card information involving our company, I have personally led the effort to ensure that we were acting swiftly, thoroughly, and responsibly to determine whether such a compromise had occurred, to protect our customers and the security of our systems, and to assist law enforcement in capturing the criminals. Because our investigation is ongoing, I may be limited in my ability to speak definitively or with specificity on some issues, and there may be some questions to which I do not have the answers. Nevertheless, it is important to us as a company to make ourselves available to you to provide whatever information we can to assist in your important work.

Our company was founded 107 years ago. One of our founding principles is based on delivering exceptional service to our customers and building long-lasting relationships with them that have spanned generations. We take this commitment to our customers very seriously. It is part of who we are and what we do daily to distinguish ourselves from other retailers.

We have never before been subjected to any sort of significant cybersecurity intrusion, so we have been particularly disturbed by this incident.

Through our ongoing forensic investigation, we have learned that the malware which penetrated our system was exceedingly sophisticated, a conclusion the Secret Service has confirmed. A recent report prepared by the Secret Service crystallized the problem when they concluded that a specific type of malware, comparable and perhaps even less sophisticated than the one in our case, according to our investigators, had a zero percent detection rate by anti-virus software.

The malware was evidently able to capture payment card data in real time, right after a card was swiped, and had sophisticated features that made it particularly difficult to detect, including some that were specifically customized to evade our multilayered security architecture that provided strong protection for our customers' data and our systems.

Because of the malware's sophisticated anti-detection devices, we did not learn that we had an actual problem in our computer system until January 2, and it was not until January 6 when the malware and its outputs had been disassembled and decrypted enough that we were able to determine that it was able to operate in our systems. Then, disabling it to ensure it was not still operating took until January 10. That day we sent out our first notices to customers potentially affected and made widely reported public statements describing what we knew at that point about the incident.

Simply put, prior to January 2, despite our immediate efforts to have two separate firms of forensic investigators dig into our systems in an attempt to find any data security compromise, no data security compromise in our systems had been identified.

Based on the current state of the evidence in the ongoing investigation: One, it now appears that the customer information that was potentially exposed to the malware was payment card information from transactions in 77 of our 85 stores between July and October 2013, at different time periods within this date range in each store; two, we have no indication that transactions on our Web sites or at our restaurants were compromised; three, PIN data was not compromised, as we do not have PIN pads and we do not request PINs; and, four, there is no indication that Social Security numbers or other personal information was exposed in any way.

We have also offered to any customer who shopped with us in the last year at either Neiman Marcus Group stores or Web sites—whether their card was exposed to the malware or not—one year of free credit monitoring and identity theft insurance. We will continue to provide the excellent service to our customers that is our hallmark, and I know that the way we responded to this situation is consistent with that commitment.

Thank you again for your invitation to testify today, and I look forward to answering your questions.

[The prepared statement of Mr. Kingston appears as a submission for the record.]

Chairman LEAHY. Thank you very much, Mr. Kingston.

And our next witness is Delara Derakhshani, who serves as policy counsel in Consumers Union's Washington office. She is the lead advocate for the organization's telecommunications, media, and privacy efforts. Consumers Union is the policy and advocacy division of *Consumer Reports*. Ms. Derakhshani graduated from the University of Virginia and earned a law degree from Catholic University's Columbus School of Law.

We are glad to have you here. Please go ahead.

STATEMENT OF DELARA DERAKHSHANI, POLICY COUNSEL, CONSUMERS UNION, WASHINGTON, DC

Ms. DERAKHSHANI. Chairman Leahy, Ranking Member Grassley, and esteemed Members of the Committee, thank you for the opportunity to testify before you today about data breaches. My name is Delara Derakhshani, and I serve as policy counsel of Consumers Union, the policy and advocacy arm of *Consumer Reports*.

This past December—at the height of the holiday shopping season—40 million unsuspecting consumers learned that criminals may have gained unauthorized access to their credit card and debit card information. Subsequently, 70 million more learned that personal information such as names, addresses, and telephone numbers may have also fallen into the hands of suspected hackers. Since then we have learned of similar breaches at other retailers: Neiman Marcus has confirmed unauthorized access to payment data, and Michaels has stated that it is investigating whether a similar breach occurred. The press is reporting that the malware that was reportedly used in the Neiman Marcus and Target breaches was sold to criminals overseas. So what we have seen thus far may just be the tip of the iceberg.

This is truly disturbing. As *Consumer Reports* and Consumers Union have reported with regularity in our publications, consumers who have their data compromised in a large-scale security breach are more likely to become victims of identity theft or fraud. And although federal consumer protection lending laws and voluntary industry standards generally protect consumers from significant out-of-pocket losses, policymakers and consumers should take these threats seriously.

Then there are the very practical and time-consuming concerns for consumers whose data has been breached. Of particular concern is debit cards, which carry fewer legal protections. And while consumers might not ultimately be held responsible if someone steals their debit card data or pin number, data thieves can still empty out a consumer's bank account and set off a cascade of bounced checks and late fees which victims will have to settle down the road.

What can happen to the data after it is stolen is disconcerting, to say the least. Sometimes data is resold to criminals outside of the country. Other times it is used to create counterfeit cards, debit cards which have direct access to your checking account. The result is decreased consumer confidence in the marketplace and uncertainty with the realization that your private financial information is out there in the ether for anybody to use for an unauthorized purpose.

When Consumers Union learned of the breach, we wrote to the CFPB and urged them to investigate the matter and for increased public disclosure. And just last week, Attorney General Eric Holder confirmed that the Department of Justice is also investigating the matter. We know that lawmakers have urged the Federal Trade Commission to investigate as well, and we are grateful for these federal agencies' efforts and State Attorneys General's efforts so that we can figure out what happened and get to the bottom of this and figure out how to come up with a solution together to prevent these breaches from occurring in the future.

We have also provided consumers with a number of tips, including checking transaction data, notifying your bank immediately of any suspicious activity; for extra protection, replacing credit cards, debit cards, and PIN numbers; placing fraud alerts and also security freezes so that lenders will be blocked from access to your credit report. And Target and affected retailers are also offering consumers credit monitoring, which we would be happy to speak about and answer questions about as well.

Many other countries have shifted or are in the process of shifting to what is known as EMV technology or chip-and-PIN technology, which uses multiple layers of security, including a computer chip in each card that stores and transmits encrypted data, as well as a unique identifier that can change with each transaction.

What we have reported in the past is that when this technology has been adopted in Europe, it has significantly decreased fraud. So we need a strong commitment from all stakeholders to adopt this technology sooner rather than later.

These incidents reinforce just how timely and relevant these issues are. We are very appreciative of the Committee's efforts and the Chairman for introducing the *Data Privacy and Security Act*. We think that the sooner consumers know their data has been compromised, the sooner they can take steps to protect themselves.

We would also urge the Committee to consider shortening the timeline for notification from the 60 days to require more immediate notification.

We do also—we would like to strengthen some provisions, including those related to preemption. We want to make sure that any national standard results in strong, meaningful protections.

In closing, we thank you for the opportunity to speak before you today. We appreciate your interest in data security, and we want to ensure that there is consumer confidence in the marketplace, and we look forward to working with you and all interested parties.

Thank you very much.

[The prepared statement of Ms. Derakhshani appears as a submission for the record.]

Chairman LEAHY. Well, thank you, and thank you for what you said about the legislation. I am hoping we can move it quickly.

Fran Rosch is the senior vice president of user protection productivity, product management, and mobility solutions at Symantec. He drives the development and execution of Symantec and Norton's endpoint and mobile management. He was vice president of identity and authentication services before that. Obviously he has a background in this field.

Please, sir, go ahead.

STATEMENT OF FRAN ROSCH, SENIOR VICE PRESIDENT, SECURITY PRODUCTS AND SERVICES, ENDPOINT AND MOBILITY, SYMANTEC CORPORATION, MOUNTAIN VIEW, CALIFORNIA

Mr. ROSCH. Thank you, and good morning. Chairman Leahy, Ranking Member Grassley, distinguished Members of the Committee, thank you for the opportunity to testify today on behalf of Symantec Corporation. We are the world's largest security software company with over 31 years of experience developing information security and management technology.

Our Global Intelligence Network is composed of millions of sensors all over the world and records thousands of events per second, and we maintain 10 Security Response Centers that operate 24/7 around the globe. This gives us a view of the entire Internet threat landscape. At Symantec, we also invest over $1 billion a year in R&D on advanced security technologies to help our customers stay ahead of the bad guys.

The hearing today is critically important and will focus attention on what businesses and consumers can do to protect themselves from cyber attacks and data breaches. Attacks on point-of-sale, or POS, devices are not new, but it does appear the pace is increasing. This increase brings with it media attention and citizen concern, but this cannot be just about one or two high-profile crimes. Not just retailers but every organization with sensitive information is at risk, because cyber crime is a big business.

In 2013, we estimate that the identities of over 435 million people were exposed, and that number is rising as new reports surface. The cost of these breaches is very real and is borne directly by both consumers and organizations.

For example, we estimate that in 2012 the global price tag of consumer cyber crime was $113 billion. The Ponemon Institute looked at the impact on companies and found that the average total cost of a breach in 2012 was $5.4 million. Ponemon also found that strong security before a breach and good incident management post-breach can dramatically cut the cost of these incidents.

These breaches are increasingly caused by targeted attacks, which were up 42 percent year over year. Some are direct attacks on a company's servers, where attackers search for unpatched vulnerabilities or undefended connections to the Internet.

All attacks have essentially one goal: to gain control of the user's computer. After infiltrating an organization, attackers can move laterally until they find what they are looking for. In the case of a retailer, this can include compromising point-of-sale systems to obtain valuable consumer information.

The best way to prevent these attacks starts with the basics. Though criminals' tactics are continually evolving, good cyber hygiene is simple and cost-effective. Strong passwords, two-factor authentication, ubiquitous encryption are important elements of any good security program.

But suboptimally deployed security can also lead to a breach, and a modern security suite that is being fully utilized is essential. Advanced security protection is much more than anti-virus software. In the past, the same piece of malware would be delivered to thousands or even millions of computers and was easily blocked through signature-based systems. Today cyber criminals can take the same malware and create unlimited unique variants that can slip past basic AV software. That is why modern security software does much more than look for known malware. It monitors your computer or mobile device, watching for unusual traffic patterns or processes that could be indicative of malicious behavior.

At Symantec we have developed and provide reputation-based and behavior-based heuristic security technologies, which can identify and block more advanced threats. These solutions put files in context, using their age, frequency, location, and other characteristics to expose emerging threats that might otherwise be missed. If a computer is trying to execute a file that we have never seen anywhere in the world and that comes from an unknown source, there is a high probability that it is malicious and it should be blocked.

Security should also be specific to the device being protected, and in some ways, point-of-sale system devices have advantages over other systems because the functions they need to perform can be narrowly defined. Allowing these devices to only run approved applications will reduce the attack surface and render many strains of malware ineffective.

Yesterday Symantec released a special report called ''Attacks on Point of Sales Systems'' that provides an overview of the methods that attackers may use and provides recommendations on how to protect these systems from attack.

Unfortunately data breaches and cyber threats are part of our day-to-day lives. We will never be able to prevent every data breach or cyber attack, but working together, industry and govern- ment can make it increasingly more difficult for cyber criminals to succeed.

Thank you again for this opportunity to be here today, and I am happy to take any questions that you may have.

[The prepared statement of Mr. Rosch appears as a submission for the record.]

Chairman LEAHY. Well, thank you very much, Mr. Rosch.

I think we are all united in the same thing. We all want to stop these attacks, number one. Number two, as you just pointed out, Mr. Rosch, we are always going to have these attacks. No matter what we do, there will be more attacks. The question is: Can we successfully stop them? And are we keeping up to date with the realities of today as compared to years ago?

Now, Mr. Mulligan, the data breach at Target, of course, became front-page news. I am not just going after your company, obviously, but it did have the potential to place one in three Americans at risk of fraud or identity theft—identity theft being probably one of the most difficult things somebody has to deal with.

So what have you found so far? Are you any closer to finding who did it? And tell us just briefly what are the steps you are taking to protect privacy.

Mr. MULLIGAN. So, Senator, as I said earlier, the intruder came in through a set of compromised vendor credentials and took two sets of data. The first set of data was malware was placed on our point-of-sale registers, and there they grabbed payment card information in the time between it being swiped from the magnetic stripe until we encrypt it within our systems. They then encrypted that and removed it from our systems.

Separately, they took information from certain personal data—name, address, phone number, email address—for up to 70 million records, similarly encrypted that, and removed that from our systems.

We have had an ongoing forensic investigation and an end-to-end review of our entire network to understand what went on. Since that time, we have removed the malware from our system. We have closed the point of entry. We have narrowed the scope of who has access to our systems. We have provided the malware to security firms for their review. And we have the ongoing end-to-end review where we will have additional learnings, and we are committed to taking additional actions.

Chairman LEAHY. You talk about discovery. As I understand it, the Justice Department told you about this on—well, you said this—on December 12 of last year. You found and removed the malware three days later, December 15. Am I correct on those dates?

Mr. MULLIGAN. That is accurate, Mr. Chairman.

Chairman LEAHY. Had you had any knowledge that malware was there before the Department of Justice gave you that notification?

Mr. MULLIGAN. We did not, Senator, Mr. Chairman. Despite the significant investment in multiple layers of detection that we had within our systems, we did not.

Chairman LEAHY. So you had all your systems in place, but you found out about it from the Department of Justice.

Mr. MULLIGAN. That is correct, Mr. Chairman.

Chairman LEAHY. But the breach did not involve online purchases or transactions. Is that correct?

Mr. MULLIGAN. That is correct. That is my understanding, Mr. Chairman.

Chairman LEAHY. And, Mr. Kingston, you testified that the breach that you saw at your company could affect 1.1 million American consumers. Is that correct?

Mr. KINGSTON. What we have learned, Mr. Chairman, in our investigation is that this malware, which was inserted into our systems by the criminals, was operating in many of our stores at certain times between July and October 2013. And the maximum number of account numbers in our stores at that time that were exposed to the malware was 1.1 million accounts. But we do believe, because the malware was only operating at certain times, that the number is actually less than that.

Chairman LEAHY. Well, when did you first find out about it? As you said, it was operating during the summer. But when did you first find out about it?

Mr. KINGSTON. The first time that we found out about the malware was when our forensic investigation teams discovered it on January 2, 2014.

Chairman LEAHY. When did you first receive information about it?

Mr. KINGSTON. The forensic investigation firm first alerted us that there was some suspicious malware that they had found as part of the investigation on our systems on January 1.

Chairman LEAHY. But didn't you say that you first received information on December 17?

Mr. KINGSTON. On December 17, we were notified by our merchant processor that MasterCard had found in its fraud systems 122 account numbers that had been fraudulently used that were used prior to that at Neiman Marcus locations.

Chairman LEAHY. Now, in the last month, since January when you first had this, have you changed any of your malware protection protocols or equipment?

Mr. KINGSTON. Yes, we have. We have actually made a number of different changes. As I mentioned in my testimony, the malware, unfortunately, was not detected by our anti-virus systems, which we maintain and keep up to date. Since then, we have shared the malware both with forensic investigations teams, the Secret Service, and our anti-virus company, and they have provided us with updated signatures so that we can remove it and disable it.

Chairman LEAHY. How has the cooperation been with law enforcement?

Mr. KINGSTON. We have been working with law enforcement all along the investigation, and they have actually been very, very helpful and very cooperative.

Chairman LEAHY. Would you say the same, Mr. Mulligan?

Mr. MULLIGAN. I would, Senator. We have a long relationship with law enforcement, and they have been—our interactions throughout this time have been very productive.

Chairman LEAHY. Thank you.

Senator Grassley.

Senator GRASSLEY. Yes, I want to associate myself with the remarks that the Chairman made just before he asked questions, and that is, I think we are all trying to find the same solution. This is not a case of a group of business people on one side and the government on the other side. We have got a major problem we have to deal with, and it is going to take cooperation. The Senator did not say it exactly that way, but I think—I hope I——

Chairman LEAHY. I agree with you.

Senator GRASSLEY. Thank you.

As we have heard today, even companies with tremendous resources and multilayered—by the way, I am going to ask Mulligan, Kingston, and Rosch this. As we have heard today, even companies with tremendous resources and multilayered security systems can be attacked and breached. This means smaller businesses are more vulnerable to similar attacks. One thing I have heard repeatedly is that businesses of all sizes need flexibility in creating and implementing their security programs. What works for one may not work for another. But companies must be proactive, and guidelines for what they should be doing are helpful.

So to you three, how can the government encourage the private sector to strengthen data security that provides businesses that flexibility and guidance that they need as opposed to burdensome government regulation?

Mr. MULLIGAN. Start with me, Senator?

Senator GRASSLEY. Yes.

Mr. MULLIGAN. We agree, Senator, that this is an evolving threat and one that is well beyond retail or Target to all industry. There were hundreds of breaches last year, and we think, therefore, the solution needs to be a combination of efforts across all participants in the space, Senator.

I think for payment card information, similarly, there are a number of participants in the payment card world, and we need to work collectively to move to chip-and-PIN technology. That would have rendered the account numbers that were taken far less useful. But it is technologies like that that we think are important, and we are committed to moving forward and accelerating our efforts in that particular area.

Senator GRASSLEY. Mr. Kingston.

Mr. KINGSTON. First of all, I think shedding light on this issue as the Committee is doing today is extremely helpful, and we appreciate that. I think one of the things that the government can do—there are a lot of actors in this ecosystem. There are technology companies. Obviously there is the private sector. There are law enforcement, government agencies. There are security experts. I think collectively all of those actors, all of those stakeholders, who have intelligence and are able to share it with the community, should be encouraged to do that. Information sharing can help us try to keep up with this problem, which is continuing to evolve and continuing to become more sophisticated.

Senator GRASSLEY. Mr. Rosch.

Mr. ROSCH. Yes, I would agree with what Mr. Kingston said. This is definitely a shared responsibility between companies and security vendors and consumers themselves to follow good practices. But we do believe it would be helpful for the government to recommend, in a very flexible way, some preventative measures that companies can take to at least give a guideline to be able to protect their systems.

You mentioned the NIST standard. We believe that is a good voluntary and flexible framework that companies can use to guide in developing good security solutions.

Senator GRASSLEY. To the three of you again, you know, and this gets back to some people, maybe, think this ought to be completely government driven, and then there are people that think it is entirely industry, government stay out of it. The Chairman and I have talked about a partnership. Recently the National Institute of Standards and Technology was just mentioned here.

So for you three, if government is going to create federal data security standards, what role, if any, should the private sector have in that process? Mr. Mulligan and then Kingston and then Rosch.

Mr. MULLIGAN. Senator, I think private industry and government have to work together here. I agree with what you have heard. It is a shared responsibility, and communication between both the private sector and the public sector is important. We have had ongoing relationships and information sharing with law enforcement. That needs to happen more broadly between our organization and private organizations more broadly and the government to find solutions here.

Senator GRASSLEY. Mr. Kingston.

Mr. KINGSTON. I think guidelines and standards are always very helpful, particularly in this case. So I would encourage that all of the stakeholders provide input into that.

Mr. ROSCH. Yes, I would agree, and I think, you know, the key word here is ''flexibility.'' I think what we have to recognize is that this is kind of an ongoing war, and the types of threats are changing all the time, and the new technology comes on the market to protect all the time. So we are constantly kind of raising the bar. So whatever gets developed needs to allow for that to happen versus locking in at any particular time what might seem acceptable.

Senator GRASSLEY. I am not going to ask a question. I did have a question, but I kind of want to make a statement that I hope that we can avoid a situation where the government says you do something and you do it, and it is abiding by the regulations and that may come up short of what we need to do. That is why I think cooperation is so important.

Thank you, Mr. Chairman.

Chairman LEAHY. And I had indicated I agree with that, because we know we are dealing with something that even with the expertise of the four of you here, you could not tell me specifically what would be the greatest threat you might face 18 months from now, because these things are evolving, just as our best intelligence agencies and others cannot either. But we want to give you a framework. We want to have a framework, one that protects consumers so they know where their rights are and being protected, but also protect our businesses, because you have to maintain the trust between both the businesses and the consumers for the good of our country. We have a fragile recovery. We are slowly recovering. But without that credibility, we cannot do it.

I am going to yield to Senator Feinstein, then Senator Hatch, and go back and forth. I have to step out for a moment. Senator Feinstein.

Senator FEINSTEIN [presiding]. Thank you very much, Mr. Chairman.

I want to begin by thanking Mr. Mulligan and Mr. Kingston for being here, because up until very recently, companies would not step forward. Companies would not make it public. I introduced the first data breach notification bill in 2003, and I could not get any cooperation in that data breach. And I pulled the record and would like to introduce the particulars of what happened in 2002 and 2003 into the record. That will be the order.

[The information referred to appears as a submission for the record.]

Senator FEINSTEIN. I am a shopper at your business then, Mr. Kingston. I do not recall getting any notice that my data may have been breached. When would I have had notice? And I would have shopped during the period of time.

Mr. KINGSTON. Senator, we have actually sent out a number of different notifications, and I will start with the 10 of January when we learned——

Senator FEINSTEIN. But you said you did not learn—the breach took place months before you actually learned then that there was a breach.

Mr. KINGSTON. It was not until January 6, actually, that we learned that this very sophisticated malware that was put in our systems had the ability to scrape card data in our systems. And then we quickly put in actions to contain and eradicate that malware, and then we immediately began notifying customers.

Senator FEINSTEIN. And you said that 1.1 million customers had been affected?

Mr. KINGSTON. During that period of time, that was the total number of accounts that we transacted in our stores.

Senator FEINSTEIN. Now, can I assume that all 1.1 million were affected and notified, so somewhere in my record I should be able to find a record of having been notified?

Mr. KINGSTON. We have notified all customers who shopped in our stores or on our Web sites, which is a greater number of customers than were affected in this 1.1 million number. We have notified all of those customers.

Senator FEINSTEIN. And when did you do that?

Mr. KINGSTON. We did that on January 22.

Senator FEINSTEIN. Okay. And, Mr. Mulligan, when did you notify your customers? And how many did you notify?

Mr. MULLIGAN. Senator, we notified—sorry, we refer to them as ''guests''—on December 19, four days after we found the malware. For those guests which we had email addresses for, we notified them by email. But given the scope, we thought it appropriate that broad disclosure was the best path to go, and so we had very broad disclosure through the media, on our Web site, through social media, a multitude of channels.

Senator FEINSTEIN. But you did not notify individual customers?

Mr. MULLIGAN. We did not have specific contact information for all——

Senator FEINSTEIN. So you were depending on the public for your notice. Can you explain to me why—see, I document cases going back to 2003 and 2002. Nobody would notify. And I had a bill that was notification, and it was fiercely fought. Companies did not want to notify their customers. And I have worked on that bill. It is not going to go anywhere because of the notice provisions. So here we are, sort of, again with respect to notices.

I believe that if somebody has an account or uses their credit at your institution and their data is breached, they should be notified so they can protect themselves.

Do you want to respond to that? I do not mean to——

Mr. MULLIGAN. No. We agree with your view completely, Senator. Our focus has been on having accurate and actionable information balanced with providing that notice as quickly as possible and ensuring that we had the capability to respond to what were going to be millions of requests for information.

We felt, given the scope of our breach, that public dissemination was appropriate and would let all of our guests know virtually immediately. And as I am sure you are aware, we were on the front page of every newspaper in this country.

Senator FEINSTEIN. But here is the problem with that. The public notification is always vague. It is sort of non-specific. You really do not know. And then you find out, kind of brutally, in other ways if you have money missing.

Now, you happen to be retail establishments. In 2003, a hacker broke into electronic records of the payroll facility for California State employees, and some 265,000 Social Security numbers were compromised. Now, you said there was no compromise of Social Security numbers. But my point is those people deserve to know that their data was hacked. And this has been the big resistance out there in the commercial community in the 11, 12 years that I have worked on this. And so as far as I am concerned, any bill that is forthcoming from this institution should provide notification of customers that their data may have been breached so they can protect themselves.

If anyone has a comment on that, if you disagree, please tell me. No comment?

Mr. KINGSTON. We agree, Senator, which is why we did exactly as you said. Once we knew that we had criminal activity inside of our systems and who was impacted, we reached out individually to customers. In fact, we reached out to more customers just to be cautious, because it is important to us that our customers understand that this is our primary concern, their privacy and their information. And so all customers that shopped the entire year in Neiman Marcus stores and Web sites were notified.

Senator FEINSTEIN. I will go home and look for my notice. Thank you very much.

Ms. DERAKHSHANI. We also agree that notification is an extremely important aspect of this discussion, and as you indicated, the sooner consumers are made aware, the sooner they can take actions to protect themselves.

Senator FEINSTEIN. Thank you very much.

Senator Hatch.

Senator HATCH. Well, thank you, Senator.

I know that many retailers are migrating toward secure point-of-sale terminals capable of processing chip-and-PIN transactions. Yet I have heard that some credit cards will only require chip and signature, not chip and PIN. Why would that be the case, especially when a chip-and-PIN credit card would be more secure for in-store purchases? Anybody who cares to answer that, I would just throw it to all of you.

Mr. MULLIGAN. Senator, it is my understanding today the standards have been set for chip-enabled card technology. The chip-and-PIN standards are not set yet. We are advocates, as you mentioned, of getting to chip-and-PIN technology. We think that is a safer form. But we think also waiting, we think making the next step is important, and getting to a place where we have guest payment devices and retailers that can read chips and cards are issued with chips so that we can begin to migrate away from magnetic strips is an important next step.

Senator HATCH. Okay. It is my understanding that chip-and-PIN technology does not make online purchases more secure. In fact, the reports confirm that as Europe transitioned to chip-and-PIN cards, fraud losses from online transactions actually increased at a greater pace. As chip-and-PIN cards make in-store transactions more secure in the United States, how will you make online sales similarly secure, Mr. Mulligan?

Mr. MULLIGAN. I think that is an excellent question, Senator, and I think, first, we need to not let the perfect get in the way of the good, so making progress in stores makes a lot of sense, and installing chip-and-PIN technology there, we think, is important.

As you said, the threat continues to evolve, and so there is a shared responsibility here and continuing to have all parties that ensure payment transactions are processed appropriately here in the U.S. be participants in moving that forward to find solutions to the online transactions. We are part of the EMV Migration Forum, and that is a topic there where all interested parties in the payment space come together and discuss that, so that we can find solutions to online. But your point is right on.

Senator HATCH. Okay. Thank you.

Mr. Kingston, you said that credit card information was scraped. What about other information like birthdays and Social Security numbers? Did the hackers—were they able to get that information, too?

Mr. KINGSTON. Senator, our investigation, which is still ongoing, has shown no evidence that other personal information outside of card holder information was scraped.

Senator HATCH. Okay. Mr. Rosch, could you please describe both the advantages and the disadvantages or shortcomings of chip-and-PIN technology as well as any alternatives that may exist that are not currently being considered? As you know, chip-and-PIN technology itself is more than 20 years old. Are there more secure alternatives that we should be considering?

Mr. ROSCH. Well, I think we would agree with the other panelists and yourself that chip and PIN is definitely a step in the right direction. While it is not a panacea, it definitely adds three primary benefits to the ecosystem: One, it is more encryption. So the credit card information would stay encrypted longer, and it would make it much more difficult for the hackers to be able to obtain that information. So that is a big benefit of chip and PIN. The second is it makes it more difficult to duplicate the card. So if the information is stolen, sometimes with the regular magstripe, it is easy enough to go and create another credit card. The fraudsters can create another credit card. Because the chip in these cards have a unique credential, they cannot be copied, so it reduces the risk of multiple cards being generated. And then I think, third, with the PIN, that combines what we call two-factor authentication, when you have something you have and something you know, the card being something you have and the PIN something you know. So if someone was to actually steal your physical card, it would do no good unless they knew your PIN.

So the three primary advantages, it definitely raises the bar on security.

Senator HATCH. Okay. Now, I have a related question about so-called mobile wallets. Although companies like Google are just starting to roll out these types of products, I have no doubt that this technology that allows you to pay by simply tapping your smartphone at a register will be widespread in just a few years. Could you describe the security features of these payment platforms and whether chip-and-PIN technology is compatible?

Mr. ROSCH. Yes, I think we would agree with you that mobile payments are certainly going to be the future. It is still yet to determine exactly which of those different models that are out there will be the future, but I think it is important to note that when you use a mobile device, that is basically a new opportunity for the criminals to be able to attack. That broadens the attack surface. So there are a lot of good technologies that can lock down these devices and keep that information safe, and those things are in progress.

Chip and PIN would not apply in that case. As you mentioned, it is really for card present when you have a swipe. But there are other ways using behavioral analysis to be able to fingerprint some of these devices and recognize a user that can add security in the mobile payments ecosystem.

Senator HATCH. Thank you. My time is up.

Senator FEINSTEIN. Thank you very much, Senator Hatch.

Senator Klobuchar.

Senator KLOBUCHAR. Thank you very much, Senator Feinstein.

As Chairman Leahy noted, these are good companies. We certainly know that in Minnesota, the home of Target. And we also know that if these companies can see these kinds of data breaches, these companies that employ so many people in our country, it can happen to anyone.

And as Senator Feinstein expressed, a lot of times when we have pushed some of these cyber bills, whether it is about government security, whether it is about private security, we get a lot of pushback. And I think that, if anything, we have learned from this major, major breach that we can no longer do nothing, that we have to take action.

And as a former prosecutor, of course, my first reaction to this is to find the crooks that did this and punish them, and I know that that investigation is continuing.

My second reaction is that we have to find the technical solutions here and that our laws have to be as sophisticated as the crooks that are breaking them, and I start there.

So I thought I would start with following up with what Senator Hatch talked about, which was this new technology that, I understand, is adopted in Europe. Is that true, Mr. Rosch?

Mr. ROSCH. Yes, it has been adopted in Europe, and it has showed some significant benefits.

Senator KLOBUCHAR. And is it true in Great Britain that they have seen a major decrease in these kinds of breaches?

Mr. ROSCH. They have seen a reduction in in-store or card-present breaches. They have also seen, however, some of that shift to the online channel where the chip and PIN does not prevent that. But it has definitely helped in reducing fraud in-store.

Senator KLOBUCHAR. Okay. And so what is stopping us from moving to this kind of technology? We have acknowledged, as Senator Hatch has, that maybe there will be some other new great thing that comes along. But what is stopping our country when they are doing this in Europe? I know, Mr. Mulligan, that Target had attempted using this technology. I think—was it back in 2003? Is that right? And so what has stopped it from being rolled out on a major basis? And how can we change that, Mr. Mulligan?

Mr. MULLIGAN. As you know, there are many participants in the payment card world that ensure transactions are processed appropriately in the U.S. As you said, we tried this in 2003. We put guest payment devices, as we call them, in our stores to read chips. We introduced a new payment card, a Target Visa card, with a chip in it. But without broad adoption, there is not significant benefits for consumers.

Senator KLOBUCHAR. And by broad adoption, you mean other retail outlets using the same card?

Mr. MULLIGAN. Other retailer outlets having the ability to read that card as well as the cards being issued with chip technology on them. So it is both pieces of the payment industry need to move together simultaneously.

We have been advocates of this, and all of us need to move together simultaneously. It is a shared responsibility.

Senator KLOBUCHAR. And how does this interact with the financial industry?

Mr. MULLIGAN. The financial industry, obviously, they are, in general, the issuers of the cards, and so, again, in partnership with them, we need to move together collectively so that the whole system is employing chip-and-PIN technology.

Senator KLOBUCHAR. And would the NIST standard we were talking about before—that is in development. Is that right?

Mr. ROSCH. Yes, the NIST standard——

Senator KLOBUCHAR. How long has it been in development?

Mr. ROSCH. It has been in development for quite some time, but it is due to be released in a week.

Senator KLOBUCHAR. Okay. Like 20 years or——

Mr. ROSCH. No. Just more on a year time frame.

Senator KLOBUCHAR. Okay, good.

Mr. ROSCH. But it is due to be released next week, so we are making good progress.

Senator KLOBUCHAR. Okay. Well, that is good timing. And so would that cover this kind of new technology and it would set a standard for these companies? Or do we need to do something more aggressive to get the new technology out there?

Mr. ROSCH. I think the NIST standard does provide some guidelines and objectives for companies to follow. It is not specific in requiring chip and PIN.

Senator KLOBUCHAR. Okay. Did you want to add anything, Mr. Kingston or Ms. Derakhshani?

Ms. DERAKHSHANI. We are definitely supportive of chip-and-PIN technology and of the efforts to—of any efforts to expedite wide adoption of this technology.

Senator KLOBUCHAR. Okay. And then I just want to go back quickly to something that was raised at the beginning, about the time in between when it was confirmed this malware was on the system and when the consumers found out about it. Mr. Mulligan, could you give me just the time in between the time it was confirmed and the time you notified customers?

Mr. MULLIGAN. We confirmed malware on our systems on December 15, and we notified customers on December 19, Senator.

Senator KLOBUCHAR. And by ''notified,'' to make clear—this was Senator Feinstein's question—it was done publicly.

Mr. MULLIGAN. Broad public disclosure, yes.

Senator KLOBUCHAR. Okay. And then, Mr. Kingston, what was your timeline?

Mr. KINGSTON. We were first notified by our forensic investigators on January 2 that they saw suspicious malware. It was not until January 6 that they understood how it operated. And then we spent the next few days containing, disabling, and removing the malware, and it was on January 10 that we started notifying the public and customers directly.

Senator KLOBUCHAR. All right. And did both companies have policies in place on how you would do this consumer notification before it started?

Mr. MULLIGAN. We have several crisis communications plans, and we enacted those immediately upon finding the malware in our systems.

Senator KLOBUCHAR. Okay. Mr. Kingston.

Mr. KINGSTON. Yes, we do.

Senator KLOBUCHAR. All right. Very good. Well, I think you know Senator Leahy has a bill that is focused on some of these notification issues, but I continue—which I think is very important, and I think some of the issues Senator Feinstein raised are worth discussing. I also think that we really have to push on this technology, understanding some of the smaller retailers are going to have different situations than the bigger retailers. But if we want to fix this going forward so this just does not keep happening and happening—we just recently found out hotel chains are now being affected by this—we are really going to have to put something in place. So thank you very much for being here today.

Senator FEINSTEIN. Thank you very much, Senator Klobuchar.

Senator Lee, Senator Hatch has asked to make just one small statement before I recognize you, if that is agreeable. Please go ahead.

Senator HATCH. Well, thank you, and thank you, Senator Lee.

Just an article that came up actually today, it starts off by saying, ''U.S. intelligence agencies last week urged the Obama administration to check its new health care network for malicious software after learning that developers linked to the Belarus Government helped produce the website.''

I will just read two other sentences. '' 'The U.S. Affordable Care Act software was written in part in Belarus by software developers under state control, and that makes the software a potential target for cyber attacks,' one official said.''

And then, ''Cybersecurity officials said the potential threat to the U.S. health care data is compounded by what they said was an Internet data 'hijacking' last year involving Belarussian state-controlled networks.''

I just wanted to bring that up because this is a really serious set of discussions, and it goes far beyond just maybe what the retail community is concerned about.

Thank you.

Senator FEINSTEIN. You are right, Senator. Thank you.

Senator Lee.

Senator LEE. Thank you, Senator Feinstein, and thanks to all of you for joining us today. This is an important topic. I know it is important to each of you and to America's consumers.

I generally trust that the marketplace will create the right kinds of incentives for retailers to protect the personal data of their consumer base. But I think the creation of those incentives really requires, as a condition, precedent that there be adequate notification procedures in place. In other words, consumers, I think, have to have received notification in order for any of this to work. They have to receive notification in order to take the steps they need to take to protect their identity, and they also need notification so that they can decide where to take their business. If they do not trust a particular business with their data, they are not going to shop there.

So I will start with you, Mr. Mulligan. What factors do you weigh in deciding at what point to notify consumers—''guests,'' as you put it. I do not want to denigrate the Target consumer base by calling them just ''consumers.'' We have to call them ''guests.'' At what point do you decide to do that? Because there are some countervailing considerations, aren't there? I mean, you do not necessarily want to notify immediately upon discovering that there is a problem.

Mr. MULLIGAN. Our view, Senator—and you are right. After 18 years, it almost rolls off my tongue without thinking about it. But our view is there is a balance to be struck here. Certainly speed is very important to let consumers know what is going on, but balancing that, as we look through the lens of our guests, is ensuring that we are providing them with accurate information so they can understand what happened, and then actionable information so they can understand what to do about it. And balancing those two factors is the lens we look through, and that ultimately led us to our time frame.

I would also add, for us in particular, given the magnitude and the size of our company, ensuring that we had the appropriate ability to respond to our guests, as we knew the questions were going to come, ensuring our call centers were staffed up and prepared with information for our guests, and that our stores were able to provide that information. So there was a large training element that also went on to ensure we were able to handle their questions and concerns appropriately. But all of that came together and balanced our decision making on how quickly to provide notification.

Senator LEE. But it could cause problems if you notified too soon. If you notified before you know the nature and extent of the threat and before you know what you are going to do about it, that could cause issues.

Mr. MULLIGAN. We believe it is important to provide accurate information once notification is made, Senator, yes, what has gone on and helping our consumers understand what to do about it.

Senator LEE. Okay. Thank you.

Mr. Kingston, one potential legislative response to all of this could involve establishing some kind of national security standard, to codify certain security standards, perhaps standards that are already accepted within the industry. I am always a little bit concerned about creating a new federal regulatory authority, in part because sometimes once you establish something like that, it quickly becomes ineffective, especially if it is in an area like this one where technological advances can very quickly render a codified national security standard irrelevant or outdated.

There is also, I think, some risk that if we create a national security standard, that would be seen not just as a floor but as a floor and a ceiling, and you could see some people complying with that, and then that creates an easy target for would-be thieves to go after, because they know what the security standards are because they are codified in law. Do you see some risks associated with adopting federal legislation that codifies a uniform security standard?

Mr. KINGSTON. I think there are going to inherently be risks for some of the reasons that you stated, Senator. I think the thing that we have to keep in mind is that the cybersecurity threat landscape continues to evolve. Every day it becomes more and more complicated. And so as soon as we establish the standards—and I think standards are helpful but as soon as we establish those, as you pointed out, the whole world knows about it and that gives them the ability to try to, as in our case, come up with ways to defeat those standards.

I think it is obviously healthy to be able to communicate to people what some of the standards and good practices are. But I agree with you; I think there are risks there as well.

Senator LEE. Okay. In the two seconds I have remaining, Mr. Rosch, I saw you nodding. Do you have anything you want to add to that?

Mr. ROSCH. Yes. I think it is not only that the cyber threats are evolving very quickly so it is difficult to lock things in; our environments are changing so quickly. If we look at what a company's infrastructure looked like five years ago, it was pretty much contained within their data centers and their devices. Today information is everywhere. It is in our data centers. It is in the cloud. It is in, you know, software that sits in the cloud on mobile devices. So the threats are exploding, but so is the attack surface. So we need to be flexible to be able to adjust, because both of those environments change.

Senator LEE. Thank you very much.

Thank you, Chair.

Senator FEINSTEIN. Thanks, Senator Lee.

Senator Franken.

Senator FRANKEN. Thank you, Madam Chair.

First of all, I think on those—Chairman Leahy has a bill that I am a cosponsor of that talks about having some standards, but I think you can write them in a flexible manner. And I see you nodding, Mr. Rosch.

As some of you may know, I am Chair of the Subcommittee on Privacy, Technology, and the Law. I think the people have a fundamental right to privacy, and for me, part of that right is knowing that your sensitive information is protected and secure. And when millions of consumers have their credit and debit card data stolen, we have a big problem. We need to fix it.

Minnesotans shop at Target all the time, as do millions of other Americans. Minnesotans shop at Neiman Marcus, too. We need to get to the bottom of these breaches.

But what is clear to me is that we are not just dealing with the problem of Target and Neiman Marcus, or Michaels, for that matter. We are dealing with a systemic problem. A big part of that problem, as we have discussed, is the security of our credit and debit cards. The U.S. has one-fourth of the world's card transactions, and yet we are victims to half of all card fraud.

Two weeks ago, I wrote to each of the Nation's largest credit and debit card companies to ask them what they were doing to make our cards safer, and their responses are due tomorrow.

The Federal Government has a role to play here, too. Congress needs to pass laws that promote data security. Right now there is no federal law setting out clear security standards that merchants and data brokers need to meet, and there is no federal law requiring companies to tell their customers when their data has been stolen. And I am glad to say that Chairman Leahy has a bill that would fix this problem, and I am glad to be a cosponsor of it. And I think it contains enough flexibility that it is not a signal to how to overcome that to criminals.

First I want to get a little better handle on how Target and Neiman Marcus had their breaches occur. Mr. Mulligan, retailers are on the front line when it comes to stopping the breach of their customers' data. I understand Target has spent considerable resources on data security systems. But a January 17 article in the *New York Times* states that your systems at Target were ''astonishingly open'' and ''particularly vulnerable to attack.''

I know that you had had independent audits before, a couple of them, saying that you had passed muster and you were among the best in the industry. Can you respond to these charges?

Mr. MULLIGAN. Sure. Respectfully, Senator, we would not share that view. Over the past several years, we have invested hundreds of millions of dollars in several areas in technology to prevent data loss. This includes segmentation, malware detection, intrusion detection and prevention, data loss prevention tools, multiple layers of firewalls. But beyond that, as you said, we have ongoing assessments and third parties coming in doing penetration testing of our systems, benchmarking us against others, assessing if we are in compliance with our own processes and control standards. And we have invested in team. We have hundreds of team members responsible for this. We go so far as training 370,000 team members annually on the importance of data security. So we have taken a holistic view of our approach to data security and invested significant resources.

Senator FRANKEN. Okay. It is kind of spy versus spy, is what we are talking about.

Mr. MULLIGAN. Yes.

Senator FRANKEN. You said in your oral testimony that you are for—and Senator Hatch brought this up—that you are for the smart chip plus PIN. And, Mr. Rosch, Visa and MasterCard are pushing to roll out smart chip cards in the U.S. in October 2015. I wish that could be hurried. It is my understanding these cards will not require or may not require PINs for every transaction, and this is surprising to me because, as we have heard from you, the incidence of fraud is far higher for signature debit transactions than for PIN debit transactions. And maybe this is for Ms. Derakhshani. Is there a reason that Visa and MasterCard do not want to put the PIN in there?

Ms. DERAKHSHANI. So we are aware of the promises that have been made to implement the technology by 2015. I think the answer comes down to money. It is expensive to update the technology at the point of sale. It is expensive to reissue cards. So we would be supportive of efforts to encourage widespread adoption of these technologies, and we think that more of a push would be a good thing.

Senator FRANKEN. Mr. Rosch, could you follow up on that? In particular, do Visa and MasterCard have a reason?

Mr. ROSCH. Sure. I think that, you know, chip and PIN, we think, is the best and most secure solution.

Senator FRANKEN. Sure.

Mr. ROSCH. I think the chip on its own still does provide more advanced security around encrypting and preventing the cloning of the cards. The PIN is just an additional thing, and we think that is the way to go.

Senator FRANKEN. Okay. Thank you.

Thank you, Madam Chair.

Senator FEINSTEIN. Senator Franken, it is my understanding it has been arranged that you chair. I must leave now.

Senator FRANKEN. Yes.

Senator FEINSTEIN. And I believe Senator Durbin is next.

Senator FRANKEN [presiding]. Yes. So go ahead, Senator Durbin. And I will move over to the chair. Senator Durbin.

Senator DURBIN. I believe under the early bird rule that Senator Coons is next.

Senator FEINSTEIN. It is not early bird. It was by seniority.

Senator DURBIN. Oh. Well, I am going to defer to Senator Coons.

Senator FRANKEN. As Chair, Senator Coons.

Senator COONS. Thank you very much, Senator Durbin and Senator Franken.

If I could just follow up on the line of questioning Senator Franken was on, first, I just want to thank all the witnesses because it is very helpful when you take the time to share with us the details of these incidents. And as we in Congress work hard to try and strike the right balance between a robust and a vibrant marketplace where we all benefit from the ease and the convenience of using credit cards and debit cards, but we also try to make sure we are sufficiently protected in our privacy and against theft and fraud. These are delicate balancing choices we have to make, and I think this has been very helpful for us to better understand standards, what is possible, what is desirable, and what it would cost and what the impact is.

So if I could just continue, Ms. Derakhshani, does the Consumers Union believe that October 2015 is a reasonable deadline for the implementation of this chip technology?

Ms. DERAKHSHANI. I think we are supportive of efforts to expedite it even more quickly.

Senator COONS. So you think it is possible for it to be done even more quickly, it is just a matter of cost?

Ms. DERAKHSHANI. Well, I would not be able to speak to the exact—you know, everything that it takes for it to be implemented. But we would like to see it be implemented more quickly.

Senator COONS. And if I understand correctly, chip plus PIN, which is now possible, a PIN is possible in many debit card cases, and there is a sevenfold increase in fraud when you use debit cards without a PIN than when you use them with a PIN. Do you believe PIN technology ought to be enabled for credit cards as well?

Ms. DERAKHSHANI. That is an interesting question. We have spoken about the differences between debit card protections and credit card protections, and I think it would be a good thing for debit card—you know, you are less protected under debit cards, and it would be a good thing for debit card technology to come in line with credit card protection.

Senator COONS. Mr. Kingston, do you have the option currently requiring customers who present a debit card at point of sale to input a PIN?

Mr. KINGSTON. We do not use PIN pads in our stores currently, and we do not require PINs.

Senator COONS. And just help me understand why not.

Mr. KINGSTON. I think the issue that we are talking about here is that there are a lot of different technologies that are available, and this is something that right now in the industry consumers actually do not really have a lot of these cards in their wallet. I am a consumer. I have several credit cards in my wallet. None of them have chips on them. So while it is an option, it is something that just has not been widely adopted by the industry at this point.

Senator COONS. But my specific question was about PINs on debit cards rather than chips, but I understand your point that the trajectory of cards with chips in them, the trajectory of that adoption is not easily predictable.

A broad question, Mr. Rosch, if I might. You testified breach notification standards are not enough. Federal legislation is needed to ensure pre-breach security measures. Can you grade the sufficiency of the cybersecurity efforts currently in place by retailers? We have talked about data security and cybersecurity. If you could give us some insight into how the PCI compliance factor weighs in to cybersecurity.

Mr. ROSCH. Yes, it is a great question, and I think, you know, there are a lot of companies that have put in very effective security solutions and some that have a ways to go. I think the trick here is—we focus very much on chip and PIN, which is just one kind of potential breach point. What companies really need to do is look at very layered securities at every part of their ecosystems and ensuring good basics, like putting stronger authentication in place so bad people cannot get into the networks, into their companies and start laying the foundation for this threat. The more we can encrypt the data throughout its entire—as it traverses around, then if the bad guys do get it, they cannot decrypt it and it is of no value to them.

We talk about anti-virus missing some of these things, and it does. Anti-virus is a great foundational technology, but there are things that we can do on top of that to recognize and stop some of these emerging threats.

So it is really about putting this layered security approach, and we think any legislation should reflect those layers.

Senator COONS. Thank you. My last question, if I might, to Mr. Mulligan and Mr. Kingston. Just if you would help us understand what are the key impediments that your companies face in trying to achieve this sort of more robust cybersecurity. Obviously it is expensive. But as you try to strike the right balance, whether it is guests or customers, those of us who enjoy shopping at your stores and enjoy the flexibility and freedom of having cards we can use anywhere also want to make sure that our data is protected and that we are not, as a country, subject to vast amounts of fraud.

What are the major impediments to your companies actually implementing stronger cybersecurity measures?

Mr. MULLIGAN. I can start. For us, we agree, layers of protection are important broadly across the entire enterprise. As we think about it, this is an evolving threat, and we think one of the keys going forward is, again, shared responsibility, to share information across the industry, not just retail but broadly across industry, and, you know, we have a history of doing that with law enforcement, but with other parts of the government, so that we can all understand the evolving threat and respond to it as we design our data security systems and protocols.

Mr. KINGSTON. I talked earlier about the importance of all the actors in this ecosystem being able to share intelligence. As we have learned, these recent cyber attacks are very, very sophisticated. Things that have not been seen before are done. So I think that is one thing.

I think the other thing that is really important is that all of the actors be able to adopt these technologies at the same time. So consumers obviously have to be able to adopt it, technology companies, financial institutions, and private sector as well.

Senator COONS. Well, thank you. I do think there is a strong federal role here in ensuring strengthening cybersecurity and privacy.

Thank you both to Senator Durbin and to Senator Franken. Thank you.

Senator FRANKEN. We actually are using the early bird rule, so you are the late bird. So we go to Senator Blumenthal.

Senator BLUMENTHAL. Thank you. Thank you all for being here. It is not easy to be the face of the industry which really bears a responsibility here for what I see as a record of failure. And this comment is not directed at Target or Neiman Marcus. It is directed at an industry, and I think you deserve a lot of credit for coming here today and representing that industry, and also for the steps that you have taken in the wake of breaches that certainly victimized you, and those measures include credit monitoring, insurance, measures that I sought for others in this industry and in other worlds to adopt voluntarily while I was Attorney General of the State of Connecticut and literally had to bludgeon and pummel them into doing—not physically but legally. And I just want to commend you for appearing here and for the proactive steps that you have taken.

But I have introduced a bill that I think builds on the very good measures that Senator Leahy and Senator Rockefeller have introduced to establish standards so that there will be, in effect, a bar— a bar that everybody has to follow, a standard of care—because this information is not yours. It is entrusted to you. It belongs to the consumers. And that kind of basic principle is the bedrock of this legislation, a standard of care applied industrywide, and enforcement, because rights are not real unless they are enforceable—so enforcement by the FTC but also by consumers themselves, a private right of action for consumers to take when they are victimized, as your stores may be victimized, by those hackers, a standard of care enforceable by an individual right of action, and a clearinghouse so that you can share the kind of information everybody has said here this morning that is so important for you to be able to exchange among yourselves and help to be flexible and raise that bar. And I do agree that the standard has to be flexible. Right now we are talking about chip and PIN, but the threats are emerging and evolving, and so does the standard in its specifics.

But, you know, I sit here with the attitude of most of your consumers, which is half the fraud occurs in the United States, but only a quarter of the credit card use. Something is wrong with this picture. Isn't that fact and the continuing series of significant, even sensational, breaches an indictment of the American retailing industry in its failure to protect consumer information? We are talking here, after all, not about some exotic, novel science fiction technology in chip and PIN? We are talking about something that is widely used in Europe and could easily have been imposed here much earlier.

So my question to you, Mr. Rosch, in light of your very welcome and important recommendations—and you have had the good sense to make them somewhat simple in a graph that is understandable to us rudimentary laymen—would your recommendations have helped to prevent this kind of massive breach at Neiman Marcus and Target?

Mr. ROSCH. Yes, well, to start out, I am unable to speak about any specifics of the incidents. You know, all the evidence based on public information is that these were very sophisticated attackers and they were very well resourced. However, in general, we do believe that, you know, if companies put in this good layered security approach while leveraging the strong authentication, the encryption, the heuristics on top of AV, the chip and PIN, all these things would contribute to a safe ecosystem.

Senator BLUMENTHAL. That is basically a yes, it would have helped prevent—I am not asking you to go into the details, but network segmentation, two-factor authentication—and you also recommend the chip and PIN or something like it—would have at least helped to prevent this kind of massive breach.

Let me ask you, gentlemen, Mr. Kingston and Mr. Mulligan, were you then in the process of adopting some of these recommendations or not knowing they were recommendations of Symantec but recommendations in substance like them? And if not then, are you now?

Mr. KINGSTON. Senator, as I said in my written statement, we actually do have a multilayered security architecture and had prior to these attacks at Neiman Marcus. Many of the technologies——

Senator BLUMENTHAL. Was this information encrypted?

Mr. KINGSTON. The information was encrypted during processing. Many of the technologies that are being discussed here today by the Committee—two-factor authentication, segmentation, network monitoring for suspicious traffic—these are all technologies that we have deployed and utilized at Neiman Marcus.

Unfortunately, the sophistication of this particular attack was able to evade detection of all of those best practices, and I think what we have learned and what is important here is that just having tools and technology is not enough in this day and age. These attackers, again, are very, very sophisticated, and they have figured out ways around that.

It is often how you are deploying those technologies and what else are you doing, which comes back to making sure that we are sharing intelligence as much as we can so that we can try to stay as close to or ahead of the attacks.

Senator BLUMENTHAL. Thank you. My time has expired, so you may be spared, Mr. Mulligan, an answer to that question. But I would like to ask both of you to provide perhaps some detailed answers in writing to the question about whether you are going beyond your present practices and procedures to adopt these steps that Symantec has recommended. I am not saying they are the only solutions, but just a kind of benchmark. And if you could provide that in writing, I would appreciate it.

[The information referred to appears as a submission for the record.]

Senator BLUMENTHAL. I also want to say that my bill would provide for mandatory notification, and I also want to thank you for the notification steps that you did take, both of your companies took to notify consumers.

Thank you very much, Mr. Chairman. Thank you, Senator Durbin.

Senator FRANKEN. Yes, just one. I know Mr. Mulligan did not answer on this, but Target, as Senator Klobuchar pointed out, 10 years ago tried to implement the EMV technology and found that so few others were doing that that they abandoned that. But that is something I want to find out from the banks and the credit card issuers and debit card issuers about how fast they can go to this technology, because right now it is October 2015.

But let us go to Senator Hirono.

Senator HIRONO. Thank you. Following what appears to be the protocol on this side of the table, I would certainly be happy to defer to Senator Durbin if he would like to ask his questions.

Senator DURBIN. Mr. Chairman, I would like to defer to everyone except Senator Whitehouse.

[Laughter.]

Senator HIRONO. Thank you.

Senator FRANKEN. I am the Chair of this Committee, and I will determine——

[Laughter.]

Senator FRANKEN. But that is about right, okay. Senator Hirono.

Senator HIRONO. I would like to thank Target and Neiman Marcus for coming here today because I think all of us—most of us shop at both of these establishments. And there has been discussion about by 2015 Visa and MasterCard are required—basically using the power of the—their power, to require that the merchants and banks agree to issue cards and you all have readers that will read cards with chips in them. So I take it that, Mr. Kingston and Mr. Mulligan, both of you are prepared to meet that deadline with the chip technology.

Mr. MULLIGAN. Senator, we have been proponents of chip and PIN, as you just heard, for a very long time. We are in the process of rolling this out in our stores. Over 300 of our stores already have, we call them, "guest payment devices," and we are accelerating that $100 million investment to get those in our stores by the fourth quarter of this year, and then the products we offer will have the chips in them early next year.

Senator HIRONO. Are you also prepared to adopt the PIN portion of what is being suggested?

Mr. MULLIGAN. We are advocates for the PIN. As the industry in total becomes capable of handling that for credit transactions, we will be ready for that as well, as we are advocates of that as a double authentication.

Senator HIRONO. What about you, Mr. Kingston?

Mr. KINGSTON. Senator, Neiman Marcus is certainly willing and will consider anything that is going to make this process and consumer information safer, including chip and PIN. As I pointed out earlier, at Neiman Marcus we do not use PIN pads today, and as a practical matter, I think it is important for the Committee to understand that while I think the industry would be safer with that, there is lots of work to do in order to make that happen. Obviously there are PIN pads that have to be able to process this. There are software changes that will have to happen. And, of course, all of the integration with the other actors, such as the banks and the merchant processors has to occur, and then finally, of course, getting all the cards with the chips in consumers' hands.

I think we are very supportive of considering those and other technologies and capabilities that will make us safer, but I think we all need to understand that there is a lot of work involved in doing that.

Senator HIRONO. Well, what I heard is that Target is prepared to establish or go with both a chip-and-PIN technology, but you are raising some concerns. So does that mean that at Neiman Marcus you would not be able to meet a 2015 deadline with both of these factors?

Mr. KINGSTON. I am not saying that we are not prepared to do it. What I am saying is that we would definitely want to evaluate that as a safer measure for our customers and move as quickly as we possibly can to do that.

Senator HIRONO. Would federal legislation help if we were to say—because right now it is just Visa and MasterCard saying here is what is going to happen in the arena. Would federal legislation that says here is what we would like to see?

Mr. KINGSTON. I think we would have to consider that. If we have to do it under the law, obviously we will follow the law.

Senator HIRONO. It may be coming down the pike. But, of course, we would want to have all the parties at the table so that we can proceed in a reasonable way. And, also, the cost was mentioned, and I do not know whether in the non-federal arena this cost was going to be borne by Target and Neiman Marcus and all the other retailers and financial institutions to comport with what MasterCard and Visa——

Mr. MULLIGAN. It is a shared responsibility and a shared interest in payment processing, and the costs will be borne by—a portion of the costs will be borne by all participants.

Senator HIRONO. Including the consumers?

Mr. MULLIGAN. No. It would be the companies involved in payment processing, Senator.

Senator HIRONO. So what would be the cost to implement this kind of technology? And perhaps Ms. Derakhshani can enlighten us on that.

Ms. DERAKHSHANI. Well, we think that it is very important for costs not to be borne by the consumer. Consumers have lost this information through no fault of their own. I think it is really important to remember that.

Senator HIRONO. So do you have any idea what the cost of putting in place a chip-and-PIN system would be?

Ms. DERAKHSHANI. I would be happy to maybe look into and get back to you all, but I do not have figures at this time.

Senator HIRONO. I know I am running out of time, but one of the areas that I was very interested in is the prevention side of things. Mr. Rosch, you mentioned that one of the first lines of defense is for the consumers to use different kinds of—that they should use certain kinds of PINs and all of that. How do we get this information out to consumers so that, as you say, they are the first line of defense in terms of prevention? What can we do to enable consumers to know that they can take some of these prevention elements into their own hands and protect themselves?

Mr. ROSCH. It is a great question. I do think that there are things that consumers can do around stronger passwords, changing them frequently, getting their credit reports, watching their bills. So I think we all have that shared responsibility to try to get that communication out. I know *Consumer Reports* is an excellent—makes excellent recommendations directly to consumers. We do that as part of our business. The Better Business Bureau has good recommendations, so I think it is just kind of that shared getting the news out there that these basic hygiene things can help keep them protected.

Senator HIRONO. I think that is very important aspect because, for a lot of consumers—and I am one of them. I am trying to simplify my life by just using very few passwords. You are suggesting the exact opposite, so I think that kind of information needs to get out and have consumers adopt the kind of suggestions you are giving.

Thank you.

Senator FRANKEN. Senator Durbin.

Senator DURBIN. Thank you very much, Mr. Chairman.

I want to return to those thrilling days of yesteryear, 2010 and the Durbin interchange fee amendment on debit cards, where we basically finally asked publicly a question about something that was known to retailers across the United States, and not very well known to anyone else, and that was the amount that was being charged on each transaction by the card issuers and banks when a retailer used the card. And what the Federal Reserve reported to us was that the average was 44 cents on transactions; the actual cost to the card issuer and the bank, seven cents. So we asked them to find some reasonable fee, interchange fee, for debit cards, and the Federal Reserve came up with about 24 cents. I do not know exactly how they made that calculation. It is currently being litigated.

Within that 24 cents, though, was one penny or one cent for fraud prevention, and it is ironic, or at least coincidental, that just weeks after this law was passed and signed by the President and implemented, we had an announcement by Visa that they were finally adopting a road map for chip card technology in the United States. They had a dedicated source coming off the interchange fee that they represented to the Federal Reserve was going to be an anti-fraud effort. So we are moving in that direction, albeit slowly, considering the circumstances we are talking about today.

It is ironic—my staff had me cover the numbers, but it is ironic that I have had a chip card in my wallet with American Express for years, and I do not know that it has ever been used for any purpose other than this, but it is clear that it is there and it has been around for a while.

So let me go to a study that came out recently in 2012. There was about $5.3 billion in credit and debit card fraud loss in the United States in 2012—$5.3 billion. One-fifth the payment card fraud loss has occurred with debit cards. The Federal Reserve found that in 2011 there were $1.38 billion in debit card fraud losses. The Fed said that card issuers bore 60 percent of these debit card fraud losses, merchants 38 percent, card holders two percent.

So, Mr. Mulligan, in light of that fact that fraud losses are divided among banks, merchants, and card holders, do you agree it is a shared responsibility to support this move toward new technology such as chip and PIN?

Mr. MULLIGAN. We absolutely agree it is a shared responsibility among all participants in ensuring payment transactions happen that are facilitated in the U.S. today. All of us have an interest in ensuring that consumers or our guests have trust in the system that they are using every day. That is why we have been proponents of moving to chip and PIN over a very long period of time, and we are currently looking to accelerate our investment to bring those devices into our stores more quickly.

Senator DURBIN. You and I had a brief conversation when we met yesterday, and one of the aspects of this is the card reader, which retailers are responsible for paying for, right?

Mr. MULLIGAN. Yes.

Senator DURBIN. So what is the—can you give me an idea of what the cost is of a card reader today versus chip and PIN?

Mr. MULLIGAN. I do not know the incremental cost, Senator. What I can tell you is that the total investment for us is about $100 million. That is split about equally between putting card readers in our point-of-sale system and reissuing the cards with the chips in them, so about 50/50 percent.

Senator DURBIN. So let me get back to the original point. Retailers, and customers in many cases, are paying an additional one cent on every transaction for anti-fraud measures, so they are, in fact, giving the issuing banks and card companies basically a subsidy to have anti-fraud technology. So it is not as if we are not paying already to move this technology forward.

Mr. MULLIGAN. The contractual arrangements provide for retailers to provide revenue into the system for the processors and the banks issuing those cards.

Senator DURBIN. And I am sure the recurring concern among members is the impact of new technology and cost of card readers on smaller retail establishments, which is something that we need to be sensitive to. But, in fact, the card issuers and banks are receiving money currently, if they are alleging to the Fed that they are using this money for anti-fraud purposes, they can be.

Now, Ms. Derakhshani—did I pronounce that correctly?

Ms. DERAKHSHANI. Perfectly, yes.

Senator DURBIN. Thank you. There are lots of legislative proposals designed to address data breach. There are fewer proposals, however, that address the underlying issue: the collection of personally identifiable information and practices governing their retention by large brokerages and corporations. That is largely unregulated.

We had a hearing a week or two ago here about the National Security Agency collecting our telephone information, literally phone numbers and what they are used for, and whether that was a breach of privacy. So the question I ask you: In an environment where sensitive consumer data is aggressively sought after by both good guys and bad guys, do you believe Congress should consider proposals that govern the collection and retention of personally identifiable information by private entities?

Ms. DERAKHSHANI. So we think of this as a separate issue, but you have touched on a lot of important things, among them the fact that there are a lot of threats out there, and we are really glad that there is attention brought to this important issue, and the issue of privacy and data security in general.

Senator DURBIN. Well, let us start with Mr. Rosch. I will bring you into the conversation.

Mr. ROSCH. Sure.

Senator DURBIN. So we are talking about how much regulation should there be on my personal information collected by a private sector entity.

Mr. ROSCH. I think that, you know, any data breach legislation should include proactive measures that companies can take to protect this information. That information should be any sensitive information, including personal about myself, my credit card information, about my financials. And, you know, having that good security approach end to end is important.

I think it is also important that we are very transparent with users, that if we are going to collect their information for a particular business, legitimate business reason, that they are aware of that and they are fully aware of how we are going to use it, how any company would use it, and then when it is no longer needed, it is eliminated.

So I think it is all these different layers, but it is definitely about, you know, giving guidelines on proactive measures to keep this information safe.

Senator DURBIN. So I guess I am trying to sort out, as I close here, who do we trust when it comes to our privacy. Clearly there is some skepticism if the government is collecting information about us, that it has more power than most to misuse it. But we are finding on the private side the collection of personal information can also be abused as well if we are dealing with malware and hackers and the like that can get into the system. And I think it is incumbent on us to really try to establish a standard so that

Americans feel confident that their personal information is being protected in a reasonable fashion.

Thank you.

Senator FRANKEN. Thank you, Senator Durbin.

Senator Whitehouse.

Senator WHITEHOUSE. Thank you, Chairman, and thank you to all the witnesses.

Let me ask Mr. Mulligan from Target, clearly you have a robust IT department. Correct?

Mr. MULLIGAN. Yes, Senator.

Senator WHITEHOUSE. And clearly had robust Internet security?

Mr. MULLIGAN. Yes.

Senator WHITEHOUSE. And yet you were unaware of this breach and were informed of it by the United States Secret Service. Correct?

Mr. MULLIGAN. The Attorney General was the first notice, but yes, Senator, that is correct.

Senator WHITEHOUSE. I hope that for folks who are watching this is really seen as an object lesson as to the vulnerability that we all have to a whole variety of Internet penetrations. I think that Target is an extraordinarily well-respected retailer and does a very efficient business. And when a company like that can be hacked without knowing it, the wrong reaction is to say, ''Oh, well, Target must have done something wrong.'' The right reaction is to say, ''Oh, my gosh, are we being hacked and do we not know it, too?'' And I think we need to pay a lot more attention in that regard.

As dangerous as this privacy breach was, as much as it is likely to lead to criminal activity in the form of identity fraud and other forms of fraud, we can thank God that you provided a vital service but you are not running the electric grid, and you are not running the servers behind all of our banks and our financial systems. There are pieces of our American critical infrastructure that are run by the private sector that are facing very much these same threats, and we need to be much more attentive to it. And if you are not doing intellectual property but if you have a—sorry, if you are not doing critical infrastructure but if you have significant intellectual property that is an important part of your business model, you better be watching out for that, too, because there are folks across the Pacific who are probably in your data already and who have a national policy of trying to break into American computers, steal our intellectual property, and give it to competitor companies in order to seek competitive advantage.

So this is a window in a much larger problem, and I just wanted to make that point. I am sorry that it was you, but I think I am very gratified that you have had the courage and the sense of what is going on around you to come here and make this more transparent. And I will close with my appreciation to Symantec. We came very close to getting a very comprehensive piece of cyber legislation through the Senate not too long ago, and some of the U.S. Internet security providers, particularly Symantec and McAfee and Mandiant, were very, very helpful in classified private briefings, walking Senators through the scale of the problem and the scope of the problem, so that a momentum could be developed toward legislation. Unfortunately the U.S. Chamber of Commerce saw things otherwise and found ways to defeat the progress that we had made. But I hope that we can, nevertheless, continue to go forward because this is a continuing threat. And I think I just—I am seeing a nod from Mr. Rosch from Symantec. Yes, this is a continuing threat?

Mr. ROSCH. Yes, continuing and growing, and we are happy to work with you and others on making the ecosystem safer.

Senator WHITEHOUSE. Your effort was very important and much appreciated.

Mr. ROSCH. Thank you.

Senator WHITEHOUSE. Thank you, Chairman.

Senator FRANKEN. Thank you, Senator Whitehouse.

I would like to thank this panel of witnesses. Thank you for your testimony and your answers. You are dismissed.

Senator FRANKEN. I would now like to call our second panel of witnesses.

I am going to ask you to stand, so you might as well not sit down.

I would like to ask the witnesses to raise their right hands. Do you swear that your testimony will be the truth, the whole truth, and nothing but the truth?

Ms. RAMIREZ. I do.

Mr. NOONAN. I do.

Ms. RAMAN. I do.

Senator FRANKEN. Thank you. You may be seated.

Chairwoman Ramirez, a Commissioner of the Federal Trade Commission since 2010, was appointed Chairwoman of the FTC in March 2013. Prior to this, Ms. Ramirez was a partner in the office of Quinn, Emanuel, Urquhart & Sullivan, LLP, in Los Angeles, where she focused her work on matters of intellectual property, antitrust, and trademark issues.

Mr. Noonan is the Deputy Special Agent in Charge for the Secret Service's Criminal Investigative Division, Cyber Operations. He has over 20 years of Federal Government experience. Throughout his career he has initiated and managed a number of high-profile fraud investigations.

Ms. Raman is the Acting Assistant Attorney General for the Criminal Division of the Department of Justice. She has worked in the Criminal Division since 2008, where she previously served as the chief of staff. Formerly, Ms. Raman served as an Assistant United States Attorney in the U.S. Attorney's Office for the District of Maryland.

Thank you all for joining us. You each have five minutes for any opening remarks you would like to make. Chairman Ramirez, would you like to begin?

Oh, I am sorry. Excuse me. I would like to recognize the Ranking Member who has something he would like to say.

Senator GRASSLEY. This will not take more than 45 seconds. I am going to submit questions for answer in writing, but also I wanted to point out two very significant things that I want to discuss. One is unrelated to this hearing, but to Chairwoman Ramirez, I sent you a letter on the LP gas shortage in the Midwest. I just want to call to your attention I have not gotten an answer yet. If you could answer that, I would appreciate it.

And then, related to this question, for Mr. Noonan, I will have a question on the fact that the morning *Washington Times* said that there was a Belarus company involved in writing some of the software for the health care reform act, and the extent to which that could be indicative of somebody having access to our records over here in the same vein that we have asked Target to respond to it.

[The questions of Senator Grassley appear as submissions for the record.]

Senator GRASSLEY. Thank you very much.

Senator FRANKEN. Sorry I did not go right to you.

Again, thank you all for joining us. Chairman Ramirez, would you like to begin?

STATEMENT OF HON. EDITH RAMIREZ, CHAIRWOMAN, FEDERAL TRADE COMMISSION, WASHINGTON, DC

Ms. RAMIREZ. Mr. Chairman, Ranking Member Grassley, and Members of the Committee, thank you for the opportunity to appear before you to discuss the Federal Trade Commission's data security enforcement program. I am pleased to be testifying here this morning with my colleagues from the Justice Department and the Secret Service.

We live in an increasingly connected world in which vast amounts of consumer data are collected. As recent breaches at Target and other retailers remind us, this data is susceptible to compromise by those who seek to exploit security vulnerabilities.

This takes place against the background of the threat of identity theft, which has been the FTC's top consumer complaint for the last 13 years.

According to estimates of the Bureau of Justice Statistics, in 2012 this crime affected a staggering seven percent of all people in the U.S. age 16 and older.

The Commission is here today to reiterate its bipartisan and unanimous call for federal data security legislation. Never has the need for such legislation been greater. With reports of data breaches on the rise, Congress needs to act. We support legislation that would strengthen existing data security standards and require companies, in appropriate circumstances, to notify consumers when there has been a breach.

Legislation should give the FTC authority to seek civil penalties where warranted to help ensure that FTC actions have an appropriate deterrent effect. It should also provide rulemaking authority under the APA and jurisdiction over nonprofits which have been the source of a large number of breaches. Such provisions would create a strong, consistent standard and enable the FTC to protect consumers more effectively.

Using its existing authority, the FTC has devoted substantial resources to encourage companies to make data security a priority. The FTC has brought 50 civil actions against companies that we alleged put consumer data at risk. We have brought these cases under our authority to combat deceptive and unfair commercial practices as well as more targeted laws such as the *Gramm-Leach-Bliley Act* and the *Fair Credit Reporting Act*.

In all these cases, the touchstone of the Commission's approach has been reasonableness. A company's data security measures must be reasonable in light of the sensitivity and volume of consumer information it holds, the size and complexity of its data operations, and the cost of available tools to improve security and reduce vulnerabilities.

The Commission has made clear that it does not require perfect security, and the fact that a breach occurred does not mean that a company has violated the law.

Significantly, a number of FTC enforcement actions have involved large breaches of payment card information. For example, in 2008, the FTC settled allegations that security deficiencies of retailer TJ Maxx permitted hackers to obtain information about tens of millions of credit and debit cards. To resolve these allegations, the retailer agreed to institute a comprehensive security program and to submit to a series of security audits. At the same time, the Justice Department successfully prosecuted a hacker behind the TJ Maxx and other breaches.

As this case illustrates well, the FTC and criminal authorities share complementary goals. FTC actions help ensure on the front end that businesses do not put their customer's data at unnecessary risk, while criminal enforcement help ensure that cyber criminals are caught and punished. This dual approach to data security leverages government resources and best serves the interests of consumers, and to that end, the FTC, the Justice Department, and the Secret Service have worked together to coordinate our respective data security investigations.

In addition to the Commission's enforcement work, the FTC offers guidance to consumers and businesses. For those consumers affected by recent breaches, the FTC has posted information online about steps they should take to protect themselves. These materials are in addition to the large stable of other FTC resources we have for ID victims, including an ID theft hotline. We also engage in extensive policy initiatives on privacy and data security issues. For example, we have recently conducted workshops on mobile security and emerging forms of ID theft, such as child ID theft and senior ID theft.

In closing, I want to thank the Committee for holding this hearing and for the opportunity to provide the Commission's views. Data security is among the Commission's highest priorities, and we look forward to working with Congress on this critical issue.

Thank you.

[The prepared statement of Ms. Ramirez appears as a submission for the record.]

Senator FRANKEN. Thank you, Madam Chairwoman.

Mr. Noonan.

STATEMENT OF WILLIAM NOONAN, DEPUTY SPECIAL AGENT IN CHARGE, CRIMINAL INVESTIGATIVE DIVISION, CYBER OPERATIONS BRANCH, U.S. SECRET SERVICE, WASHINGTON, DC

Mr. NOONAN. Good afternoon, Mr. Chairman and distinguished Members of the Committee. Thank you for the opportunity to testify on behalf of the Department of Homeland Security regarding the ongoing trends of criminals exploiting cyberspace to obtain financial and identity information as part of a complex criminal scheme to defraud our Nation's payment systems.

Our modern financial system depends heavily on information technology for convenience and efficiency. Accordingly, criminals, motivated by greed, have adapted their methods and are increasingly using cyberspace to exploit our Nation's financial payment systems to engage in fraud and other illicit activities. The widely reported data breaches of Target and Neiman Marcus are just recent examples of this trend. The Secret Service is investigating these recent data breaches, and we are confident that we will bring the criminals responsible to justice.

However, data breaches like these recent events are part of a long trend. In 1984, Congress recognized the risks posed by the increase use of information technology and established 18 U.S.C. Sections 1029 and 1030 through the Comprehensive Crime Control Act. These statutes defined access to vice fraud and misuse of computers as federal crimes and explicitly assigned the Secret Service authority to investigate these crimes.

It is a part of the Department of Homeland Security's mission to safeguard cyberspace. The Secret Service investigates cyber crime through the efforts of our highly trained special agents and the work of our growing network of 33 Electronic Crimes Task Forces, which Congress assigned the mission of preventing, detecting, and investigating various forms of electronic crimes.

As a result of our cyber crime investigations, over the past four years the Secret Service has arrested nearly 5,000 cyber criminals. In total, these criminals were responsible for over $1 billion in fraud losses, and we estimate our investigations prevented over $11 billion in fraud losses.

Data breaches like the recently reported occurrences are just one part of a complex criminal scheme executed by organized cyber crime. These criminal groups are using increasingly sophisticated technology to conduct conspiracy consisting of five parts: One, gaining unauthorized access to computer systems carrying valuable protected information; two, deploying specialized malware to capture and exfiltrate this data; three, distributing or selling this sensitive data to the criminal associates; four, engaging in sophisticated and distributed frauds using the sensitive information obtained; and five, laundering the proceeds of this illicit activity.

All five of these activities are criminal violations in and of themselves. And when conducted by sophisticated transnational networks of cyber criminals, this scheme has yielded hundreds of millions of dollars in illicit proceeds.

The Secret Service is committed to protecting our Nation from this threat. We disrupt every step of their five-part criminal scheme through proactive criminal investigations and defeat these transnational cyber criminals through coordinated arrests and seizure of assets.

Foundational to these efforts are our private industry partners as well as our close partnerships with State, local, federal, and international law enforcement. As a result of these partnerships, we were able to prevent many cyber crimes by sharing criminal intelligence regarding the plans of cyber criminals and minimizing financial losses by stopping their criminal scheme.

Through our Department's National Cybersecurity and Communications Integration Center, the NCCIC, the Secret Service also quickly shares technical cybersecurity information while protecting civil rights and civil liberties in order to allow organizations to reduce their cyber risks by mitigating technical vulnerabilities. We also partner with the private sector and academia to research cyber threats and publish information on cyber crime trends through reports like the *Carnegie Mellon CERT Insider Threat Study*, the *Verizon Data Breach Investigations Report*, and the *Trustwave Global Security Report*.

The Secret Service has a long history of protecting the Nation's financial system from threats. In 1865, the threat we were founded to address was that of counterfeit currency. As our financial payments system has evolved from paper to plastic, now digital information, so too has the investigative mission. The Secret Service is committed to protecting our Nation's financial system even as criminals increasingly exploit it through cyberspace.

Through the dedicated efforts of the Electronic Crimes Task Forces and by working in close partnership with the Department of Justice, in particular the Criminal Division and local U.S. Attorney's Offices, the Secret Service will continue to bring cyber criminals that perpetrate major data breaches to justice.

Thank you for the opportunity to testify on this important topic, and we look forward to your questions.

[The prepared statement of Mr. Noonan appears as a submission for the record.]

Senator FRANKEN. Thank you, Mr. Noonan.

Ms. Raman.

STATEMENT OF MYTHILI RAMAN, ACTING ASSISTANT ATTORNEY GENERAL, CRIMINAL DIVISION, UNITED STATES DEPARTMENT OF JUSTICE, WASHINGTON, DC

Ms. RAMAN. Good afternoon, Mr. Chairman and Members of the Committee. Thank you for the opportunity to appear before the Committee today to discuss the Department of Justice's fight against cyber crime.

Cyber crime has increased dramatically over the last decade, and our financial infrastructure has suffered repeated cyber intrusions.

The recent reports about the massive data breaches at Target, which the Justice Department is investigating alongside the Secret Service, have underscored that cyber crime is a real, present threat and one that is growing. Cyber criminals create botnets to systematically steal the personal and financial information of Americans, they carry out Distributed Denial of Service attacks on networks, and they steal sensitive corporate and military data.

The Justice Department is vigorously responding to this threat through the work of the Criminal Division's Computer Crime and Intellectual Property Section, or CCIPS, which partners with U.S. Attorney's Offices across the country as part of a network of almost 300 Justice Department cyber crime prosecutors.

In addition, the FBI has made combating cyber threats one of its top priorities, working through cyber task forces in its 56 field offices, and continuing to strengthen the National Cyber Investigative Joint Task Force. Every day our prosecutors and agents strive to hold to account cyber criminals who victimize Americans using all the tools available to us to identify these criminals wherever in the world they are located, break up their networks, and bring them to justice.

We are developing meaningful partnerships with foreign law enforcement and with industry to strengthen our collective capacity to fight and protect against cyber crime. And we use our tools responsibly and consistent with the important long-established legal safeguards that protect against abuse.

As just one example of our work in this area, just last week CCIPS, the U.S. Attorney's Office in Atlanta, and the FBI announced the guilty plea of a Russian citizen named Aleksandr Panin, who admitted to developing and distributing sophisticated malware called ''SpyEye.'' The SpyEye malware created botnets, or networks of secretly hacked computers, by surreptitiously infecting victims' computers, enabling cyber criminals to remotely control the computers through command and control servers. In that way, the criminals were able to steal personal and financial information such as credit card information, banking credentials, user names, and passwords. Panin offered and sold this botnet software, including specially tailormade versions of the malware, to at least 154 of his criminal clients, who in turn used it to infect an estimated 1.4 million computers around the world. Panin will be sentenced in April.

The Panin case is only the latest of our recent successes against cyber criminals. Others include, for example, a 15-year sentence handed down in September to a Romanian cyber criminal who led a multimillion-dollar scheme to hack into U.S. merchants' payment card data; an 88-month sentence handed down last April to a Russian hacker who used online forums to sell stolen credit and debit card information to purchasers around the world; and the indictment last year of a China-based manufacturer of wind turbines, which is alleged to have stolen trade secrets from an American company, causing over $800 million in losses.

But without the tools that we have been provided, we would not be able to bring such offenders to justice, and we must ensure that the statutes we enforce keep up with technology so that we can keep pace with the cyber criminals who are constantly developing new tactics and methods.

The Administration is proposing several statutory provisions to keep federal criminal laws up to date.

First, we recommend the establishment of a strong, uniform federal standard requiring certain types of businesses to report data breaches. Businesses should be required to provide prompt notice to consumers in the wake of a breach and to notify the Federal Government of breaches so that law enforcement can pursue and catch the perpetrators.

Our prosecutors also rely on substantive criminal statutes to bring cyber criminals to justice. One of the most important of these is the *Computer Fraud and Abuse Act*, also known as the CFAA. The Administration proposed several revisions to the CFAA in May 2011, and we continue to support changes like those to keep federal criminal law up to date. We also look forward to working with Congress to address the CFAA's application to insiders, such as bank employees or government employees, who access computers in violation of their authorization and then steal or misuse the information contained in the computers.

Finally, we recommend several statutory amendments, including a proposal to address the proliferation of botnets, which are described at greater length in my written testimony.

I very much appreciate the opportunity to discuss the Justice Department's efforts to protect American citizens by aggressively investigating and prosecuting hackers. We are committed to using the full range of investigative tools and laws available to us to fight these crimes and to do so vigorously and responsibly.

Thank you for the opportunity to discuss the Department's work, and I look forward to answering your questions.

[The prepared statement of Ms. Raman appears as a submission to the record.]

Senator FRANKEN. Thank you all.

I think we will go to Senator Klobuchar. Since I am chairing this, I will be here to the end, so I can ask my questions at the end. Senator.

Senator KLOBUCHAR. Okay. Very good. Thank you very much. Thank you all for coming today.

I think while we all know why we are here with the breaches that we have seen and we just heard about with the last panel at Target, Neiman Marcus, and Michaels, now hotel chains, are there any other similar breaches that have occurred? Do you see industries that are more targeted than others? And, Ms. Ramirez, how successful has your agency been in getting criminal hackers extradited from foreign countries? And what challenges do you see when dealing with extradition issues?

Ms. RAMIREZ. Let me start by answering your initial question. I cannot speak about any particular companies or breaches. We cannot disclose information relating to non-public investigations. But what I can tell you is that the FTC has been very active in this area, having just announced last week our 50th data security case.

We believe that the FTC's action has had an important and sent an important signal to the marketplace, but based on the information that we have available to us, including the *Verizon Data Breach Report*, which Mr. Noonan referenced in his opening remarks, by those indications it is clear that companies need to do a lot more, that they continue to make very basic mistakes when it comes to data security, so this is an area where the Federal Trade Commission unanimously believes there needs to be congressional action and, in particular, a strong federal law that imposes robust standards for data security and also for breach notification.

Senator KLOBUCHAR. So this is what we have been talking about earlier with the NIST standards and then taking this out with the chip and PIN and those kinds of things. Is that what you are talking about?

Ms. RAMIREZ. At the FTC we do not advocate for particular technologies. We rather take a process-based approach in light of the fact that the threats, as were identified in the prior panel, are constantly changing and evolving. So we recommend a process-based approach to attacking this problem.

Senator KLOBUCHAR. Okay. The extradition question, the reason I asked that is I think we already have learned that a young Russian already claimed to be co-author of the malware used in the attack with Target, and I think we know there is no shortage of these crimes internationally. I wonder if the U.S. should be asking that.

Ms. RAMIREZ. I will defer on that question to my colleagues and the criminal authorities who are dealing with those issues.

Senator KLOBUCHAR. Okay.

Ms. RAMAN. You point out one of our extraordinary challenges in cyber crime cases, and that is that some of the most notorious hackers are living halfway across the world, and sometimes in countries with which we do not have extradition relationships. And so that is a challenge that we have in a number of these cases. We try to be as creative as we can to ensure that we are able to catch the wrongdoers, and we have had significant success. The Panin case that I just mentioned in my opening statement is an example of a success, a Russian hacker who had developed the SpyEye malware, and he pleaded guilty just last week. And we have had numerous such successes. Sometimes it just takes patience.

Senator KLOBUCHAR. OkayK. Mr. Noonan.

Mr. NOONAN. Yes, ma'am, the Secret Service has had a unique success in this field. We have been able to arrest and extradite a number of significant cyber criminals abroad with the help of the Department of Justice, the Office of International Affairs, and the State Department. Just to name a few, the Dave and Buster's intrusion happened in 2007, we were successful in arresting Maksym Yastremskiy, and in that intrusion we also actually arrested and extradited Aleksandr Suvorov. In the Carder.su case that we had in 2007, we were successful in extraditing Sergei Litvinenko. There are a number of other successes that we have had of high-value targets, of high-value hackers that have been attacking our financial infrastructure that, with the assistance of international law enforcement and relationships, we have been able to arrest those people and bring them to justice here domestically.

Senator KLOBUCHAR. You know, one of the things we talked about earlier was the time between the companies confirming the breaches and then letting customers know and how quickly they can find out what their policies are. And I assume, Ms. Ramirez, that you would want that to happen as soon as possible. But one of the questions I want to know, having been in this law enforcement before, there is also this thing where you want to catch people. And I would think when a data breach is this big, you come down on the side of letting the public know immediately. But how do you strike that balance with putting information out there but then also trying to find the perpetrators and not tipping them off? Anyone can answer.

Ms. RAMIREZ. Let me, if I may, start off the discussion on this point. "Balancing" is exactly the right word. In our view, a company should notify affected consumers as reasonably practicable as possible. In other words, there should be enough time for the company to assess the relevant breach, examine exactly what took place, which customers were affected. But we think that it is important that customers be notified reasonably promptly, and we believe that the outside limit for that ought to be 60 days.

At the same time, I will also note that when the FTC is looking at these issues, we do coordinate very closely with colleagues at the Department of Justice and Secret Service and also at the FBI. And so if there is a need for there to be certain delay due to the needs of these criminal investigations, we think that that is also appropriate.

Senator KLOBUCHAR. Okay.

Mr. NOONAN. Yes, ma'am, it is a coordinated effort actually between the Secret Service, our law enforcement, and the U.S. Attorney's Office as well. But it is very important for us in a timely manner to take what we know from an investigation as far as the cybersecurity pieces of that, and then to get that and share it out to greater infrastructure. We use the Department of Homeland Security's NCCIC, which is the National Cybersecurity Communications and Integration Center. We take information that we learn from the malware and hacking tools and such. We share that with the NCCIC, who then does some reverse engineering, and they are able to push that out to the greater infrastructure.

We also partner through our Electronic Crimes Task Forces—we have 33 of those—in which we are able to take that same type of information and put it out to our trusted partners that are out in the community, out in the infrastructure, as well and we also partner with various ISACs. Specifically in the lane of financial services, we partner with the FS-ISAC to get that information out to the industry, to be able to assist them in finding and mitigating what other attacks may be happen to themselves.

Senator KLOBUCHAR. Okay.

Ms. RAMAN. Going back to your original question, we do believe that the Administration's data breach notification proposal allows the flexibility that would allow us to delay consumer notification in small increments if there is a law enforcement reason for that. There may be an undercover operation that is necessary or other covert investigative steps that can be taken immediately after a breach, and there may be certain circumstances where delayed notification is appropriate.

But that being said, we do believe that prompt notification to consumers is important and prompt notification to law enforcement is important.

Senator KLOBUCHAR. Thank you very much.

Senator FRANKEN. Thank you, Senator Klobuchar.

Senator Whitehouse.

Senator WHITEHOUSE. Thank you again, Chairman.

Let me address myself briefly to the two law enforcement witnesses who we have here. The theft of intellectual property from American corporations purely across cyber networks by hacking into corporate networks and exfiltrating their data has been described on multiple occasions as "the greatest illicit transfer of wealth in history." Has any indictment yet resulted from that conduct, foreign hackers purely through cyber networks hacking into an American corporation's intellectual property and exfiltrating it for competitive purposes?

Ms. RAMAN. Well, I will say, Senator, that the threat that you described is one that we are very aware of and we are focused on. Last year, there was an——

Senator WHITEHOUSE. Has there been an indictment of anyone in such a case?

Ms. RAMAN. Last year, in a similar case, there was an indictment of Sinovel Corporation and about five of its executives—that is a Chinese corporation and five of its executives—for stealing the proprietary information of an American company.

Senator WHITEHOUSE. How had they stolen it?

Ms. RAMAN. I am sorry?

Senator WHITEHOUSE. How had they stolen it? Was it through a cyber hack? Or did it involve human——

Ms. RAMAN. A combination, but also an insider at the American company.

Senator WHITEHOUSE. Yes.

Ms. RAMAN. But I think that kind of case, where it would show that we are willing to indict a Chinese company and Chinese nationals, including the insider here, shows our resolve to get to the bottom of these issues.

Senator WHITEHOUSE. Actually the numbers involved show anything but resolve, and I hope that there will be more attention paid to this. And I say this with full appreciation of how very, very challenging and difficult these cases are, from a forensic point of view, from locating the foreign defendant point of view, from an interference with intelligence and diplomatic relations point of view, from a security point of view. I mean, there is a whole array of reasons that these are immensely difficult and complicated cases. But when we are on the losing end of what has been on multiple occasions described as ''the greatest illicit transfer of wealth in history,'' I think one case that actually was not that, because it involved a human exchange as well, just is not an adequate response. So I urge you guys to improve your game on that, and if you are getting pushback from the intelligence communities and from the State Department and other people, push back harder, because I think an indictment has a clarifying effect.

The other thing that has come up recently has been that Chairwoman Mikulski of the Appropriations Committee, who is also the Chairman in charge of your appropriations at the Subcommittee level, has put into the omnibus spending bill that we just passed a requirement that the Department of Justice provide a multiyear strategic plan for cyber within 120 days. That is not a long window. It is going to require the DOJ, the FBI, the Secret Service, probably folks within FEMA and Homeland Security, and certainly OMB, without whom no budget-related discussion is possible, to get together and start to figure out what we look like three, four, five years out, 10 years out, in terms of the structure.

We have the FBI deeply involved in this, and we have the Secret Service deeply involved in this. We have two different sections of the Department of Justice separately involved in this. The different programs that we enforce and the different strategies seem to be changing every six months or so as I have pursued this. I think a lot of that is necessary and reflects a sensible and good adaptation to an emerging threat.

But I think that we are a long way from having a clear sense of what our cyber law enforcement structure should look like. We are still, I think, evolving, and it has been hard for me to find any place in which the thinking about what it should look like three or four or five years out is taking place.

So could you give me a moment on what you are doing right now to respond to the 120-day requirement for a multiyear strategic plan?

Ms. RAMAN. Well, we are very aware, Senator Whitehouse, of the 120-day requirement, and thankfully, even before that requirement was put into place, we had been endeavoring for several months to go through the exercise of putting on paper a strategy for the Justice Department's cyber program. That involves some of the issues that you have already touched on, which is how we integrate all of our various capabilities.

I think that the way that the responsibilities are divided now, which is the Criminal Division, the National Security Division, and the FBI, works well together, and the reason that we are able to work well together is that we communicate literally on a daily basis, sometimes an hourly basis, about how to respond to particular threats.

But, together, I am certain that we will be able to comply with the 120-day requirement. We have been working on it, and we will continue to work to meet that deadline.

Senator WHITEHOUSE. Good. Well, I am very glad that you work well together. I would hazard the thought that working well together and having the proper administrative structure are two different questions. And I would offer as an example the challenge of trying to get the civil botnet takedown capability, which the Department has demonstrated on several occasions, properly integrated into the criminal and national security and intelligence elements of this. I think it is a bigger challenge than just having people work well together.

Ms. RAMAN. I agree with you, Senator. On the botnet capabilities that we used in the Coreflood takedown, that was civil authority, but the Criminal Division, along with the U.S. Attorney's Office in Connecticut, used those civil authorities, and we were able to do so because of the specific way that botnet was structured. But botnets are high on our list of priorities. We know that every botnet is different, and we know that behind every botnet is an individual or individuals. And so we are focused both on getting those individuals and finding ways, creative ways, to dismantle botnets.

Senator WHITEHOUSE. Good. My concern was that it is my understanding that after the Coreflood botnet takedown, the group, the kind of ad hoc group from different organizations and the U.S. Attorney's Office and Main Justice that had gotten together to accomplish the Coreflood botnet more or less disintegrated back into their original positions, and that there is not a robust and integrated ongoing administrative structure for integrating those botnet takedowns. They seem to be more episodic and to grab people from out of the Department for that one event, and then they got a big award from the Attorney General—which they merited. I was delighted that that happened. But then I think the structure of it evaporated or disintegrated.

So the structure question, I think, is one we can continue to work on. Thank you.

Senator FRANKEN. Thank you, Senator Whitehouse, for your continued focus on cybersecurity.

I have a question for either Mr. Noonan or Ms. Raman. Can you walk me through how a criminal could go about harvesting the data on a magnetic stripe card and how they go about using and selling that data once it is stolen?

Mr. NOONAN. Yes, sir. If we are talking about the intrusions that we are here today to discuss, it is generally—it is not one criminal we are talking about. We are talking about a sophisticated network of cyber criminals. I use the analogy sometimes the movie "Ocean's Eleven." This is an organization that has specific skills when brought together, so they will have their person that is looking for access in the systems. They will have their people that are controlling the bulletproof hosting system. They will have people that are working on extracting the information from the network. They will have wholesalers and vendors of that data. And then ultimately there will be end users that take the data, use it on a street level through either making counterfeit credit cards and going into retail stores, buying goods and fencing that. And then there is a money-laundering system as well in this.

I think it is also important to understand that we are not talking about currencies here. We are talking about virtual currencies in which a lot of this money is moved, so in the criminal underground, they are moving their money back and forth through virtual currency, which is hard for U.S. law enforcement and for others in the government to be able to trace and track those finances.

Ms. RAMAN. I agree with that description. I think the additional element I would add is that oftentimes after there is this kind of harvesting of personal information through the use of malware, often through botnets, the stolen information is then sold in carding sites around the world and to other criminals who may use it for their own financial profit, sometimes for other purposes. And so that is also another chain in the threats that we are seeing.

Senator FRANKEN. It sounds like there is real justification for putting the RICO piece in Chairman Leahy's bill, that this is coordinated organized crime.

Right now the information on most cards in the United States is static. It stays the same until the card is canceled. What does that mean for criminals wanting to make counterfeit cards? It will make it easier and more effective.

Mr. NOONAN. Sure, so your question is that it is static data that is coming across?

Senator FRANKEN. Yes.

Mr. NOONAN. Right. You have got to understand that the magstripe data is roughly 30-year-old technology, so I would agree with the fact that a 30-year-old technology is perhaps a little bit more easy for them to utilize and put on to readily available magnetic cards or magnetic stripe cards that are available in industry today.

Senator FRANKEN. We have been talking today about going to the EMV technology and going to the EMV with a PIN. Do you all agree here that that would be extremely helpful?

Mr. NOONAN. We believe that anything that would assist in the security of our Nation's payment systems would be a benefit to the industry, of course.

Senator FRANKEN. Okay. Thank you.

Chairwoman Ramirez, when a company has really poor digital security practices, the FTC can initiate an enforcement action against the company for committing what is called an "unfair trade practice," and the Commission has used this authority admirably in the past. At the same time, there is no comprehensive federal law that sets up a data security standard for companies that store data, the data of tens of thousands of customers.

Do you think that the Commission's existing authority in this space precludes the need for a federal data security and data breach law?

Ms. RAMIREZ. No, I do not. We have used our authority under Section 5 of the FTC Act barring deceptive or unfair commercial practices, and we think we have used that authority effectively. But I think we could be even more effective in this area if there were a federal data security law that the FTC could enforce. And, in particular, we think there are three areas where we could use additional authority. We would like to see legislation that would give the FTC civil penalty authority. We think this would enable us to deter more effectively. We also believe that we need jurisdiction over nonprofits. We have found that a number of breaches occur at nonprofits, and currently we lack authority over nonprofits, so that is a gap that we would like to see filled. And, in addition, in order to implement a data security law effectively, we believe that it would be appropriate to give the FTC APA rule-making authority to enable us to deal with the evolving risks and harms that one sees in this area.

Senator FRANKEN. Well, thank you. This is why it is so important that we get to data privacy legislation. I look forward to doing that.

I want to ask one—and then I see Senator Blumenthal has arrived, is back. This is a little unrelated, but it is something I have been interested in. Ms. Raman, in your written testimony you said that the Department could use better tools to go after the operators of cell phone spy software. This software is a huge problem. Every year tens of thousands of women are stalked through the use of what are called "stalking apps." These are apps specifically designed to facilitate stalking. An abuser will install one of these apps on a victim's phone and be able to track her whereabouts at all times. We have received testimony, my Subcommittee, on this time and again.

These apps can be found within minutes through a Web search. One is called "FlexiSPY." It brags, "FlexiSPY gives you total control over your partner's phone without them knowing it. See exactly where they are, or were at any given date in time. Buy now and start spying on a cell phone in minutes."

Another is called "SpyEra." It says, "The target user is never interrupted from what they're doing and won't notice a thing … . You'll not only know what is being said and done, but you'll also know exactly when and where."

I have a privacy bill specifically aimed at shutting these apps down, and so I want to work with you to give you all the tools that we need to do that. So can you and I work together on this?

Ms. RAMAN. Absolutely. We appreciate any support that you can give us in this area. As you describe, it is an incredibly frightening capability. We are focused on the criminal threat, but one of the tools that we think could be helpful in our fight against this kind of software is civil authority to forfeit proceeds of the crime, and we would be happy to speak further with you and your staff about those particulars.

Senator FRANKEN. Thank you.

Senator Blumenthal.

Senator BLUMENTHAL. Thank you, Senator Franken.

Thank you all for your great work in this area, and thank you, Chairman Ramirez, for your focus and your interest in additional authority, which I agree is important. I think the FTC has broad authority now to impose some rules and take some enforcement action when there has been a failure to impose sufficiently stringent safeguards to protect consumer information, but certainly clarifying that authority and expanding it in the ways you have suggested makes a lot of sense. And, in fact, I have just introduced a bill that would provide for rulemaking authority, but also stiff penalties, and possibly even stringent penalties if the Congress would go along with them, because I think that the potential damage to consumers is so horrific from identity theft and associated wrongs that emanate from these hacking and abusive activities.

It also provides for mandatory notification, a clearinghouse, and, in my view, very importantly, a private right of action as well as jurisdiction for Attorneys General to enforce these rules.

What do you think about a private right of action and the authority of Attorneys General to impose these rules?

Ms. RAMIREZ. The Commission has not taken a position on the issue of a private right of action, but as regards concurrent State enforcement, we believe that that is absolutely critical. The States have done very important work in this arena, and we think it is vital for them to continue to be involved.

Senator BLUMENTHAL. What has been the reaction of nonprofits? Have they been ahead of the for-profit sector or behind?

Ms. RAMIREZ. Well, I think we see problems amongst all companies, including nonprofits, and that is an area where we currently lack jurisdiction, and we think it is a gap that needs to be rectified so that we do have jurisdiction. But as I mentioned earlier, the data that we have available today—and I specifically referenced the Verizon Data Breach Investigation Report that is issued annually. It continues to indicate that companies need to do a lot more in this area, that very fundamental mistakes are being made when it comes to data security. And so that signals to me that action, further action, needs to be taken. And, of course, this is a very complex problem, multifaceted problem that requires a multifaceted solution.

Senator BLUMENTHAL. Am I right in thinking that the United States is behind a lot of the rest of the world in its data security safeguards? We heard testimony earlier about the lack of use of chip-and-PIN methodologies, which is now prevalent in Europe, and maybe the lack of use of it here is a reason not only for the Neiman Marcus and Target breaches, but also for the fact that almost half the world's credit card fraud occurs here but only a quarter of credit card use. So there seems a disparity that indicates we are behind the rest of the world.

Ms. RAMIREZ. Let me say that while at the FTC we do not prescribe or recommend particular technologies, it is of concern to me that our payment card systems really do need improvement. So in my view, more work can be done in that area. It is absolutely critical from my perspective that payment card systems be secure and protect consumer information, and I really think it is important that all of the players in the ecosystem—retailers, banks, payment card networks—all work together to find solutions.

Senator BLUMENTHAL. Any of the other witnesses have perspectives on these questions?

Mr. NOONAN. Yes, sir, I have a perspective in the fact that you can come up with devices that will secure credit card data, but it does not alleviate the fact that we are talking about it is still criminals that are doing it. These criminals are motivated by money. They are financially motivated. They are going to use whatever they have at their disposal to still go after the pot of gold which is held in the payment card systems piece.

So it does not take away the criminal element, but it does add a layer, potentially could add a layer of security. So I just wanted to make the point that, again, when we are talking about the criminal element, it is law enforcement and the work that is being done between the Department of Justice and law enforcement that is going at the criminal to try to take them and put them behind bars, taking the virtual world and making it reality with handcuffs, if you will.

Ms. RAMAN. I agree that securing data is obviously incredibly important for all American consumers. From a law enforcement point of view, anything that strengthens our ability to secure that data is a good thing. It makes our—frankly, it makes us less necessary if there are fewer breaches and if there are fewer attempts to try to get at sensitive data. But that having been said, Mr. Noonan is absolutely right. Malware adapts every day. Botnets adapt every day. Criminals are early adopters of almost every kind of technology, and our challenge is to stay ahead of them.

Senator BLUMENTHAL. Well, there is an arms race. There always has been, not only in this area but in so many others. Having done a bit of law enforcement work myself, both federal and State, I am well aware that there will never be the foolproof safeguard or the impenetrable lock on the door. But if you leave the door completely unlocked, it is almost an invitation to the bad guys. And I do not want to say we have left the door unlocked in the retail industry, but certainly the locks are a lot less sophisticated than the technology available would provide. And you may not have been here earlier, but I think that the industry—or maybe I should say industries—have some real soul searching to do about whether they have been sufficiently protective of consumer information, because as we know, you can apprehend, investigate, prosecute criminals, but rarely does that compensate them when they are victims of identity theft. And that is just the stark, tragic fact of the matter, that preventing these crimes is often the only way to really protect consumers, because you can prosecute them, if you can apprehend them and investigate them. We are talking about global criminal activity here. But the victims of identity theft are often really marred and scarred for life.

So, you know, I respect your point of view, but I do think that stronger preventive action that would come with rulemaking authority, stiffer penalties on the retailers which provides an incentive to do the right thing I think are very much needed.

Thank you all. Thank you, Mr. Chairman.

Senator FRANKEN. Thank you, and thank you all. I think following up on what Senator Blumenthal just said, today's hearing has made it clear that we are dealing with a systemic data security problem in this country, and we received testimony in the first panel that our credit and debit cards just are not secure enough, and we have no federal standard for data security and breach notification. We have to update our card technology and our laws to address these 21st century threats to our data security. When millions of American consumers have their data breached, we really cannot afford not to.

That is why I have been pressing credit and debit card companies on their plans to enhance card security through improvements like smart chip technology and chip and PIN, and that is why I was proud to join Chairman Leahy on his *Data Privacy and Security Act*. I think it is just common sense that the consumers should be told when their data has been stolen and that we do everything we can to secure it before that happens.

I want to thank the witnesses for their testimony today. You have helped us understand not only how these breaches occurred but how we can move forward from this point to better protect consumers and better enforce our laws.

The record will be held open until February 11th for questions and any further materials. You are now dismissed, and this hearing is adjourned.

[Whereupon, at 1:07 p.m., the Committee was adjourned.]

A P P E N D I X

UPDATED Witness List

Hearing before the
Senate Committee on the Judiciary

On

"Privacy in the Digital Age: Preventing Data Breaches and Combating Cybercrime"

Tuesday, February 4, 2014
Dirksen Senate Office Building, Room 226
10:15 a.m.

Panel I

Delara Derakhshani
Policy Counsel
Consumers Union
Washington, DC

Michael R. Kingston
Senior Vice President and Chief Information Officer
The Neiman Marcus Group
Dallas, TX

John J. Mulligan
Executive Vice President and Chief Financial Officer
Target Corporation
Minneapolis, MN

Fran Rosch
Senior Vice President
Security Product and Services, Endpoint and Mobility
Symantec Corporation
Mountain View, CA

Panel II

The Honorable Edith Ramirez
Chairwoman
Federal Trade Commission
Washington, DC

William Noonan
Deputy Special Agent in Charge

Criminal Investigative Division, United States Secret Service
Washington, DC

Mythili Raman
Acting Assistant Attorney General
Criminal Division, United States Department of Justice
Washington, DC

**Statement Of Senator Patrick Leahy (D-Vt.),
Chairman, Senate Judiciary Committee
Hearing on "Privacy in the Digital Age:
Preventing Data Breaches and Combating Cybercrime"
February 4, 2014**

Today, the Judiciary Committee meets to examine how we can protect Americans from the growing dangers of data breaches and cybercrime in the digital age. Safeguarding American consumers and businesses from data breaches and cybercrime has been a priority of this Committee since 2005. For years, I have worked closely with Members on both sides of the aisle to advance meaningful data privacy legislation. I thank Senator Grassley for working closely with me on this hearing. I hope we can continue working together to advance the Personal Data Privacy and Security Act that I recently reintroduced to protect American consumers.

Like many Americans, I am alarmed by the recent data breaches at Target, Neiman Marcus, and Michaels Stores. The investigations into those cyberattacks are ongoing. Yet, it is already clear that these attacks have compromised the privacy and security of millions of American consumers — potentially putting one in three Americans at risk of identity theft and other cybercrimes.

Public confidence is crucial to our economy. If consumers lose faith in business' ability to protect their personal information, our economic recovery will falter. Unfortunately, in the digital age, major data breaches involving our private information are not uncommon. The threat and dangers of data breaches are also not unique to the retail industry. There have been significant data breaches involving Sony, Epsilon, and Coca-Cola, as well as Federal government agencies, such as the Departments of Veterans Affairs and Energy. In the past few days, we have also learned of data breaches at Yahoo! and White Lodging, the hotel management company for national hotel chains such as Marriott and Starwood.

According to the Privacy Rights Clearinghouse, more than 662 million records have been involved in data breaches since 2005. A 2013 Verizon report also found that there were more than 600 publicly disclosed data breaches just last year.

No one would dispute that businesses need to thoroughly assess the damage when a cyberattack is discovered. But time is of the essence for law enforcement seeking to catch the perpetrators, and also for consumers who want to protect themselves against further exposure. American consumers deserve to know when their private information has been compromised and what a business is doing in response to a cyberattack.

We should remember that the businesses that suffer cyberattacks are also often the victims of a cybercrime. A recent study sponsored by Symantec found that data breaches involving malicious cyberattacks are the most costly data breaches around the globe. The per capita cost of such cyberattacks in the United States was $277 per compromised record in 2013 — the highest cost for any nation surveyed, according to the report. This high cost is especially alarming in the midst of the fragile economic recovery.

Before the Judiciary Committee today are representatives of Target and Neiman Marcus, as well as Consumers Union and Symantec. Later, we will also hear from the United States Secret Service, the Department of Justice, and the Federal Trade Commission, who are here to provide insight into how our government is protecting American consumers and businesses from the growing threats of data breaches and cybercrime.

In the digital age, Americans face threats to their privacy and security unlike any time before in Nation's our history. I hope that all Members of the Committee will join me in responding to this urgent problem by supporting my data privacy legislation. I thank all of our witnesses for being with us today.

# # # # #

PREPARED STATEMENT OF RANKING MEMBER CHUCK GRASSLEY

**Statement of Ranking Member Grassley of Iowa
Senate Committee on the Judiciary Hearing,
"Privacy in the Digital Age: Preventing Data Breaches and Combating Cybercrime"
Tuesday, February 4, 2014.**

Mr. Chairman, thank you for holding today's hearing to examine the well-publicized recent commercial data breaches. We're still learning all the details, but it's clear these and other breaches have potentially impacted millions of consumers nationwide.

Today we have the opportunity to learn about the challenges that both industry and law enforcement face in combatting cyber-attacks from well organized criminals. The witnesses have a unique ability to provide us various important perspectives as we consider the government's role in securing sensitive data and crafting a breach notification standard.

I hope to learn where the Committee's expertise could be helpful in combatting future attacks. Furthermore, I'd like to use this hearing to explore areas of common ground, so we can determine what might be accomplished quickly.

In most cases, thankfully, businesses are able to prevent the relentless attacks against their networks. This is due to comprehensive security programs coupled with law enforcement's diligent work. However, the data breaches at Target and Neiman Marcus demonstrate that even companies with vast resources can suffer serious attacks with the potential to harm their customers.

One defensive tool that's been discussed is updating payment card technology. Retailers and card issuers are preparing to transition away from decades-old technology. This is a positive step in the right direction. However, it's a bit troubling that it's taken so long to implement this technology. Many fraudulent transactions might have been prevented had this occurred already. But this alone won't provide complete security, as I'm sure we'll hear today.

Criminal hackers aren't quitters. They continue to find ways to break into company networks. As the Federal Bureau of Investigation has warned, attacks like those recently suffered will continue. So companies must be vigilant in defending their systems, as well as in taking steps after an attack to warn customers and limit the damage.

Unfortunately, it may be days, weeks, or months before a business realizes it's been attacked. And if a hacker can breach a large business's security system, then it's obvious that smaller businesses are threatened as well. It's important we remain mindful of the differences in businesses and the resources they have available as we go forward.

It's been a couple of years since the committee last considered data security legislation. In that time, we've learned a lot about this subject thanks to the broader cybersecurity conversation. The proposals offered by the Administration and Congress, along with other government initiatives, can be helpful for us as we consider how to proceed on legislation.

Currently, there are at least four pieces of data security and breach notification legislation in the Senate, with possibly more to come as other committees begin their work. While these bills would establish national security standards, they take different approaches. This offers us the chance to examine the effects of each, which is a good thing.

In the past, I've expressed concern with approaches that don't provide businesses the flexibility they need to secure their data. We must avoid creating a one-size-fits-all security requirement, particularly if it fails to account for businesses of different sizes and resources. An inflexible approach could lead to businesses focusing on merely completing a checklist of requirements in order to avoid liability, instead of doing what makes sense to secure customer information in their particular circumstances.

On this point, I hope to learn how the government can better partner with the private sector and law enforcement to strengthen data security. The government has a strong interest to work together with industry, given the impact cyber-attacks have on the Nation's economy.

Fostering a greater public-private approach to cybersecurity was recognized in last year's Executive Order from the President on Improving Critical Infrastructure Cybersecurity. The Executive Order stated that strengthening cybersecurity can be achieved through government partnership with private business.

As a result of the Executive Order, we should review the National Institute of Standards and Technology ongoing partnership with owners of critical infrastructure. This partnership will create standards, guidelines, and best practices for businesses to implement on a voluntary basis.

There's already bipartisan support for this approach. Senators Rockefeller and Thune have introduced a bill to enshrine the National Institute of Standards and Technology role in creating a cybersecurity framework. This is just one model for government action focused on securing critical infrastructure. It's worth considering how this approach might work in this particular context.

The recent breaches also draw attention to the need for a uniform, federal notification standard. There's been little suggestion that the public failed to receive news about these recent breaches. However, we once again see the difficulties faced with a patchwork of state laws. Companies must ensure compliance, while also investigating ongoing threats.

I've supported creating a federal notification standard to replace the laws in 46 states and the District of Columbia. It makes sense. If done correctly, it would ease compliance costs for businesses, particularly since the current laws are ever changing. A federal standard would also ensure consumers are notified of breaches that could result in financial harm or identity theft.

But if the standard for notification is crafted too broadly or the penalties for failure to notify are too harsh, there's a risk for consumer over-notification. Businesses may choose to issue notice of even trivial breaches. Just as there's a potential for harm when a victim is not notified of a breach, over-notification can lead to harm or apathy.

Further, a notification law must recognize the resources available to different businesses. While companies like those before us today were quickly able to comply with existing law, many smaller businesses would face a more difficult experience.

There's widespread support for a national breach notification standard. As a result, we should ask whether it's appropriate to separate this issue from other aspects of the ongoing data security debate. This might provide the chance to take action quickly, as we continue work on other issues.

Thank you again, Mr. Chairman. I look forward to exploring these issues and working with you and others.

PREPARED STATEMENT OF JOHN MULLIGAN

WRITTEN TESTIMONY

BEFORE THE

SENATE COMMITTEE ON THE JUDICIARY

HEARING ON

PRIVACY IN THE DIGITAL AGE:

PREVENTING DATA BREACHES AND COMBATING CYBERCRIME

FEBRUARY 4, 2014

TESTIMONY OF

JOHN MULLIGAN

EXECUTIVE VICE PRESIDENT AND CHIEF FINANCIAL OFFICER

TARGET

I. Introduction

Good morning Chairman Leahy, Ranking Member Grassley, and Members of the Committee. My name is John Mulligan and I am the Executive Vice President and Chief Financial Officer of Target. I appreciate the opportunity to be here today to discuss important issues surrounding data breaches and cybercrime.

As you know, Target recently experienced a data breach resulting from a criminal attack on our systems. To begin, I want to say how deeply sorry we are for the impact this incident has had on our guests – your constituents. We know this breach has shaken their confidence in Target, and we are determined to work very hard to earn it back.

At Target we take our responsibility to our guests very seriously, and this attack has only strengthened our resolve. We will learn from this incident and as a result, we hope to make Target, and our industry, more secure for consumers in the future.

I'd now like to explain the events of the breach as I currently understand them. Please recognize that I may not be able to provide specifics on certain matters because the criminal and forensic investigations remain active and ongoing. We are working closely with the U.S. Secret Service and the U.S. Department of Justice on the investigation – to help them bring to justice the criminals who perpetrated this wide-scale attack on Target, American business and consumers.

II.   What We Know

On the evening of December 12, we were notified by the Justice Department of suspicious activity involving payment cards used at Target stores. We immediately started our internal investigation.

On December 13, we met with the Justice Department and the Secret Service. On December 14, we hired an independent team of experts to lead a thorough forensic investigation.

On December 15, we confirmed that criminals had infiltrated our system, had installed malware on our point-of-sale network and had potentially stolen guest payment card data. That same day, we removed the malware from virtually all registers in our U.S. stores.

Over the next two days, we began notifying the payment processors and card networks, preparing to publicly notify our guests and equipping our call centers and stores with the necessary information and resources to address the concerns of our guests.

On December 18 we disabled malware on about 25 additional registers which were disconnected from our system when we completed the initial malware removal on December 15. As a result, we determined that fewer than 150 additional guest accounts were affected.

Our actions leading up to our public announcement on December 19 – and since – have been guided by the principle of serving our guests, and we have been moving as quickly as possible to share accurate and actionable information with the public. When we announced the intrusion on December 19 we used multiple forms of communication, including a mass-scale public announcement, email, prominent notices on our website, and social media channels.

What we know today is that the breach affected two types of data: payment card data which affected approximately 40 million guests and certain personal data which affected up to 70 million guests. The theft of the payment card data affected guests who shopped at our U.S. stores from November 27 through December 18. The theft of partial personal data included name, mailing address, phone number or email address.

We now know that the intruder stole a vendor's credentials to access our system and place malware on our point-of-sale registers. The malware was designed to capture payment card data from the magnetic strip of credit and debit cards prior to encryption within our system.

As the forensic investigation continued, we learned that the malware also captured some strongly encrypted PIN data. We publicly shared this information on December 27, reassuring our guests that they would not be responsible for any fraudulent charges that may occur as a result of the breach.

When we subsequently confirmed the theft of partial personal data on January 9, we used various channels of communication to notify our guests on January 10 and provide them with tips to guard against possible scams.

III. Protecting Our Guests

From the outset, our response to the breach has been focused on supporting our guests and strengthening our security. In addition to the immediate actions I already described, we are taking the following concrete actions:

- First, we are undertaking an end-to-end review of our entire network and will make security enhancements, as appropriate.

- Second, we increased fraud detection for our Target REDcard guests. To date, we have not seen any fraud on our Target proprietary credit and debit cards due to this breach. And we have seen only a very low amount of additional fraud on our Target Visa card.

- Third, we are reissuing new Target credit or debit cards immediately to any guest who requests one.

- Fourth, we are offering one year of free credit monitoring and identity theft protection to anyone who has ever shopped at our U.S. Target stores. This protection includes a free credit report, daily credit monitoring, identity theft insurance and unlimited access to personalized assistance from a highly trained fraud resolution agent.

- Fifth, we informed our guests that they have zero liability for any fraudulent charges on their cards arising from this incident. We encouraged them to monitor their accounts and promptly alert either Target or their issuing bank of any suspicious activity.

- Sixth, Target is accelerating our investment in chip technology for our Target REDcards and stores' point-of-sale terminals. We believe that chip-enabled technologies are critical to providing enhanced protection for consumers, which is why we are a founding, and steering committee, member of the EMV Migration Forum at the SmartCard Alliance.

- Seventh, Target initiated the creation of, and is investing $5 million in, a campaign with Better Business Bureau, the National Cyber Security Alliance and the National Cyber-Forensics & Training Alliance to advance public education around cybersecurity and the dangers of consumer scams.

- And, eighth, last week Target helped launch a retail industry Cybersecurity and Data Privacy Initiative that will be focused on informing public dialogue and enhancing practices related to cybersecurity, improved payment security and consumer privacy. Target will be an active leader in this effort.

For many years, Target has invested significant capital and resources in security technology, personnel and processes. We had in place multiple layers of protection, including firewalls, malware detection software, intrusion detection and prevention capabilities and data loss prevention tools. We perform internal and external validation and benchmarking assessments. And, as recently as September 2013, our systems were certified as compliant with the Payment Card Industry Data Security Standards.

But, the unfortunate reality is that we suffered a breach, and all businesses – and their customers -- are facing increasingly sophisticated threats from cyber criminals. In fact, recent news reports have indicated that several other companies have been subjected to similar attacks.

IV. Moving Forward

To prevent this from happening again, none of us can go it alone. We need to work together.

Updating payment card technology and strengthening protections for American consumers is a shared responsibility and requires a collective and coordinated response. On behalf of Target, I am committing that we will be an active part of that solution.

Senators -- to each of you, and to all of your constituents and our guests, I want to say once again how sorry we are that this has happened. We will work with you, the business community, and other thought leaders to find effective solutions to this ongoing and pervasive challenge. Thank you very much for your time today.

PREPARED STATEMENT OF MICHAEL R. KINGSTON

Written Testimony of Michael R. Kingston
Senior Vice President & Chief Information Officer, Neiman Marcus Group

Before the Senate Judiciary Committee
February 4, 2014

Mr. Chairman, Senator Grassley, members of the Committee, I want to thank you for your invitation to appear today to share with you our experiences regarding the recent criminal cybersecurity incident at our company.

For over 20 years, I have held numerous positions in the information technology field, and since April 2012 I have been proud to serve as Chief Information Officer of Neiman Marcus Group. We are in the midst of an ongoing forensic investigation that has revealed a cyber attack using very sophisticated malware. From the moment I learned that there might be a compromise of payment card information at our company, I have personally led the effort, in conjunction with others in senior management, outside consultants, and counsel, to ensure that we were acting swiftly, thoroughly, and responsibly to determine whether such a compromise had occurred, to protect our customers and the security of our systems, and to assist law enforcement in capturing the criminals. Because our investigation is ongoing, I may be limited in my ability to speak definitively or with specificity on some issues, and there may be some questions to which I do not have the answers. Nevertheless, it is important to us as a company to make ourselves available to you to provide whatever information we can, as you attempt to address this important problem that confronts so many corporate and governmental entities around the world.

Introduction

Our company was founded 107 years ago. One of our founding principles is based on delivering exceptional service to our customers and building long lasting relationships with them that have spanned generations. We take this commitment to our customers very seriously. It is part of who we are and what we do daily to distinguish ourselves from other retailers.

We have never before been subjected to any sort of significant cybersecurity intrusion, so we have been particularly disturbed by this incident. It is clear that we are not alone, and that numerous retailers and others in the United States have been recently subjected to sophisticated attacks on their computer systems in an attempt to steal their customers' payment card information. The problem is clearly widespread. And the sophistication of these unprecedented cyber attacks makes the problem very challenging.

Through our ongoing forensic investigation, we have learned that the malware which penetrated our system was exceedingly sophisticated, a conclusion the Secret Service has confirmed with us. The malware was evidently able to capture payment card data in real time right after a card was swiped, and had sophisticated features that made it particularly difficult to detect. These features included some that were specifically customized to evade our multi-layered security architecture that provided strong protection of our systems and customer data. Our security measures included numerous firewalls at the corporate and store level, network segmentation, a customized tokenization tool, numerous encryption methods, an intrusion detection system, a two-factor authentication requirement, and use of industry-standard and centrally-managed enterprise anti-virus software. However, no system – no matter how sophisticated – is completely immune from cyber attack. A recent report prepared by the Secret Service and others in federal law enforcement crystallized the problem when they concluded that comparable RAM scraping malware (perhaps less sophisticated than the one in our case, according to our investigators) had a *zero percent* anti-virus detection rate.

Because of the malware's sophisticated anti-detection devices, we did not learn that we had an actual problem in our computer system until *January 2*, and it was not until *January 6* when the malware and its outputs had been disassembled and decrypted enough that we were able to determine how it operated. Then, disabling it to ensure it was not still operating took until *January 10*. That day we sent out our first notices to customers potentially affected and made widely-reported public statements describing what we knew at that point about the incident.

Simply put, prior to January 2, despite our immediate efforts to have two separate firms of forensic investigators dig into our systems in an attempt to find any data security compromise, no data security compromise in our systems had been identified. A more detailed chronology of the period before January 2 is set out later in my testimony, but specifically:

Tues. Dec.17: We receive a "CPP report" from MasterCard showing 122 payment cards with confirmed fraud use, suggesting that the "common point of purchase" (CPP) _may_ have been one Neiman Marcus store where these cards had been previously used over a several-month period.

Wed. Dec. 18: We call forensic investigative firms in order to start an investigation, consistent with the card brand protocol. A new CPP report is received showing 74 cards.

Fri. Dec. 20: We hire a leading forensic investigative firm to conduct a thorough investigation. They start immediately. A new CPP report is received showing 26 cards.

Mon. Dec. 23: We notify federal law enforcement. They follow up with us shortly thereafter and we have been working with them since then. A new CPP report is received showing 2,185 cards.

Sun. Dec. 29: The forensic investigation has not turned up any evidence of a data compromise, and we decide to bring on a second leading forensic investigative firm to accelerate the investigation and help us determine whether we have a problem.

Wed. Jan. 1: For the first time, the forensic investigators find preliminary indications of malware that may have the capability to "scrape" or capture payment card data. This is confirmed on January 2, but it remains unknown whether the malware was able to function on our systems.

Mon. Jan. 6: After days of highly technical work disassembling, decrypting, and decoding the malware and its output files, the investigators conclude that the malware appeared to have been capturing payment card data at numerous stores. The immediate focus of the Neiman Marcus team turns to containing and disabling the malware as it is unknown whether the malware is still capturing card data.

Fri. Jan. 10: The malware appears to be contained and disabled. Neiman Marcus issues public statements identifying the data security incident and begins sending notices to customers on the CPP reports. Prominent coverage follows. We subsequently send out additional notices on our website and to all customers who shopped in any Neiman Marcus store or website during 2013, whether or not potentially exposed to the malware.

Based on the current state of the evidence in the ongoing investigation: (i) it now appears that the customer information that was potentially exposed to the malware was payment card account information from transactions in 77 of our 85 stores between July and October 2013, at different time periods within this date range in each store; (ii) we have no indication that transactions on our websites or at our restaurants were compromised; (iii) PIN data was not compromised, as we do not have PIN pads and do not request PINs; and (iv) there is no indication that social security numbers or other personal information were exposed in any way.

The policies of payment card brands protect our customers from any liability for any unauthorized charges if the fraudulent charges are reported in a timely manner. Nonetheless, we have now offered to any customer who shopped with us in the last year at either Neiman Marcus Group stores or websites – whether their card was exposed to the malware or not – one year of free credit monitoring and identity-theft insurance. We will continue to provide the excellent service to our customers that is our hallmark, and I know that the way we responded to this situation is consistent with that commitment.

December: CPP Reports and Forensic Investigation

This malware was discovered as a result of forensic investigative efforts by two of the leading computer forensic firms, hired by us upon receiving very limited information suggesting that there might have been a compromise regarding payment card data.

Specifically, on the evening of Friday, December 13, we were contacted by our merchant processor that Visa had identified an unknown number of fraudulently-reported credit cards with a possible common point of purchase at a small number of Neiman Marcus stores. The merchant processor provided no details concerning the number of cards affected, the credit card account numbers, or prior Neiman Marcus transactions. This initial report did not provide any indication of a cyber-incident or that our network may have been penetrated, but because even this limited information raised a potential concern, we immediately began an internal investigation to determine what could be responsible for the card fraud and whether our systems had been compromised in any way.

Despite repeated requests to our merchant processor over that weekend and on Monday for more information, we did not receive any additional information until Tuesday, December 17. On that date, we received a Common Point of Purchase ("CPP") report listing 122 MasterCard cards that had been used in one Neiman Marcus store and had subsequently been used fraudulently elsewhere.[1]

On December 18, we received another CPP report, this one listing 74 Visa cards. That day, consistent with Visa's protocols, we began contacting forensic investigative firms. On December 20, we engaged a leading forensic investigative firm to immediately start a thorough investigation of our systems in order to determine whether there was any evidence of a data compromise that might indicate the potential theft of payment card data.

---

[1] As we understand the general practice, accounts listed on CPP reports are accounts for which the issuing bank and the cardholder are both already aware that the card has been used fraudulently. These CPP reports provide some indication that a particular merchant *may* have a compromise regarding payment card data, based on analysis by the banks and the card brands. This analysis is tentative, not definitive. The reports indicate a level of suspicion that a problem may exist but do not establish that there actually is a problem, or the nature of the problem – including whether the potential theft of the cards relates to cybercrime or more traditional criminal methods. Nevertheless, our internal investigation focused on this information immediately.

Also on December 20, we received additional CPP reports listing a total of 26 Visa and MasterCard cards, bringing the total number of cards on the CPP reports to 222, which had been used at Neiman Marcus over a period of several months. Although we take any indication of potential payment-card theft seriously, this appeared to be a very small number of cards on CPP reports, especially in light of the millions of transactions Neiman Marcus Group conducts annually. News of the Target data security incident and its potential effect on 40 million payment cards was being reported, and this added to the uncertainty about whether the source of any payment card theft was within our system. And we had not received any CPP reports listing any American Express or Neiman Marcus private label credit card accounts.

On Monday, December 23, we received another CPP report which listed 2,185 MasterCard accounts relating to transactions at numerous Neiman Marcus stores. That day, we notified federal law enforcement of the situation, even though the forensic investigators had not found anything significant. In addition to giving them notice of our situation, we wanted to see if they could shed any light on areas where we should focus our attention and to determine if they had seen anything in their other investigations that would assist us in determining whether a compromise had occurred. The Secret Service followed up with us shortly thereafter, and we have been working closely with them since then.

Meanwhile, the investigation continued but was not turning up any evidence of a data compromise. This forensic work involved, among other things, experienced computer investigators looking at hundreds of thousands of files, logs, and other items of data in our system in an attempt to find anything out of the ordinary. However, by December 28, after a week of forensic investigative work, it was still not clear whether there was a problem in our system.

The next day, December 29, we decided to bring in a second leading computer forensic investigative firm to begin conducting an additional, independent investigation. Although the first firm had not found any evidence of a data compromise in our system that appeared in any way related to the potential theft of credit card information, we wanted another expert team to examine our system. Simply put, we wanted to accelerate the investigation and ensure that we were taking the best steps to protect our customers and to learn if our systems had been compromised.

January: Discovery and containment of the malware,
and notice to the public and our customers

On January 1, the first investigative firm reported that they had discovered malware that they suspected to have card "scraping" functionality (malware that attempts to fraudulently obtain or capture payment card data). On January 2, the investigators reported that the malware appeared to actually have this functionality. However, they could not say whether the malware had functioned at all in our system, whether it had the capability to successfully capture and exfiltrate card data (that is, send data to an outside source), or whether exfiltration had actually occurred. For the next several days, the two investigative firms engaged in the difficult work of trying to learn what they could about the malware and look for evidence of its operation in different parts of our systems.

Attempting to figure out how the malware functioned was complicated work, requiring the investigators to disassemble the malware program and run tests in our technology labs to try to recreate its functionality. After some time they determined that the malware's output files were encrypted. They then developed a custom decoder to decrypt the output files. They also created a custom-coded scanning tool to determine where and how the malware was operating.

By January 6, we had succeeded in decrypting the output files and in locating the malware at various points on our system. As a result, certain observations about the malware could be made for the first time: the malware apparently operated at point-of-sale registers in multiple stores, and it appeared to have been successful in "scraping" and capturing payment card data at the moment a card is swiped through our Point of Sale system. However, it was unknown whether the malware had actually managed to steal data, the dates when it had been operating, and the full scope of how and where it had been operating.

In addition, our expert computer forensic investigators told us that the malware was highly sophisticated and was different than any other malware they had ever analyzed. Its complex, specialized elements helped to explain how the malware had successfully evaded detection, despite all of the security measures we had in place, in at least five different ways. First, the malware was apparently not known to the anti-virus community and had been written to evade anti-virus signatures. Second, the malware erased its tracks by removing the disk file that had caused it to run, even while the program itself was still running in memory – a highly unusual and difficult-to-achieve feature. Third, when the malware scraped and captured card data, it created encrypted output files, so the output files did not exhibit evidence of card-scraping activity – until they were decrypted. Fourth, the malware appeared to have features that were custom-built as a result of reconnaissance efforts within our systems that appear to have been clandestinely conducted earlier in 2013. Finally, the malware carefully covered its tracks with a built-in capability that wiped out files evidencing its operation by overwriting them with random data – making forensic detection much more difficult.

Although the investigators knew more about the malware by January 6, they did not know whether the malware was still scraping and capturing card data, and they were concerned that additional customer card data might be getting captured on an ongoing basis. The investigators discussed with us an immediate problem: since the malware was not yet contained, if the attacker learned that we had discovered the malware, there was a significant risk that the attacker might accelerate efforts to obtain captured account numbers, or that other cyber criminals might be encouraged to test our systems for vulnerabilities. Thus, our top priority at that point became disabling the malware.

From January 7 through January 10, we took a variety of steps in an attempt to ensure that the malware could not function. Since we did not yet know the full contours of how the malware functioned, designing a containment strategy was highly challenging. Nevertheless, by January 10, the investigators had a substantial level of confidence that the malware had been disabled.

That day, January 10, Neiman Marcus announced publicly that we had suffered a data security incident and that some customers' payment card information had been potentially compromised. This announcement was widely disseminated by the media in prominent print and broadcast coverage, and appeared on social media. We also sent email notices that same day to all customers whose payment cards were listed on the CPP reports (about 2,400) for whom we had email addresses. The next business day we sent letter notices to all customers in that group for whom we had postal addresses.

On January 16, our CEO Karen Katz issued a public letter, posted on our website with a prominent link from our home page, explaining that we had been the subject of a data security incident, and offering free credit monitoring and identity-theft insurance for one year to any customer who had used any payment card to conduct any transaction during the past year at any Neiman Marcus Group store or website.

Around this time, the investigators became confident that the dates during which the card-scraping malware had been active was July 16 to October 30, 2013. The number of unique payment cards used at all Neiman Marcus Group stores during this period was approximately 1,100,000. However, the ongoing investigations have not found evidence of the malware operating in all Neiman Marcus Group stores, and it appears that the malware was probably not operating each day during this period based on current evidence. Thus, the number of payment cards that were potentially exposed during this period appears to be lower than 1,100,000, although we have not yet determined how much lower. Because the investigation is ongoing, this information is preliminary.

On January 22, we issued an updated public notice on our website explaining the July 16 – October 30 period and stating that 1,100,000 payment card accounts were potentially exposed. The same day, we sent out individual email and letter notices about the incident to any customer who used a payment card at any time in the past year for any Neiman Marcus Group purchase – whether in one of our stores or on our websites – and for whom we had address information. Our individual notices again provided information about the offer of free credit monitoring and identity-theft insurance.

Notably, we sent this notice – and offered free credit monitoring and identity-theft insurance – to a much larger group than the cardholders whose information appears to have been potentially exposed. Our expanded group included anyone who had used a payment card over a much longer period of time (one year), and website customers (who do not appear to have been exposed to the malware). We took these steps in an abundance of caution because of the ongoing nature of the investigation, and because we want all of our customers to know that we place the highest priority on the security of their personal information.

The ongoing investigation

As with other investigations, computer forensic investigations into data security incidents evolve over time, sometimes in unpredictable ways. We remain in close contact with law enforcement. My statements today are based on the current evidence from the investigations into this recent incident, and therefore should be considered tentative and subject to change. But even though we are still in the midst of discovering the facts, we are pleased to have had the opportunity to provide information to this Committee.

Thank you for your invitation to testify today, and I look forward to answering your questions.

ConsumersUnion

POLICY & ACTION FROM CONSUMER REPORTS

STATEMENT OF

DELARA DERAKHSHANI

CONSUMERS UNION

BEFORE THE

UNITED STATES SENATE COMMITTEE ON THE JUDICIARY

ON

"PRIVACY IN THE DIGITAL AGE: PREVENTING DATA
BREACHES AND COMBATING CYBERCRIME"

FEBRUARY 4, 2013

Chairman Leahy, Ranking Member Grassley, and esteemed members of the Committee. Thank you for the opportunity to testify before you today about data breaches. My name is Delara Derakhshani, and I serve as policy counsel for Consumers Union, the policy and advocacy arm of Consumer Reports.

This past December – at the height of the holiday shopping season – 40 million unsuspecting consumers learned that criminals may have gained unauthorized access to their credit and debit card numbers. Subsequently, 70 million more Target customers learned that personal information such as names, home addresses and telephone numbers may have also fallen into the hands of suspected criminal hackers. We now also know of similar breaches at other retailers: Neiman Marcus confirmed unauthorized access to payment data, and – most recently – Michael's has reported that it is investigating whether a similar breach occurred. The press is reporting that this may be the tip of the iceberg because versions of the malware that was reportedly used in the Target and Neiman Marcus cyberattacks was sold to cybercriminals overseas.

This is truly disturbing. The threats from such breaches are real – and they are serious. As Consumer Reports and Consumers Union have reported with regularity in our publications, consumers who have their data compromised in a large-scale security breach are more likely to become victims of identity theft or fraud. Although federal consumer protection lending laws and voluntary industry practices generally protect consumers from significant out-of-pocket losses, consumers, policymakers, and regulators should take this threat seriously – not only to prevent fraudulent charges which in the end could wind up coming out of the pockets of the retailers, but also because a security breach exposes consumers to unpredictable risks that their personal data will be used without their authorization and for nefarious purposes.

Then there are the very practical and time-consuming concerns for consumers whose personal data has been breached. Consumers have to cancel cards, and must monitor their credit reports and continue to do so in the future. Even though millions have not yet experienced a problem, the threat and uncertainty are there. Of particular concern are debit cards which carry fewer legal protections. While consumers might not ultimately be held responsible if someone steals their debit card and pin number, data thieves can still empty out consumers' bank accounts and set off a cascade of bounced checks and late fees which victims will have to settle down the road.

Clearly, the burden is being put on consumers to be vigilant to prevent future fraudulent use of their information.

What can happen to the data after it's stolen is disconcerting, to say the least. Sometimes, data is resold to criminals outside of the country. Other times, it is used to create counterfeit credit cards or debit cards with direct access to your checking account. Even if you do not wind up becoming a victim of identity theft or have your card used for fraudulent purposes, the result is decreased consumer confidence in the marketplace and uncertainty with the realization that your private financial data is in the ether, and could one day be accessible to individuals for any purpose whatsoever.

Furthermore, in the wake of these breaches, a number of scam artists are trying to take advantage of the situation. What is happening is that scammers are trying to prey on concerns about compromised data. These scammers are attempting to gather consumers' personal and credit information – sometimes through a method called "phishing." We have urged consumers to verify the authenticity of any breach-related messages they receive, and to be wary of emails and phone calls offering identity theft or fraud protection.

When Consumers Union learned of the breach, we wrote to the CFPB, urging them to investigate the matter and for increased public disclosure. Just last week, Attorney General Eric Holder confirmed that the Department of Justice is also investigating the matter. We know lawmakers have urged the Federal Trade Commission to investigate as well. We are grateful that the federal agencies – and State Attorneys General – are on the case, so that we can get to the bottom of who did this and how it happened. And together we can formulate policies and procedures to prevent data breaches from occurring in the future.

Consumers Union and Consumer Reports have also provided consumers with a number of tips to protect themselves – such as closely monitoring their accounts, checking their financial statements frequently, and notifying their financial institutions of any suspicious card activity immediately. For extra protection, consumers can replace credit card numbers as well as debit cards and PIN numbers. We explained that consumers affected by a breach can go online and request a 90-day fraud alert on their credit reports with the three national credit bureaus – Equifax, Experian, and TransUnion – so that they can be notified if thieves try to open up a new credit account in their name. This type of new account fraud is rare and requires a Social Security number – and there's no evidence at this time that hackers have access to consumers' Social Security numbers. But consumers should know that this additional protection is available to them if they want it. Consumers may also want to place a security freeze on their credit report – which blocks access to your credit file by lenders who don't already do business with you. Finally, we have urged consumers not to waste $120 to $300 a year on so-called identity theft protection services. As we've pointed out, consumers can protect themselves for little or nothing. Some of these services use deceptive marketing to sell overpriced and useless products to consumers.

Target and affected retailers are also offering consumers credit monitoring. We believe there are some things that consumers should consider before they enroll in these services. First, consumers should recognize that these services are only free for a year. Although Target assures consumers that they will not be automatically re-enrolled, consumers may get sales solicitations when the free period ends. Second, as some consumer advocates have pointed out, in order to sign up, consumers have to agree to mandatory arbitration, which means that they waive their right to go to court should a dispute arise.

It is important to point out that we should also focus on what needs to be done to help avoid data breaches in the first place. The credit cards and debit cards most Americans use are surprisingly vulnerable to fraud, relying on decades-old technology that makes them susceptible. American credit and debit card data are usually stored unencrypted on a magnetic stripe on the back of each card. Thieves can cheaply and easily "skim" the data off of this magnetic stripe when a credit or debit card is swiped and create a counterfeit card that can access a cardholder's account at an ATM.

Many other countries have shifted or are in the process of shifting to what is known as EMV "smart cards" – or chip and pin technology, which utilizes multiple layers of security – including a computer chip in each card that stores and transmits encrypted data, as well as a unique identifier that can change with each transaction. Cardholders also enter a PIN to authorize transactions. Total fraud losses dropped by 50 percent and card counterfeiting fell by 78 percent in the first year after EMV smart cards were introduced in France in 1992. The United States has lagged behind because replacing all payment cards, updating ATMs to accept the new cards, and updating the terminals in retail stores all cost money. Some financial institutions have indicated that they will switch over to this new technology in the next few years. We need a stronger commitment from all stakeholders to adopt this technology sooner rather than later. We believe it is money well-spent, and it is a penny-wise pound-foolish philosophy to wait any longer, particularly when the burden of guarding against harm following a breach falls most squarely on the shoulders of innocent consumers whose data was compromised.

Policymakers must also take action to encourage investments in new technology to help financial institutions tighten up the own security to help prevent fraud. We need to make sure that we don't fall further behind the rest of the world in fraud protection.

These incidents reinforce just how timely and relevant this Committee's efforts are to guard against data breaches and to quickly help consumers should a breach occur. We appreciate the efforts of Chairman Leahy and the Committee on data breaches, and we recognize the long history of involvement in the topic.

The current legislation introduced by the Chairman, the Personal Data Privacy and Security Act of 2014, would encourage companies to be proactive about safeguarding the data that is entrusted to them.

We applaud the sponsors' desire to ensure that consumers are notified when a breach occurs. We believe that the sooner consumers know that their data has been compromised, the sooner they can take steps to protect themselves. We would therefore urge the Committee to consider shortening the timeline for notification from the 60 days currently in the bill to require more immediate notification. We appreciate the bill's provisions to require companies to identify security vulnerabilities, and periodically assess whether their data privacy and security programs are able to address current threats.

We are also pleased that the bill grants enforcement power to both the Federal Trade Commission and State Attorneys General. The enforcement provisions of the bill are a crucial element of a data security framework, and as we have stated previously – we strongly believe that State Attorneys General must be involved in such enforcement. State Attorneys General have been at the forefront of notice and data breach issues and have played an invaluable role in the efforts to address identity theft and data breaches.

In testimony to Congress on this matter, Consumers Union has repeatedly pointed out that the strongest state notice of breach laws do not require a finding of risk before requiring notification to consumers. Although Consumers Union would prefer that consumers receive notification anytime their personal information is compromised – if there is to be a standard for risk, then Consumers Union would prefer the approach taken by this bill – in which the risk is considered an exemption rather than an affirmative trigger. Under this exemption approach, insufficient information about the level of risk does not eliminate a company's obligation to tell consumers about the breach.

Nevertheless, we would like to strengthen some provisions in the bill, including those related to pre-emption. We want to make sure that any national standard results in strong, meaningful protections for consumers – but that any federal standard does not tie the hands of states or limit their ability to adopt additional protective measures for consumers. Our organization supported the California breach law passed in 2002 and enacted in 2003, and we have a long history of working with state legislatures to pass initiatives that would protect consumers. As a result, we would certainly urge that any federal law addressing data breach and notification set out a floor – not a ceiling – allowing states the freedom to innovate in order to address new threats to consumers.

In closing, thank you for the opportunity to speak before you today. We appreciate the Committee's interest in data security, and we encourage policymakers and regulators to continue to press for responsible data security practices with a new urgency. We all want to ensure consumer confidence in the marketplace. Data breaches undermine that confidence and place unfair burdens on consumers. We look forward to working with the Committee and other stakeholders to make sure that consumers – and their information – are protected adequately. Thank you.

Prepared Testimony and
Statement for the Record of

Fran Rosch
Senior Vice President
Security Products and Services, Endpoint and Mobility
Symantec Corporation

Hearing on

"Privacy in the Digital Age:
Preventing Data Breaches and Combating Cybercrime"

Before the

U.S. Senate
Committee on the Judiciary

February 4, 2014

226 Dirksen Senate Office Building

Chairman Leahy, Ranking Member Grassley, distinguished members of the Committee, thank you for the opportunity to testify today on behalf of Symantec Corporation.

My name is Fran Rosch, and I am the Senior Vice President, Security Products and Services, Endpoint and Mobility at Symantec. In this role I drive the development and execution of Symantec and Norton's endpoint and mobile management and protection strategy. I joined Symantec in 2010 through the acquisition of VeriSign's security business, and during my twelve-year career with VeriSign I worked with the company's largest customers to design and deploy effective security solutions to solve business challenges.

Symantec protects much of the world's information, and is a global leader in security, backup and availability solutions. Symantec is the largest security software company in the world, with over 31 years of experience developing Internet security technology and helping consumers, businesses and governments secure and manage their information and identities. Our products and services protect people and information in any environment – from the smallest mobile device, to the enterprise data center, to cloud-based systems. We have established some of the most comprehensive sources of Internet threat data in the world through our Global Intelligence Network, which is comprised of millions of attack sensors, and we maintain 10 Security Response Centers. These sensors record thousands of events per second. In addition, every day we process billions of e-mail messages and web requests across our 14 global data centers. These resources allow us to capture worldwide security intelligence data that give our analysts a unique view of the entire Internet threat landscape.

The hearing today is not only timely – given the recent high profile data breaches – but it is a critically important discussion that will help focus attention on what businesses can do to protect themselves from similar attacks. Symantec welcomes the opportunity to provide comments to the Committee as it looks at how to prevent data breaches, combat cybercrime, and protect privacy.

In my testimony today, I will discuss:

- The need for basic computer hygiene;
- Recent statistics on data breaches;
- How breaches are happening, including the methods criminals are using to steal data;
- Security measures to protect data and prevent breaches; and
- Key elements for data breach legislation.

Computer Hygiene as a Basic Layer of Defense

Preventing data breaches and protecting privacy starts with basic computer hygiene such as having security software installed, good patch management practices, using strong passwords, and not responding to suspicious emails. But that is just the start, because sophisticated, well-funded attackers are persistent and highly skilled. Anti-virus software (AV) should be part of any security program and will stop known malicious software (malware), but it is just one element. Today, even moderately sophisticated pieces of malware have unique signatures and can slip past systems that are using only AV software. Thus, strong security is layered security – in addition to basic computer hygiene and AV software, organizations need comprehensive protection that includes intrusion protection, reputation-based security, behavioral-based blocking, and data loss prevention tools. These advanced tools look not just for known threats, but they can check the reputation of any file that is loaded on a computer and look for other behavior that could indicate the presence of previously unknown malware.

The kinds of attacks on point-of-sale (PoS) devices that this hearing is looking at are not new, but it does appear the pace is increasing. The increase in successful attacks brings with it media attention and citizen concern, but it is critically important that the public conversation we are now having *not* just be about one attack or one company. Every retailer is at risk, and over time we often learn that the most widely reported victim was not the one hit hardest. So the conversation should be about breaches – plural – not just one breach; it should be about how they are happening, how government can go after the sophisticated criminal enterprises that steal the data, and what organizations can do to prevent and minimize the risk of a successful attack.

Data Breaches by the Numbers

For organizations that have critical information assets such as customer data, intellectual property, trade secrets, and proprietary corporate data, the risk associated with a data breach is now higher than ever before. Simply put, stealing data is big business; most major breaches are part of sophisticated criminal enterprises that trade on stolen identities and credit card numbers. The cost impacts of and the metrics associated with worldwide data breaches are significant.

In 2013, we estimate that the identities of over 435 million people were exposed, and that number is rising as new reports surface. For comparison, our estimate for 2012 was 93 million, and for 2011 was 232 million.[1] In fact, a recent report by the Online Trust Alliance indicates that of the top ten breaches in history, 40% occurred in 2013.[2] Of course, the total number of identities exposed is cumulative – once a person's identity has been exposed, it does not get "unexposed" when the calendar changes. So in the most basic of terms, as a result of breaches over the past three years, the personal information of up to 750 million individuals is or could be for sale on the criminal black market to be used for identity theft, credit card fraud, and countless other illegal activities.

It is important to remember that not every one of these victims will have his or her identity stolen or bank account raided. In fact, a low percentage of them will actually suffer that kind of direct loss. But every one of them is at risk for it because once your personal information is outside of your control your options are limited. You can start credit monitoring and get new credit cards, but to a large degree your best hope is that the information becomes stale before someone tries to use it themselves or sell it on the thriving black market.

The cost of these breaches is very real and is borne directly by both consumers and organizations:

- In our 2013 Norton Report, we estimated the global price tag of consumer cybercrime was $113 billion annually;[3]
- We estimate that there are 378 million victims of consumer cybercrime per year (1 million victims per day, 12 per second);[4]
- The Ponemon Institute estimates that in 2012, the cost to US companies was $188 per identity

[1] *Symantec Internet Security Threat Report* XVIII (April 2013), 17.
http://www.symantec.com/security_response/publications/threatreport.jsp
[2] *2014 OTA Data Breach Guide*, 4. https://otalliance.org/breach.html
[3] *2013 Norton Cybercrime Report* (October 2013), 8.
http://www.symantec.com/about/news/resources/press_kits/detail.jsp?pkid=norton-report-2013
[4] *Id.* at 10.

compromised;[5]

- Ponemon's survey concluded that the average total cost of a breach in 2012 was $5.4 million;[6] and
- Attackers are increasingly targeting smaller businesses, 71% of which say their operations are somewhat or very dependent on the Internet.[7]

The Ponemon survey also found that an ounce of prevention is worth a pound of cure. Strong security protocols before a breach and good incident management policies can dramatically cut the cost of a breach. Similarly, more consumers than ever are taking basic security measures such as using security software and deleting suspicious emails.

How Data Breaches are Occurring

While the continuing onslaught of data breaches is well documented, what is less understood is why data breaches happen and what can be done to prevent them. The main causes for breaches are targeted attacks and human error.

Targeted attacks are indeed an increasing cause of data breaches. According to our 2013 Internet Security Threat Report (ISTR), 40% of data breaches were caused by hackers.[8] Some are direct attacks on a company's servers, where attackers search for unpatched vulnerabilities on websites or undefended connections to the Internet. But most rely on social engineering – in the simplest of terms, tricking people into doing something they would not do if fully aware of the consequences of their actions. Email is still a major attack vector and can take the form of broad mailings ("phishing") or highly targeted messages ("spear phishing"). More and more we see the latter variety, with publicly available information used to craft an email designed to dupe a specific victim or group of victims. The goal of both varieties is to get victims to open an infected file or go to a malicious or compromised website. While good security will stop most of these attacks – which often seek to exploit older, known vulnerabilities – many organizations do not have up-to-date security, do not make full use of the security tools available to them, or have it unevenly applied throughout their enterprise.

Another major cause of breaches is a lack of basic computer hygiene practices, often in the form of company employees who do not follow data security policies. Even today – despite the recent focus on the loss of personal information – a large segment of the workforce handles sensitive information on unprotected mobile devices, servers, desktops, and laptops. Ironically, in many ways this is the natural result of a highly productive workforce. One of the most common types of data breach occurs when sensitive data that an employee stores, sends, or copies is not encrypted. If a laptop is lost or stolen – or a hacker gains access to a network – these files are left unprotected. And while most large companies have policies requiring encryption or other security precautions for sensitive data, many employees either do not have the tools available or they ignore or are unaware of the policies.

Email, web mail, and removable storage devices are another major source of breaches. Most of us at one time or another have emailed something to our personal email address from our office so that we can work on it later. If our email accounts or home computers are compromised, or if we misplace the thumb drive we use to

---

[5] *Cost of Data Breach Study: Global Analysis*, Ponemon Institute (May 2013), 1.
http://www.symantec.com/about/news/resources/press_kits/detail.jsp?pkid=ponemon-2013
[6] *Id.* at 1.
[7] *Symantec 2012 National Small Business Study Fact Sheet*, National Cybersecurity Alliance & Symantec Corporation, 1.
http://www.staysafeonline.org/stay-safe-online/resources/
[8] *ISTR XVIII*, 19.

transport files, any sensitive, unencrypted data we sent is now lost and our company has had a data breach. Data breaches also can occur through outright theft, often by a fired or disgruntled employee.

Cybercriminals are also targeting the places where we "live and play" online in order to get at sensitive personal data. Social media is an increasingly sinister tool for cybercriminals. It is particularly effective in direct attacks, as people tend to trust things that appear to come from a friend's social media feed. But social media is also widely used to conduct reconnaissance for spear phishing or other targeted attacks; it often provides just the kind of personal details that a skilled attacker can use to get a victim to let his or her guard down. The old cliché is true when it comes to cyber attacks: we have to be right 100% of the time in protecting ourselves, while the attacker only has to get it right once.

We are also seeing the rapid growth of "watering hole" attacks on Internet sites. Like the lion in the wild who stalks a watering hole for unsuspecting prey, cybercriminals have become adept at lying in wait on legitimate websites and using them to try to infect visitors' computers. They do so by compromising legitimate websites that their victims are likely to visit and modifying them so that they will surreptitiously try to deliver malware to every visitor. For example, one attacker targeted mobile app developers by compromising a site that was popular with them. In another case, we saw employees from 500 different companies visit one compromised site in just 24 hours, each running the risk of infection.[9] Cybercriminals gain control of these websites through many of the same tactics described above – spear phishing and other social engineering attacks on the site managers, developers, or owners. Many of these websites were compromised through known attack vectors, meaning that good security practices could have prevented them from being compromised, and sensitive data on users systems would have been protected.

All of these attacks have essentially one goal: to get control of the user's computer, because once they have gained this foothold they can use the system for virtually any criminal purpose (including stealing data). When infiltrating a company, once inside, attackers typically will conduct reconnaissance of the system and then move laterally within it until they find what they want to take. In the case of a retailer, this can include compromising PoS devices and stealing information in bulk from them. In the case of an attack on an individual, the criminal will install malware that allows them to steal information or otherwise take control of the computer for future use.

Protecting Data and Preventing Breaches

Basic Security Steps - i.e., Closing the Door.

When it comes to security, it starts with the basics. Though criminals' tactics are continually evolving, good cyber hygiene, as discussed previously, is still the simplest and most cost-effective first step. Strong passwords remain the foundation of good security – on home and work devices, email, social media accounts, or whatever you use to communicate (or really anything you log into). And these passwords must be different, because using a single password means that a breach of one account exposes all of your accounts. Using a second authentication factor (whether through a text message, a smart card, biometrics, or a token with a changing numeric password) significantly increases the security of a login.

Patch management is also critical. Individuals and organizations should not delay installing patches, or software updates, because the same patch that closes a vulnerability on one computer can be a roadmap for a

---

[9] *Id.* at 21.

criminal to exploit that vulnerability and compromise any unpatched devices. The reality is that a large percentage of computers around the world, including some in large organizations, do not get patched regularly, and cybercriminals count on this. While so-called "zero day exploits" – previously unknown critical vulnerabilities – get the most press, it is older, unpatched vulnerabilities that cause most systems to get compromised.

Modern Security Software – i.e., Bolting the Doors and Windows

But poor or insufficiently deployed security can also lead to a breach, and a modern security suite that is being fully utilized is also essential. While most people still commonly refer to security software as "anti-virus" or AV, advanced security protection is much more than that. In the past, the same piece of malware would be delivered to thousands or even millions of computers. Today, cybercriminals can take the same malware and create unlimited unique variants that can slip past basic AV software. If all your security software does is check for signatures (or digital fingerprints) of known malware, you are by definition not protected against even moderately sophisticated attacks. Put differently, a check-the-box security program that only includes installation of basic AV software may give you piece of mind – but that is about all it will give you.

Modern security software does much more than look for known malware: it monitors your computer, watching for unusual internet traffic, activity, or system processes that could be indicative of malicious activity. At Symantec we also use what we call *Insight* and *SONAR*, which are reputation-based and behavior-based heuristic security technologies. Insight is a reputation-based technology that uses our Global Intelligence Network to put files in context, using their age, frequency, location and other characteristics to expose emerging threats that might otherwise be missed. If a computer is trying to execute a file that we have never seen anywhere in the world and that comes from an unknown source, there is a high probability that it is malicious – and Insight will either warn the user or block it. SONAR is behavior-based protection that uses proactive local monitoring to identify and block suspicious processes on computers.

Tailoring Security to the Device – i.e., Locking Your Valuables in a Safe

Security should also be specific to the device being protected, and in some ways PoS devices have advantages over other systems. For while a modern PoS system is typically at its core just a computer running a mainstream operating system, the functions it needs to perform can be narrowly defined. Because a user on such a device typically does not browse the web, send emails, or open shared drives, the functionally of the machine and the files that actually need to be on it are limited. This allows businesses to reduce the attack surface by locking down the system and using application control tools, as well as controlling which devices and applications are allowed to access the network. Doing so can render many strains of malware useless because they would not be allowed to run on the devices.

In addition, payment card system infrastructure is highly complex and threats can be introduced at any number of points within the system. The special report we released yesterday, *Attacks on Point of Sales Systems*, provides an overview of the methods that attackers may use to gain entry into a system.[10] It also describes the steps that retailers and other organizations can use to protect PoS systems and mitigate the risk of an attack.

---

[10] *Special Report on Attacks on Point of Sales Systems*, Symantec Security Response (February 2014). http://www.symantec.com/content/en/us/enterprise/media/security_response/whitepapers/attacks_on_point_of_sale_systems.pdf

Encrypting Data – i.e., Hiding Family Treasures in a Secret Compartment in your Safe

Encryption also is key to protecting your most valuable data. Even the best security will not stop a determined attacker, and encrypting your sensitive data provides defense in breadth, or across many platforms. Good encryption ensures that any data stolen will be useless to virtually all cybercriminals. The bottom line in computer security is no different from physical security – nothing is perfect. We can make it hard, indeed very hard, for an attacker, but if resourced and persistent criminals want to compromise a particular company or site, with time they are probably going to find a way to do it. Good security means not just doing the utmost to keep them out, but also to recognize that you must take steps to limit any damage they can do should they get in.

Responding to a Breach

The criminal organizations that carry out many of the major targeted attacks are well funded, sophisticated, and persistent. In the face of this onslaught, even the most security conscious organizations can have a data breach. Every organization needs to be prepared to manage the effects of one, because deploying an effective incident management plan after a breach can help mitigate the damage of the data loss. Organizations need to be prepared to react on several different fronts, beginning with an incident response team that represents all functional groups within an organization and a response plan that has been exercised before an incident has occurred. Lastly, organizations need to be prepared to bring in law enforcement and, as expeditiously as possible, notify anyone impacted and communicate timely information to them.

In the longer term, effective sharing of actionable information among the public and private sectors on cyber threats, vulnerabilities, and incidents is an essential component of improving overall cybersecurity and combatting cybercrime. At Symantec, we participate in various industry organizations, as well as public-private partnerships in the US and globally with all levels of government. We share high-level cybercrime and cyber threat trends and information on a voluntary basis through a number of different fora to help protect our customers and their networks. Among our partners are the National Cyber-Forensics and Training Alliance (NCFTA), which includes more than 80 industry partners and law enforcement from around the world, and the Information Technology (IT) Information Sharing and Analysis Center (ISAC), which is comprised of 27 leading IT vendors and contributes to cyber risk management of the other 15 critical infrastructure sectors through the National Council of ISACs.

Data Breach Legislation

In the United States today, there are at least 48 state-specific data breach notification laws. This creates an enormous compliance burden, particularly for smaller companies, and does little to actually protect consumers. Symantec supports a national standard for data breach notification, built on three principles:

1. Data security legislation should apply equally to all. The scope of any legislation should include all entities that collect, maintain, or sell significant numbers of records containing sensitive personal information. Requirements should impact government and the private sector equally, and should include educational institutions and charitable organizations as well. By the same token, any new legislation should consider existing federal regulations that govern data breach for some sectors and not create duplicative, additional, or conflicting rules.

2. Implementing pre-breach security measures should be a part of any legislation. As the Ponemon survey demonstrates, breaches are much less costly for companies that are proactive. New legislation should not simply require notification of consumers in case of a data breach, but should seek to minimize the likelihood of a breach by pushing organizations to take reasonable security measures to ensure the confidentiality and integrity of sensitive personal information. Numerous standards, best practices, and guidelines already exist to help organizations establish a cybersecurity program or improve an existing one. The Cybersecurity Framework that NIST will issue next week is the result of a lengthy and successful public-private partnership and if it is consistent with the drafts we have seen will be a flexible, scalable tool that organizations of all sizes and sophistication levels can use to secure their environments and protect critical infrastructure.

3. The use of encryption or other security measures that render data unreadable and unusable should be a key element in establishing the threshold for the need for notification. Any notification scheme should minimize "false positives" – notices to individuals who are later shown *not* to have been impacted by a breach because their data was rendered unusable before it was stolen. A clear reference to the "usability" of information should be considered when determining whether notification is required in case of a breach. Promoting the use of encryption as a best practice would significantly reduce the number of "false positives," thus reducing the burden on consumers and business.

Conclusion

This hearing is a key part of an important conversation that we need to have as a nation. Data breaches and cyber threats are a part of every American's day-to-day lives, and will be even more so in the years to come. We will never be able to prevent every data breach or every cyber attack, but working together, industry and government can make it increasingly more difficult – and more expensive – for cybercriminals to succeed.

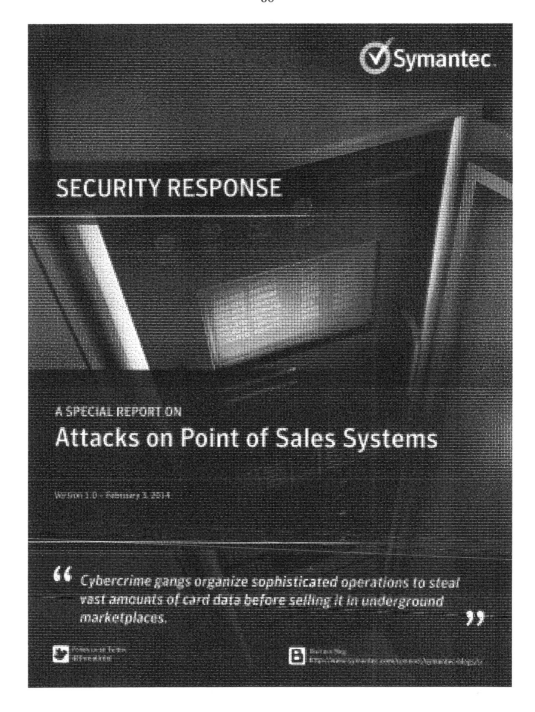

Symantec.

SECURITY RESPONSE

A SPECIAL REPORT ON

Attacks on Point of Sales Systems

Version 1.0 – February 3, 2014

" Cybercrime gangs organize sophisticated operations to steal vast amounts of card data before selling it in underground marketplaces. "

CONTENTS

OVERVIEW

Credit and debit card data theft is one of the earliest forms of cybercrime and persists today. Cybercrime gangs organize sophisticated operations to steal vast amounts of data before selling it in underground marketplaces. Criminals can use the data stolen from a card's magnetic strip to create clones. It's a potentially lucrative business with individual cards selling for up to US$130.

There are several routes attackers can take to steal this data. One option is to gain access to a database where card data is stored. But another option is to target the point at which a retailer first acquires that card data – the point-of-sale (POS) system.

Point-of-sale malware is now one of the biggest sources of stolen payment cards for cybercriminals. Although it hit the headlines over the past year, the POS malware threat has been slowly germinating since 2005. Attackers have honed their methods, paving the way for the mega-breaches of 2013 and 2014, which compromised approximately 100 million payment cards in the US.

The massive scale of attacks is explained in part because POS malware kits are now widely available on the cybercrime underground. For a modest investment, attackers can buy tools that can potentially net them millions.

Despite improvements in card security technologies and the requirements of the Payment Card Industry Data Security Standard (PCI DSS), there are still gaps in the security of POS systems. This coupled with more general security weaknesses in corporate IT infrastructure means that retailers find themselves exposed to increasingly resourceful and organized cybercriminal gangs.

Many US retailers are still vulnerable to point-of-sale malware attacks and are likely to remain so until the complete transition to more secure payment card technologies in 2015.

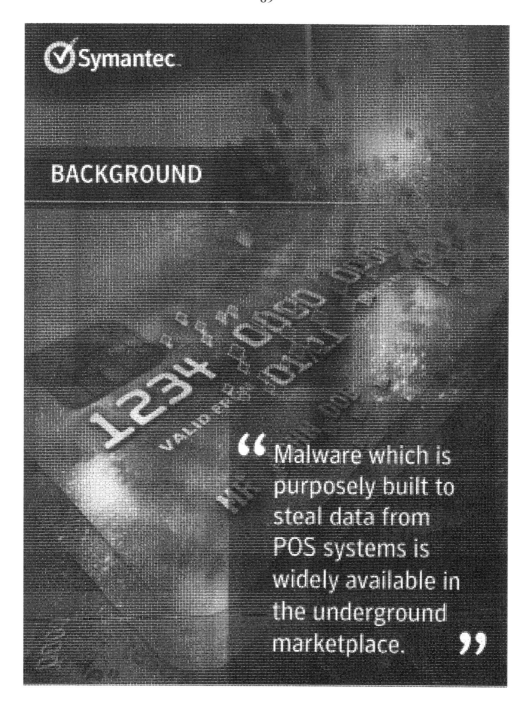

Background

The term POS (Point of Sale) device most commonly refers to the in-store systems where customers pay merchants for goods or services. While many POS transactions are in the form of cash, many of these payments are made by customers swiping their cards through a card reader. These card readers may be standalone devices but modern POS systems, particularly those in larger retailers, are all-in-one systems which can handle a variety of customer transactions such as sales, returns, gift cards and promotions. Most importantly from a security standpoint, they can handle multiple payment types.

Given the sensitive financial and sometimes, personal data to which modern POS systems have access, it is an obvious but not always well recognized fact that the security of these systems is of utmost importance.

POS security issues

Many all-in-one POS systems are based on general purpose operating systems such as Windows Embedded, Windows XP and later versions, and Unix operating systems including Linux. Consequently, these systems are susceptible to a wide variety of attack scenarios which could lead to large scale data breaches.

Accessibility

All organizations that handle payment card data are required to implement safeguards set down in the Payment Card Industry (PCI) Data Security Standard (DSS). These standards help organizations to ensure that their systems and procedures are properly secured. The standard describes a concept known as the cardholder data environment (CDE) and the need to protect it. This is defined as "The people, processes and technology that store, process or transmit cardholder data or sensitive authentication data, including any connected system components."

The current standards recommend, but do not require the CDE to be network-segmented from other non-POS systems and the public Internet. While a strictly controlled and completely isolated POS system network would be quite secure, it is too impractical for serious consideration. The POS systems must be accessible for software updates and maintenance, allow business data to be exported to other systems (e.g. purchasing data and inventory), to export system and security logs, have access to required support systems such as network time protocol (NTP) servers (as required by PCI standards), and have connectivity to external payment processors.

Despite lacking a rule for segmentation, the PCI standards do mandate certain levels of access security, for example, if remote access from a public network is allowed, the access must employ two-factor authentication. In most mature retail environments, the CDE is appropriately segmented to reduce risk. However, in these environments pathways still exist from the general corporate network to the CDE.

While previous breaches have occurred by gaining direct access to POS systems, the most common attack route against POS systems is through the corporate network. Once an attacker gains access to the corporate network, for example through a vulnerable public facing server or spearphishing email, the attacker could traverse the network until they gain access to an entry point to the POS network. This entry point is often the same as a corporate administrator would utilize to maintain the POS systems.

Lack of point to point encryption (P2PE)

When an individual pays by swiping a card credit at a POS system, data contained in the card's magnetic stripe is read and then passed through a variety of systems and networks before reaching the retailer's payment processor. When this data is transmitted over a public network, the data must be protected using network level encryption (e.g. secure socket layer (SSL)).

However, within internal networks and systems, the credit card number is not required to be encrypted except when stored. Albert Gonzalez famously took advantage of this weakness in 2005 by infiltrating many retail networks and installing network sniffing tools allowing him to collect over a hundred million credit card numbers as they passed through internal networks.

In response, many retailers today use network level encryption even within their internal networks. While that change protected the data as it travelled from one system to another, the credit card numbers are not encrypted in the systems themselves, and can still be found in plain text within the memory of the POS system and other computer systems responsible for processing or passing on the data. This weakness has led to the emergence of "RAM scraping" malware, which allows attackers to extract this data from memory while the data is being processed inside the terminal rather than when the data is travelling through the network.

Secure card readers (SCR) exist and have been implemented in some environments enabling P2PE, this can defeat RAM scraping attacks that work by searching the memory of the POS system for patterns of digits that matches those of payment card numbers. Such card readers encrypt the card data at time of swipe and the credit card number remains encrypted throughout the process even within the memory and underneath network level encryption.

Using P2PE within POS environments is not a new concept. Items such as PINs, when used with debit cards must be encrypted at the PIN pad terminal. When provisioning terminals, a payment processor or sponsor must provision the terminal by performing "key injection" where a unique encryption key is deployed directly to the device. With this scheme, the PIN remains encrypted at all times.

Software vulnerabilities

The majority of POS systems are running the older Windows XP version of Windows Embedded. This older version is more susceptible to vulnerabilities and therefore more open to attack. It should also be noted that support for Windows XP will end on April 8, 2014. In practice this means, no more patches will be issued for any software vulnerabilities found in the operating system from the cutoff date. This event will certainly place POS operators under increased risk of a successful attack and POS operators should already have mitigation plans in place to meet this coming deadline.

Susceptibility to malicious code

As many POS systems are running a version of Windows, they are also capable of running any malware that runs on Windows. This means that attackers do not need specialized skills in order to target POS systems and malware that were not specifically designed for use on POS systems could be easily repurposed for use against them.

92

Slow adoption of EMV

Europay, Mastercard and VISA (EMV) is a set of standards for card payments. It is often referred to as "Chip and PIN" and is a replacement for traditional magnetic stripe based cards. EMV cards contain embedded microprocessors that provide strong transaction security features. EMV never transmits the credit card data in the clear mitigating many common POS attacks. EMV cards are also less attractive to attackers as they are difficult to clone.

While EMV is commonly used in some parts of the world such as Europe, US merchants in particular have been slow to adopt the EMV standard and will not start implementing it until 2015.

Typical anatomy of attacks against POS systems

Attacks against POS systems in mature environments are typically multi-staged. First, the attacker must gain access to the victim's network. Usually, they gain access to an associated network and not directly to the CDE. They must then traverse the network, ultimately gaining access to the POS systems. Next, they will install malware in order to steal data from the compromised systems. As the POS system is unlikely to have external network access, the stolen data is then typically sent to an internal staging server and ultimately exfiltrated from the retailer's network to the attacker.

Infiltration

There are a variety of methods an attacker can use to gain access to a corporate network. They can look for weaknesses in external facing system, such as using an SQL injection on a Web server or finding a periphery device that still uses the default manufacturer password. Alternatively they can attack from within by sending a spearphishing email to an individual within the organization. The spearphishing email could contain a malicious attachment or a link to a website which installs a back door program onto the victim's machine.

Network traversal

Once inside the network, the attackers need to gain access to their ultimate targets – the POS systems. Attackers will typically use a variety of tools to map out the network in order to locate systems within the CDE. While they may use vulnerabilities or other techniques to gain access to these systems, often the simplest, yet effective method of gaining access is by obtaining user credentials. User credentials may be obtained through keylogging Trojans, password hash extraction, cracking, and/or replaying captured login sequences, or even brute force. Eventually, administrative level credentials may be obtained. Attackers may even gain control of a domain controller, giving them full access to all computers in the network. Once in control, they can then gain access to the CDE even if it is in a segmented network by using network and data pathways established for existing business purposes. Once inside the CDE, they then install malware which allows them to steal card data from the POS systems.

Data-stealing tools

Malware which is purposely built to steal data from POS systems is widely available in the underground marketplace. In some attacks, network sniffing tools are used to collect credit card numbers as they traversed internal unencrypted networks. Other times, RAM scraping malware is used to collect credit numbers as they are read into computer memory. Any collected data is then stored in a file locally until time for exfiltration. Often, this data file needs to be transferred to multiple computers hopping through the internal network until reaching a system that has access to external systems.

Persistence and stealth

Because the attacker is targeting a POS system and these attacks take time to gather data, they will need their code to remain persistent. Unlike database breaches where millions of records are accessible immediately, POS system breaches require the attacker to wait until transactions happen and then collect the data in real-time as each credit card is used. Because of this, early discovery of the attack can limit the extent of the damage. Malware persistence can be achieved using simple techniques to ensure the malware process is always running and restarts on any system restart.

Stealth techniques used will vary from simplistic obfuscation of filenames and processes to specific security software bypass techniques. In more secure environments, in order for attackers to succeed, they will likely already have access to compromised administrative credentials and can use them to scrub logs, disable monitoring software and systems, and even modify security software configuration (e.g. change file signing requirements or modify whitelisting entries) to avoid detection.

Exfiltration

The attackers may hijack an internal system to act as their staging server. They will attempt to identify a server that regularly communicates with the POS systems and piggyback on normal communications to avoid detection. Any data collected by the RAM-scraping malware will be sent to this staging server where it stored and aggregated until a suitable time to transmit to the attacker. At the appropriate time, the attackers may transfer the collected data through any number of other internal systems before finally arriving at an external system such as a compromised FTP server belonging to a third party. By using compromised servers from legitimate sites to receive the stolen data, the traffic to these sites are less likely to arouse suspicion on the part of the compromised retailer, particularly if they are sites that are often visited by users within the victim organization.

Symantec.

Protecting POS systems from attack

There are many steps that POS operators can take to reduce the risk of attacks against POS systems. The following diagram illustrates the typical infrastructure of payment card systems and the threats against them, along with mitigation strategies that can be employed at various points in the system.

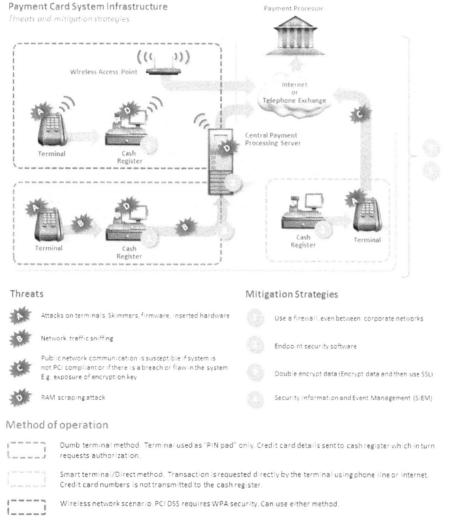

Payment Card System infrastructure
Threats and mitigation strategies

Threats

A   Attacks on terminals. Skimmers, firmware, inserted hardware

B   Network traffic sniffing

C   Public network communication is susceptible if system is not PCI compliant or if there is a breach or flaw in the system. E.g. exposure of encryption key

D   RAM scraping attack

Mitigation Strategies

Use a firewall, even between corporate networks

Endpoint security software

Double encrypt data (Encrypt data and then use SSL)

Security Information and Event Management (SIEM)

Method of operation

Dumb terminal method. Terminal used as "PIN pad" only. Credit card details sent to cash register which in turn requests authorization.

Smart terminal/Direct method. Transaction is requested directly by the terminal using phone line or internet. Credit card numbers is not transmitted to the cash register.

Wireless network scenario. PCI DSS requires WPA security. Can use either method.

Figure: Threat to payment card system and possible mitigation strategies

Practical steps to take

- Implementation of PCI Security Standards
  - Install and maintain a firewall to facilitate network segmentation
  - Change default system passwords and other security parameters
  - Encrypt transmission of cardholder data across open, public networks
  - Encrypt stored primary account number (PAN) and do not store sensitive authentication data
  - Use and regularly update security software
  - Use intrusion protection system (IPS) at critical points and the perimeter of the CDE
  - Use file integrity and monitoring software
  - Use strong authentication including two-factor authentication for remote systems
  - Monitor all network and data access (SIEM)
- Test security systems, perform pen-testing, and implement a vulnerability management program
- Maintain security policies and implement regular training for all personnel
- Implement multi-layered protections including outside the CDE. Typically, the attacker will need traverse multiple networks and layers of security before reaching a POS system. Any single layer that the attacker is unable to bypass prevents successful data exfiltration.
- Implement P2PE or EMV ("Chip and PIN")
- Increase network segmentation and reduce pathways between the CDE and other networks.
- Maintain strict auditing on connections to between the CDE and other networks. Reduce the number of personnel who have access to systems that have access to both the CDE and other networks.
- Employ two-factor authentication at all entry points to the CDE and for any personnel with access rights to the CDE
- Employ two-factor authentication for all system configuration changes within the CDE environment
- Implement system integrity and monitoring software to leverage features such as system lockdown, application control, or whitelisting

97

About Symantec

Symantec protects the world's information and is the global leader in security, backup, and availability solutions. Our innovative products and services protect people and information in any environment—from the smallest mobile device to the enterprise data center to cloud-based systems.

Our industry-leading expertise in protecting data, identities, and interactions gives our customers confidence in a connected world. More information is available at www.symantec.com or by connecting with Symantec at go.symantec.com/socialmedia.

Headquartered in Mountain View, Calif., Symantec has operations in 40 countries. More information is available at www.symantec.com.

Follow us on Twitter
@threatintel

Visit our Blog
http://www.symantec.com/connect/symantec-blogs/sr

For specific country offices and contact numbers, please visit our website.

Symantec World Headquarters
350 Ellis St.
Mountain View, CA 94043 USA
+1 (650) 527-8000
1 (800) 721-3934
www.symantec.com

PREPARED STATEMENT OF

THE FEDERAL TRADE COMMISSION

on

Privacy in the Digital Age: Preventing Data Breaches and Combating Cybercrime

Before the

COMMITTEE ON THE JUDICIARY

UNITED STATES SENATE

Washington, D.C.

February 4, 2014

I. INTRODUCTION

Chairman Leahy, Ranking Member Grassley, and members of the Committee, I am Edith Ramirez, Chairwoman of the Federal Trade Commission ("FTC" or "Commission").[1] I appreciate the opportunity to present the Commission's testimony on data security.

We live in an increasingly connected world, and information is the new currency. Businesses in this data-driven economy are collecting more personal information about consumers than ever before, and storing and transmitting across their own systems as well as the Internet. But, as recent publicly announced data breaches remind us,[2] these vast systems of data are susceptible to being compromised. Hackers and others seek to exploit vulnerabilities, obtain unauthorized access to consumers' sensitive information, and potentially misuse it in ways that can cause serious harms to consumers as well as businesses.

All of this takes place against the background of the threat of identity theft, a pernicious crime that harms both consumers and financial institutions. The Bureau of Justice Statistics estimates that 16.6 million persons – or 7 percent of all U.S. residents ages 16 and older – were victims of identity theft in 2012.[3]

As the nation's leading privacy enforcement agency, the FTC is committed to protecting consumer privacy and promoting data security in the private sector and has settled 50 law

---

[1] This written statement presents the views of the Federal Trade Commission. My oral statements and responses to questions are my own and do not necessarily reflect the views of the Commission or of any other Commissioner.

[2] *See* Elizabeth A. Harris & Nicole Perlroth, *For Target, the Breach Numbers Grow*, N.Y. Times, Jan. 10, 2014, *available at* http://www.nytimes.com/2014/01/11/business/target-breach-affected-70-million-customers.html (discussing recently-announced breaches involving payment card information by Target and Neiman Marcus); Nicole Perlroth, *Michaels Stores Is Investigating Data Breach*, N.Y. Times, Jan. 25, 2014, *available at* http://www.nytimes.com/2014/01/26/technology/michaels-stores-is-investigating-data-breach.html (discussing Michaels Stores' announcement of potential security breach involving payment card information).

[3] *See* Bureau of Justice Statistics, *Victims of Identity Theft, 2012* (Dec. 2013), *available at* http://www.bjs.gov/content/pub/pdf/vit12.pdf.

enforcement actions against businesses that we alleged failed to protect consumers' personal information appropriately. Data security is of critical importance to consumers. If companies do not protect the personal information they collect and store, that information could fall into the wrong hands, resulting in fraud and other harm, along with a potential loss of consumer confidence in particular business sectors or entities, payment methods, or types of transactions. Accordingly, the Commission has undertaken substantial efforts for over a decade to promote data security in the private sector through civil law enforcement, education, policy initiatives, and recommendations to Congress to enact legislation in this area. The FTC has also worked with the Department of Justice and criminal investigative agencies, as well as state Attorneys General, to coordinate efforts and leverage government resources more effectively.

The Commission is here today to reiterate its longstanding bipartisan call for enactment of a strong federal data security and breach notification law. Never has the need for legislation been greater. With reports of data breaches on the rise, and with a significant number of Americans suffering from identity theft, Congress needs to act. This testimony provides an overview of the Commission's efforts and restates the Commission's support for data security legislation.

II.   THE COMMISSION'S DATA SECURITY PROGRAM

A.   Law Enforcement

To promote data security, the Commission enforces several statutes and rules that impose obligations upon businesses that collect and maintain consumer data. The Commission's Safeguards Rule, which implements the Gramm-Leach-Bliley Act ("GLB Act"), for example, provides data security requirements for non-bank financial institutions.[4] The Fair Credit

---

[4] 16 C.F.R. Part 314, implementing 15 U.S.C. § 6801(b).

Reporting Act ("FCRA") requires consumer reporting agencies to use reasonable procedures to ensure that the entities to which they disclose sensitive consumer information have a permissible purpose for receiving that information,[5] and imposes safe disposal obligations on entities that maintain consumer report information.[6] The Children's Online Privacy Protection Act ("COPPA") requires reasonable security for children's information collected online.[7]

In addition, the Commission enforces the proscription against unfair or deceptive acts or practices in Section 5 of the FTC Act.[8] If a company makes materially misleading statements or omissions about a matter, including data security, and such statements or omissions are likely to mislead reasonable consumers, they can be found to be deceptive in violation of Section 5.[9] Using its deception authority, the Commission has settled more than 30 matters challenging companies' express and implied claims that they provide reasonable security for consumers' personal data when, the Commission charged, the companies failed to employ available, cost-effective security measures to minimize or reduce data risks.

Further, if a company's data security practices cause or are likely to cause substantial injury to consumers that is neither reasonably avoidable by consumers nor outweighed by countervailing benefits to consumers or to competition, those practices can be found to be unfair and violate Section 5.[10] Congress expressly codified these criteria in Section 5.[11] The

---

[5] 15 U.S.C. § 1681e.

[6] *Id.* at § 1681w. The FTC's implementing rule is at 16 C.F.R. Part 682.

[7] 15 U.S.C. §§ 6501-6506; *see also* 16 C.F.R. Part 312 ("COPPA Rule").

[8] 15 U.S.C. § 45(a).

[9] *See* Federal Trade Commission Policy Statement on Deception, *appended to Cliffdale Assocs., Inc.,* 103 F.T.C. 110, 174 (1984).

[10] *See* Federal Trade Commission Policy Statement on Unfairness, *appended to Int'l Harvester Co.,* 104 F.T.C. 949, 1070 (1984) ("FTC Unfairness Statement").

[11] 15 U.S.C. § 5(n).

Commission has settled over 20 cases alleging that a company's failure to reasonably safeguard consumer data was an unfair practice.[12]

In the data security context, the FTC conducts its investigations with a focus on reasonableness – a company's data security measures must be reasonable in light of the sensitivity and volume of consumer information it holds, the size and complexity of its business, and the cost of available tools to improve security and reduce vulnerabilities. The Commission examines such factors as whether the risks at issue were well known or reasonably foreseeable, the costs and benefits of implementing various protections, and the tools that are currently available and used in the marketplace. This same reasonableness requirement is the basis for sectoral laws that have data security requirements, including the GLB Act and the FCRA.

Since 2001, the Commission has used its authority under these laws to settle 50 cases against businesses that it charged with failing to provide reasonable and appropriate protections for consumers' personal information.[13] The practices at issue were not merely isolated mistakes. In each of these cases, the Commission examined a company's practices as a whole and challenged alleged data security failures that were multiple and systemic. And through these settlements, the Commission has made clear that it does not require perfect security; that reasonable and appropriate security is a continuous process of assessing and addressing risks; that there is no one-size-fits-all data security program; and that the mere fact that a breach occurred does not mean that a company has violated the law.

---

[12] Some of the Commission's data security settlements allege both deception and unfairness.

[13] *See* Commission Statement Marking the FTC's 50th Data Security Settlement, Jan. 31, 2014, *available at* http://www.ftc.gov/system/files/documents/cases/140131gmrstatement.pdf.

In its most recent case, the FTC settled allegations that GMR Transcription Services, Inc., and its owners violated Section 5 of the FTC Act.[14] According to the complaint, GMR provides audio file transcription services for their clients, which include health care providers, and relies on service providers and independent typists to perform this work. GMR exchanged audio files and transcripts with customers and typists by loading them on a file server. As a result of GMR's alleged failure to implement reasonable and appropriate security measures or to ensure its service providers also implemented reasonable and appropriate security, at least 15,000 files containing sensitive personal information – including consumers' names, birthdates, and medical histories – were available to anyone on the Internet. The Commission's order resolving the case prohibits GMR from making misrepresentations about privacy and security, and requires the company to implement a comprehensive information security program and undergo independent audits for the next 20 years.

The FTC also recently announced its first data security settlement concerning the "Internet of Things" – *i.e.*, Internet-connected refrigerators, thermostats, cars, and many other products and devices which can communicate with each other and/or consumers. The TRENDnet settlement involved a video camera designed to allow consumers to monitor their homes remotely.[15] The complaint alleges that TRENDnet marketed its SecurView cameras for purposes ranging from home security to baby monitoring, and claimed in numerous product descriptions that they were "secure." However, the cameras had faulty software that left them open to online viewing, and in some instances listening, by anyone with the cameras' Internet

---

[14] *GMR Transcription Servs., Inc..*, Matter No. 112-3120 (F.T.C. Dec. 16, 2013) (proposed consent order), *available at* http://www.ftc.gov/news-events/press-releases/2014/01/provider-medical-transcript-services-settles-ftc-charges-it.

[15] *TRENDnet, Inc.*, No. 122-3090 (Sept. 4, 2013), *available at* http://www.ftc.gov/opa/2013/09/trendnet.shtm.

address. This resulted in hackers posting 700 consumers' live feeds on the Internet. Under the FTC settlement, TRENDnet must maintain a comprehensive security program, obtain outside audits, notify consumers about the security issues and the availability of software updates to correct them, and provide affected customers with free technical support for the next two years.

Finally, the FTC has also brought a number of cases alleging that unreasonable security practices allowed hackers to gain access to consumers' credit and debit card information, leading to many millions of dollars of fraud loss.[16] For example, the Commission alleged that TJX's failure to use reasonable and appropriate security measures resulted in a hacker obtaining tens of millions of credit and debit payment cards, as well as the personal information of approximately 455,000 consumers who returned merchandise to the stores.[17] Banks also claimed that tens of millions of dollars in fraudulent charges were made, and cancelled and reissued millions of cards. Meanwhile, criminal law enforcement authorities investigated and prosecuted the hackers involved in this and other data breaches.[18] As this matter illustrates, the goals of FTC and federal criminal agencies are complementary: FTC actions send a message that businesses need to protect their customers' data on the front end, and actions by criminal agencies send a message to identity thieves that their efforts to victimize consumers will be punished.

---

[16] *See, e.g., Dave & Busters, Inc.*, No. C-4291 (F.T.C. May 20, 2010), *available at* http://www.ftc.gov/enforcement/cases-and-proceedings/cases/2010/06/dave-busters-incin-matter; *DSW, Inc.*, No. C-4157 (F.T.C. Mar. 7, 2006), *available at* http://www.ftc.gov/enforcement/cases-and-proceedings/cases/2006/03/dsw-incin-matter; *BJ's Wholesale Club, Inc.*, No. C-4148 (F.T.C. Sept. 20, 2005), *available at* http://www.ftc.gov/enforcement/cases-and-proceedings/cases/2005/09/bjs-wholesale-club-inc-matter.

[17] *The TJX Cos., Inc.*, No. C-4227 (F.T.C. July 29, 2008), *available at* http://www.ftc.gov/enforcement/cases-and-proceedings/cases/2008/08/tjx-companies-inc-matter.

[18] *See, e.g.*, Kim Zetter, *TJX Hacker Gets 20 Years in Prison*, Wired, Mar. 25, 2010, *available at* http://www.wired.com/threatlevel/2010/03/tjx-sentencing/.

B. Policy Initiatives

The Commission also undertakes policy initiatives to promote privacy and data security, including by hosting workshops on emerging business practices and technologies affecting consumer data. This testimony describes two such recent initiatives that addressed information security issues.

In November, the FTC held a workshop on the "Internet of Things."[19] The workshop brought together academics, industry representatives, and consumer advocates to explore the security and privacy issues from increased connectivity in everyday devices, in areas as diverse as smart homes, health and fitness devices, and cars.

Last June, the Commission hosted a public forum on mobile security issues, including potential threats to U.S. consumers and possible solutions to them.[20] As the use of mobile technology increases at a rapid rate and consumers take advantage of the technology's benefits in large numbers, it is important to address threats that exist today as well as those that may emerge in the future. The forum brought together technology researchers, industry members and academics to explore the security of existing and developing mobile technologies and the roles various members of the mobile ecosystem can play in protecting consumers from potential security threats.

The Commission has also hosted programs on emerging forms of identity theft, such as child identity theft[21] and senior identity theft.[22] In these programs, the Commission discussed

---

[19] FTC Workshop, *Internet of Things: Privacy & Security in a Connected World* (Nov. 19, 2013), *available at* http://www.ftc.gov/bcp/workshops/internet-of-things/.

[20] FTC Workshop, *Mobile Security: Potential Threats and Solutions* (June 4, 2013), *available at* http://www.ftc.gov/bcp/workshops/mobile-security/.

[21] FTC Workshop, *Stolen Futures: A Forum on Child Identity Theft* (July 12, 2011), *available at* http://www.ftc.gov/news-events/events-calendar/2011/07/stolen-futures-forum-child-identity-theft.

unique challenges facing children and seniors, and worked with stakeholders to develop outreach messages and plans for these two communities. Since the workshops took place, the Commission has continued to engage in such tailored outreach.

C. Consumer Education and Business Guidance

The Commission also promotes better data security practices through consumer education and business guidance. On the consumer education front, the Commission sponsors OnGuard Online, a website designed to educate consumers about basic computer security.[23] OnGuard Online and its Spanish-language counterpart, Alerta en Línea,[24] average more than 2.2 million unique visits per year.

As directed by Congress, the Commission maintains the nation's main repository of identity theft complaints, housed within our Consumer Sentinel consumer complaint database, and provides centralized resources for victims of identity theft.[25] Identity theft has been the top consumer complaint to the FTC for 13 consecutive years, and tax identity theft – which often begins by thieves obtaining Social Security numbers and other personal information from consumers in order to obtain their tax refund – has been an increasing share of the Commission's identity theft complaints.[26] To address these concerns, Commission staff have worked with members of Congress to host numerous town hall meetings on identity theft in order to educate their constituents. And, just last month, the FTC hosted 16 events across the country, along with

---

[22] FTC Workshop, *Senior Identity Theft: A Problem in This Day and Age* (May 7, 2013), *available at* http://www.ftc.gov/news-events/events-calendar/2013/05/senior-identity-theft-problem-day-and-age.

[23] *See* http://www.onguardonline.gov.

[24] *See* http://www.alertaenlinea.gov.

[25] 18 U.S.C. § 1028 note.

[26] In 2012, tax identity theft accounted for more than 43% of the identity theft complaints, making it the largest category of identity theft complaints by a substantial margin. *See* Press Release, *FTC Releases Top 10 Complaint Categories for 2012* (Feb. 26, 2013), *available at* http://www.ftc.gov/news-events/press-releases/2013/02/ftc-releases-top-10-complaint-categories-2012.

a series of national webinars and Twitter chats as part of Tax Identity Theft Awareness Week.[27]
The events were designed to raise awareness about tax identity theft and provide consumers with
tips on how to protect themselves, and what to do if they become victims. For consumers who
may have been affected by the recent Target and other breaches, the FTC posted information
online about steps they should take to protect themselves.[28]

The Commission directs its outreach to businesses as well. The FTC widely disseminates
a business guide on data security,[29] along with an online tutorial based on the guide.[30] These
resources are designed to provide diverse businesses – and especially small businesses – with
practical, concrete advice as they develop data security programs and plans for their companies.
The Commission has also released articles directed towards a non-legal audience regarding basic
data security issues for businesses.[31] For example, because mobile applications ("apps") and
devices often rely on consumer data, the FTC has developed specific security guidance for
mobile app developers as they create, release, and monitor their apps.[32] The FTC also creates

---

[27] Press Release, *FTC's Tax Identity Theft Awareness Week Offers Consumers Advice, Guidance* (Jan. 10, 2014), *available at* http://www.ftc.gov/news-events/press-releases/2014/01/ftcs-tax-identity-theft-awareness-week-offers-consumers-advice.

[28] *See* Nicole Vincent Fleming, *An Unfortunate Fact About Shopping*, FTC Consumer Blog, http://www.consumer.ftc.gov/blog/unfortunate-fact-about-shopping (Jan. 27, 2014); Nicole Vincent Fleming, *Are you affected by the recent Target hack?*, FTC Consumer Blog, https://www.consumer.ftc.gov/blog/are-you-affected-recent-target-hack. In addition to these materials posted in response to recent breaches, the FTC has long published a victim recovery guide and other resources to explain the immediate steps identity theft victims should take to address the crime; how to obtain a free credit report and correct fraudulent information in credit reports; how to file a police report; and how to protect their personal information. *See* http://www.consumer.ftc.gov/features/feature-0014-identity-theft.

[29] *See Protecting Personal Information: A Guide for Business*, *available at* http://business.ftc.gov/documents/bus69-protecting-personal-information-guide-business.

[30] *See Protecting Personal Information: A Guide for Business (Interactive Tutorial)*, *available at* http://business.ftc.gov/multimedia/videos/protecting-personal-information.

[31] *See generally* http://www.business.ftc.gov/privacy-and-security/data-security.

[32] *See Mobile App Developers: Start with Security* (Feb. 2013), *available at* http://business.ftc.gov/documents/bus83-mobile-app-developers-start-security.

business educational materials on specific topics – such as the risks associated with peer-to-peer ("P2P") file-sharing programs and companies' obligations to protect consumer and employee information from these risks[33] and how to properly secure and dispose of information on digital copiers.[34]

III.   DATA SECURITY LEGISLATION

The FTC supports federal legislation that would (1) strengthen its existing authority governing data security standards on companies and (2) require companies, in appropriate circumstances, to provide notification to consumers when there is a security breach.[35] Reasonable and appropriate security practices are critical to preventing data breaches and protecting consumers' data from identity theft and other harm. Where breaches occur, notifying consumers helps them protect themselves from any harm that is likely to be caused by the misuse of their data. For example, in the case of a breach of Social Security numbers, notifying consumers will enable them to request that fraud alerts be placed in their credit files, obtain

---

[33] *See Peer-to-Peer File Sharing: A Guide for Business* (Jan. 2010), *available at* http://business.ftc.gov/documents/bus46-peer-peer-file-sharing-guide-business.

[34] *See Copier Data Security: A Guide for Business* (Nov. 2010), *available at* http://business.ftc.gov/documents/bus43-copier-data-security.

[35] *See, e.g.,* Prepared Statement of the Federal Trade Commission, "Privacy and Data Security: Protecting Consumers in the Modern World," Before the Senate Committee on Commerce, Science, and Transportation, 112th Cong., June 29, 2011, *available at* http://www.ftc.gov/sites/default/files/documents/public_statements/prepared-statement-federal-trade-commission-privacy-and-data-security-protecting-consumers-modern/110629privacytestimonybrill.pdf; Prepared Statement of the Federal Trade Commission, "Data Security," Before Subcommittee on Commerce, Manufacturing, and Trade of the House Committee on Energy and Commerce, 112th Cong., June 15, 2011, *available at* http://www.ftc.gov/sites/default/files/documents/public_statements/prepared-statement-federal-trade-commission-data-security/110615datasecurityhouse.pdf; FTC, *Security in Numbers, SSNs and ID Theft* (Dec. 2008), *available at* http://www.ftc.gov/sites/default/files/documents/reports/security-numbers-social-security-numbers-and-identity-theft-federal-trade-commission-report/p075414ssnreport.pdf; President's Identity Theft Task Force, *Identity Theft Task Force Report* (Sept. 2008), *available at* http://www.ftc.gov/sites/default/files/documents/reports/presidents-identity-theft-task-force-report/081021taskforcereport.pdf.

copies of their credit reports, scrutinize their monthly account statements, and take other steps to protect themselves. And although most states have breach notification laws in place, having a strong and consistent national requirement would simplify compliance by businesses while ensuring that all consumers are protected.

Legislation in both areas – data security and breach notification – should give the FTC rulemaking authority under the Administrative Procedure Act, jurisdiction over non-profits, and the ability to seek civil penalties to help deter unlawful conduct. Enabling the FTC to bring cases against non-profits[36] would help ensure that whenever personal information is collected from consumers, entities that maintain such data adequately protect it.[37] In addition, under current laws, the FTC only has the authority to seek civil penalties for data security violations involving companies that fail to protect children's information provided online in violation of the COPPA Rule or credit report information in violation of the FCRA.[38] We urge Congress to allow the FTC to seek civil penalties against other companies to ensure that FTC actions can deter unreasonable data security practices in all appropriate instances.

VI.   CONCLUSION

Thank you for the opportunity to provide the Commission's views on data security. The FTC remains committed to promoting reasonable security for consumer data and we look forward to continuing to work with Congress on this critical issue.

---

[36] Non-profits are generally outside the FTC's jurisdiction. 15 U.S.C. §§ 44 & 45(a).

[37] A substantial number of reported breaches have involved non-profit universities and health systems. *See* Privacy Rights Clearinghouse Chronology of Data Breaches (listing breaches including breaches at non-profits, educational institutions, and health facilities), *available at* http://www.privacyrights.org/data-breach/new.

[38] The FTC can also seek civil penalties for violations of administrative orders. 15 U.S.C. § 45(*l*).

William Noonan

Deputy Special Agent in Charge
United States Secret Service
Criminal Investigative Division
Cyber Operations Branch

Prepared Testimony

Before the

United States Senate Committee on
The Judiciary

February 3, 2014

Good afternoon Chairman Leahy, Ranking Member Grassley, and distinguished Members of the Committee. Thank you for the opportunity to testify on the risks and challenges the Nation faces from large-scale data breaches like those that have been recently reported and are of great concern to our Nation. The U.S. Secret Service (Secret Service) has decades of experience investigating large-scale criminal cyber intrusions, in addition to other crimes that impact our Nation's financial payment systems. Based on investigative experience and the understanding we have developed regarding transnational organized cyber criminals that are engaged in these data breaches and associated frauds, I hope to provide this committee useful insight into this issue from a federal law enforcement perspective to help inform your deliberations.

The Role of the Secret Service

The Secret Service was founded in 1865 to protect the U.S. financial system from the counterfeiting of our national currency. As the Nation's financial system evolved from paper to plastic to electronic transactions, so too has the Secret Service's investigative mission. Today, our modern financial system depends heavily on information technology for convenience and efficiency. Accordingly, criminals have adapted their methods and are increasingly using cyberspace to exploit our Nation's financial payment system by engaging in fraud and other illicit activities. This is not a new trend; criminals have been committing cyber financial crimes since at least 1970.[1]

Congress established 18 USC § 1029-1030 as part of the Comprehensive Crime Control Act of 1984; these statutes criminalized unauthorized access to computers[2] and the fraudulent use or trafficking of access devices[3]—defined as any piece of information or tangible item that is a means of account access that can be used to obtain money, goods, services, or other thing of value.[4] Congress specifically gave the Secret Service authority to investigate violations of both statutes.[5]

Secret Service investigations have resulted in the arrest and successful prosecution of cyber criminals involved in the largest known data breaches, including those of TJ Maxx, Dave & Buster's, Heartland Payment Systems, and others. Over the past four years Secret Service cyber crime investigations have resulted in over 4,900 arrests, associated with approximately $1.37 billion in fraud losses and the prevention of over $11.24 billion in potential fraud losses. Through our work with our partners at the Department of Justice (DOJ), in particular the local U.S. Attorney Offices, the Computer Crimes and Intellectual Property section (CCIPS), the International Organized Crime Intelligence and Operations Center (IOC-2), and others, we are confident we will continue to bring the cyber criminals that perpetrate major data breaches to justice.

---

[1] Beginning in 1970, and over the course of three years, the chief teller at the Park Avenue branch of New York's Union Dime Savings Bank manipulated the account information on the bank's computer system to embezzle over $1.5 million from hundreds of customer accounts. This early example of cyber crime not only illustrates the long history of cyber crime, but the difficulty companies have in identifying and stopping cyber criminals in a timely manner—a trend that continues today.

[2] *See* 18 USC § 1030

[3] *See* 18 USC § 1029

[4] *See* 18 USC § 1029(e)(1)

[5] *See* 18 USC § 1029(d) & 1030(d)(1)

The Transnational Cyber Crime Threat

Advances in computer technology and greater access to personally identifiable information (PII) via the Internet have created a virtual marketplace for transnational cyber criminals to share stolen information and criminal methodologies. As a result, the Secret Service has observed a marked increase in the quality, quantity, and complexity of cyber crimes targeting private industry and critical infrastructure. These crimes include network intrusions, hacking attacks, malicious software, and account takeovers leading to significant data breaches affecting every sector of the world economy. The recently reported data breaches of Target and Neiman Marcus are just the most recent, well-publicized examples of this decade-long trend of major data breaches perpetrated by cyber criminals who are intent on targeting our Nation's retailers and financial payment systems.

The increasing level of collaboration among cyber-criminals allows them to compartmentalize their operations, greatly increasing the sophistication of their criminal endeavors and allowing for development of expert specialization. These specialties raise both the complexity of investigating these cases, as well as the level of potential harm to companies and individuals. For example, illicit underground cyber crime market places allow criminals to buy, sell and trade malicious software, access to sensitive networks, spamming services, credit, debit and ATM card data, PII, bank account information, brokerage account information, hacking services, and counterfeit identity documents. These illicit digital marketplaces vary in size, with some of the more popular sites boasting membership of approximately 80,000 users. These digital marketplaces often use various digital currencies, and cyber criminals have made extensive use of digital currencies to pay for criminal goods and services or launder illicit proceeds.

The Secret Service has successfully investigated many underground cyber criminal marketplaces. In one such infiltration, the Secret Service initiated and conducted a three-year investigation that led to the indictment of 11 perpetrators allegedly involved in hacking nine major U.S. retailers and the theft and sale of more than 40 million credit and debit card numbers. The investigation revealed that defendants from the United States, Estonia, China and Belarus successfully obtained credit and debit card numbers by hacking into the wireless computer networks of major retailers — including TJ Maxx, BJ's Wholesale Club, Office Max, Boston Market, Barnes & Noble, Sports Authority and Dave & Buster's. Once inside the networks, these cyber criminals installed "sniffer" programs[6] that would capture card numbers, as well as password and account information, as they moved through the retailers' credit and debit processing networks. After the data was collected, the conspirators concealed the information in encrypted computer servers that they controlled in the United States and Eastern Europe. The credit and debit card numbers were then sold through online transactions to other criminals in the United States and Eastern Europe. The stolen numbers were "cashed out" by encoding card numbers on the magnetic strips of blank cards. The defendants then used these fraudulent cards to withdraw tens of thousands of dollars at a time from ATMs. The defendants were able to conceal and launder their illegal proceeds by using anonymous Internet-based

---

[6] Sniffers are programs that detect particular information transiting computer networks, and can be used by criminals to acquire sensitive information from computer systems.

digital currencies within the United States and abroad, and by channeling funds through bank accounts in Eastern Europe.[7]

In data breaches like these the effects of the criminal acts extended well beyond the companies compromised, potentially affecting millions of individual card holders. Proactive and swift law enforcement action protects consumers by preventing and limiting the fraudulent use of payment card data, identity theft, or both. Cyber crime directly impacts the U.S. economy by requiring additional investment in implementing enhanced security measures, inflicting reputational damage on U.S. firms, and direct financial losses from fraud—all costs that are ultimately passed on to consumers.

Secret Service Strategy for Combating this Threat

The Secret Service proactively investigates cyber crime using a variety of investigative means to infiltrate these transnational cyber criminal groups. As a result of these proactive investigations, the Secret Service is often the first to learn of planned or ongoing data breaches and is quick to notify financial institutions and the victim companies with actionable information to mitigate the damage from the data breach and terminate the criminal's unauthorized access to their networks. One of the most poorly understood facts regarding data breaches is that it is rarely the victim company that first discovers the criminal's unauthorized access to their network; rather it is law enforcement, financial institutions, or other third parties that identify and notify the likely victim company of the data breach by identifying the common point of origin of the sensitive data being trafficked in cyber crime marketplaces.

A trusted relationship with the victim is essential for confirming the crime, remediating the situation, beginning a criminal investigation, and collecting evidence. The Secret Service's worldwide network of 33 Electronic Crimes Task Forces (ECTF), located within our field offices, are essential for building and maintaining these trusted relationships, along with the Secret Service's commitment to protecting victim privacy.

In order to confirm the source of data breaches and to stop the continued theft of sensitive information and the exploitation of a network, the Secret Service contacts the owner of the suspected compromised computer systems. Once the victim of a data breach confirms that unauthorized access to their networks has occurred, the Secret Service works with the local U.S. Attorney's office, or appropriate state and local officials, to begin a criminal investigation of the potential violation of 18 USC § 1030. During the course of this criminal investigation, the Secret Service identifies the malware and means of access used to acquire data from the victim's computer network. In order to enable other companies to mitigate their cyber risk based on current cyber crime methods, we quickly share information concerning the cybersecurity incident with the widest audience possible, while protecting grand jury information, the integrity of ongoing criminal investigations, and the victims' privacy. We share this cybersecurity information through:

---

[7] Additional information on the criminal use of digital currencies can be referenced in testimony provided by U.S. Secret Service Special Agent in Charge Edward Lowery before the Senate Homeland Security and Governmental Affairs Committee in a hearing titled, "Beyond Silk Road: Potential Risks, Threats, and Promises of Virtual Currencies" (November 18, 2013).

- ➢ Our Department's National Cybersecurity & Communications Integration Center (NCCIC);
- ➢ The Information Sharing and Analysis Centers (ISAC);
- ➢ Our ECTFs;
- ➢ The publication of joint industry notices;
- ➢ Our numerous partnerships developed over the past three decades in investigating cyber crimes; and,
- ➢ Contributions to leading industry and academic reports like the Verizon Data Breach Investigations Report, the Trustwave Global Security Report, and the Carnegie Mellon CERT Insider Threat Study.

As we share cybersecurity information discovered in the course of our criminal investigation, we also continue our investigation in order to apprehend and bring to justice those involved. Due to the inherent challenges in investigating transnational crime, particularly the lack of cooperation of some countries with law enforcement investigations, occasionally it takes years to finally apprehend the top tier criminals responsible. For example, Dmitriy Smilianets and Vladimir Drinkman were arrested in June 2012, as part of a multi-year investigation Secret Service investigation, while they were traveling in the Netherlands thanks to the assistance of Dutch law enforcement. The alleged total fraud loss from their cyber crimes exceeds $105 million.

As a part of our cyber crime investigations, the Secret Service also targets individuals who operate illicit infrastructure that supports the transnational organized cyber criminal. For example, in May 2013 the Secret Service, as part of a joint investigation through the Global Illicit Financial Team, shut down the digital currency provider Liberty Reserve. Liberty Reserve is alleged to have had more than one million users worldwide and to have laundered more than $6 billion in criminal proceeds. This case is believed to be the largest money laundering case ever prosecuted in the United States and is being jointly prosecuted by the U.S. Attorney's Office for the Southern District of New York and DOJ's Asset Forfeiture and Money Laundering Section. In a coordinated action with the Department of the Treasury, Liberty Reserve was identified as a financial institution of primary money laundering concern under Section 311 of the USA PATRIOT Act, effectively cutting it off from the U.S. financial system.

Collaboration with Other Federal Agencies and International Law Enforcement

While cyber-criminals operate in a world without borders, the law enforcement community does not. The increasingly multi-national, multi-jurisdictional nature of cyber crime cases has increased the time and resources needed for successful investigation and adjudication. The partnerships developed through our ECTFs, the support provided by our Criminal Investigative Division, the liaison established by our overseas offices, and the training provided to our special agents via Electronic Crimes Special Agent Program are all instrumental to the Secret Service's successful network intrusion investigations.

One example of the Secret Service's success in these investigations is the case involving Heartland Payment Systems. As described in the August 2009 indictment, a transnational organized criminal group allegedly used various network intrusion techniques to breach security and navigate the credit card processing environment. Once inside the networks, they installed "sniffer" programs to capture card numbers, as well as password and account information. The

Secret Service investigation, the largest and most complex data breach investigation ever prosecuted in the United States, revealed that data from more than 130 million credit card accounts were at risk of being compromised and exfiltrated to a command and control server operated by an international group directly related to other ongoing Secret Service investigations. During the course of the investigation, the Secret Service uncovered that this international group committed other intrusions into multiple corporate networks to steal credit and debit card data. The Secret Service relied on various investigative methods, including subpoenas, search warrants, and Mutual Legal Assistance Treaty (MLAT) requests through our foreign law enforcement partners to identify three main suspects. As a result of the investigation, these primary suspects were indicted for various computer-related crimes. The lead defendant in the indictment pled guilty and was sentenced to twenty years in federal prison. This investigation is ongoing with over 100 additional victim companies identified.

Recognizing these complexities, several federal agencies are collaborating to investigate cases and identify proactive strategies. Greater collaboration within the federal, state and local law enforcement community enhances information sharing, promotes efficiency in investigations, and facilitates efforts to de-conflict in cases of concurrent jurisdiction. For example, the Secret Service has collaborated extensively with DOJ's CCIPS, which "prevents, investigates, and prosecutes computer crimes by working with other government agencies, the private sector, academic institutions, and foreign counterparts."[8] The Secret Service's ECTFs are a natural complement to CCIPS, resulting in an excellent partnership over the years. In the last decade, nearly every major cyber investigation conducted by the Secret Service has benefited from CCIPS contributions.

The Secret Service also maintains a positive relationship with the DOJ's Federal Bureau of Investigation (FBI). The Secret Service has a permanent presence at the National Cyber Investigative Joint Task Force (NCIJTF), which coordinates, integrates, and shares information related to investigations of national security cyber threats. The Secret Service also often partners with the FBI on various criminal cyber investigations. For example, in August 2010, a joint operation involving the Secret Service, FBI, and the Security Service of Ukraine (SBU), yielded the seizure of 143 computer systems – one of the largest international seizures of digital media gathered by U.S. law enforcement – consisting of 85 terabytes of data, which was eventually transferred to law enforcement authorities in the United States. The data was seized from a criminal Internet service provider located in Odessa, Ukraine, also referred to as a "Bullet Proof Hoster." Thus far, the forensic analysis of these systems has already identified a significant amount of criminal information pertaining to numerous investigations currently underway by both agencies, including malware, criminal chat communications, and PII of U.S. citizens.

The case of Vladislav Horohorin is another example of successful cooperation between the Secret Service and its law enforcement partners around the world. Mr. Horohorin, one of the world's most notorious traffickers of stolen financial information, was arrested on August 25, 2010, pursuant to a U.S. arrest warrant issued by the Secret Service. Mr. Horohorin created the first fully-automated online store which was responsible for selling stolen credit card data. Both CCIPS and the Office of International Affairs at DOJ played critical roles in this apprehension.

---

[8] U.S. Department of Justice. (n.d.). *Computer Crime & Intellectual Property Section: About CCIPS.* Retrieved from http://www.justice.gov/criminal/cybercrime/ccips.html

Furthermore, as a result of information sharing, the FBI was able to bring additional charges against Mr. Horohorin for his involvement in a Royal Bank of Scotland network intrusion. This type of cooperation is crucial if law enforcement is to be successful in disrupting and dismantling criminal organizations involved in cyber crime.

This case demonstrates the importance of international law enforcement cooperation. Through the Secret Service's 24 international field offices the Service develops close partnerships with numerous foreign law enforcement agencies in order to combat transnational crime. Successfully investigating transnational crime depends not only on the efforts of the Department of State and the DOJ's Office of International Affairs to establish and execute MLATs, and other forms of international law enforcement cooperation, but also on the personal relationships that develop between U.S. law enforcement officers and their foreign counterparts. Both the CCIPS and the Office of International Affairs at DOJ played critical roles in this apprehension. Furthermore, as a result of information sharing, the FBI was able to bring additional charges against Mr. Horohorin for his involvement in a Royal Bank of Scotland network intrusion. This type of cooperation is crucial if law enforcement is to be successful in disrupting and dismantling criminal organizations involved in cyber crime.

Within DHS, the Secret Service benefits from a close relationship with Immigration and Customs Enforcement's Homeland Security Investigations (ICE-HSI). Since 1997, the Secret Service, ICE-HSI, and IRS-CI have jointly trained on computer investigations through the Electronic Crimes Special Agent Program (ECSAP). ICE-HSI is also a member of Secret Service ECTFs, and ICE-HSI and the Secret Service have partnered on numerous cyber crime investigations including the recent take down of the digital currency Liberty Reserve.

To further its cybersecurity information sharing efforts, the Secret Service has strengthened its relationship with the National Protection and Programs Directorate (NPPD), including the NCCIC. As the Secret Service identifies malware, suspicious IPs and other information through its criminal investigations, it shares information with our Department's NCCIC. The Secret Service continues to build upon its full-time presence at NCCIC to coordinate its cyber programs with other federal agencies.

As a part of these efforts, and to ensure that information is shared in a timely and effective manner, the Secret Service has personnel assigned to the following DHS and non-DHS entities:

- NPPD's National Cybersecurity & Communications Integration Center (NCCIC);
- NPPD's Office of Infrastructure Protection;
- DHS's Science and Technology Directorate (S&T);
- DOJ National Cyber Investigative Joint Task Force (NCIJTF);
- Each FBI Joint Terrorism Task Force (JTTF), including the National JTTF;
- Department of the Treasury - Office of Terrorist Financing and Financial Crimes (TFFC);
- Department of the Treasury - Financial Crimes Enforcement Network (FinCEN);
- Central Intelligence Agency;
- DOJ, International Organized Crime and Intelligence Operations Center (IOC-2);
- Drug Enforcement Administration's Special Operations Division;
- EUROPOL; and

- INTERPOL.

The Secret Service is committed to ensuring that all its information sharing activities comply with applicable laws, regulations, and policies, including those that pertain to privacy and civil liberties.

Secret Service Framework

To protect our financial infrastructure, industry, and the American public, the Secret Service has adopted a multi-faceted approach to aggressively combat cyber and computer-related crimes.

Electronic Crimes Task Forces

In 1995, the Secret Service New York Field Office established the New York Electronic Crimes Task Force (ECTF) to combine the resources of academia, the private sector, and local, state and federal law enforcement agencies to combat computer-based threats to our financial payment systems and critical infrastructures. In 2001, Congress directed the Secret Service to establish a nationwide network of ECTFs to "prevent, detect, and investigate various forms of electronic crimes, including potential terrorist attacks against critical infrastructure and financial payment systems."[9]

Secret Service field offices currently operate 33 ECTFs, including two based overseas in Rome, Italy, and London, England. Membership in our ECTFs includes: over 4,000 private sector partners; over 2,500 international, federal, state and local law enforcement partners; and over 350 academic partners. By joining our ECTFs, our partners benefit from the resources, information, expertise and advanced research provided by our international network of members while focusing on issues with significant regional impact.

Cyber Intelligence Section

Another example of our partnership approach with private industry is our Cyber Intelligence Section (CIS) which analyzes evidence collected as a part of Secret Service investigations and disseminates information in support of Secret Service investigations worldwide and generates new investigative leads based upon its findings. CIS leverages technology and information obtained through private sector partnerships to monitor developing technologies and trends in the financial payments industry for information that may be used to enhance the Secret Service's capabilities to prevent and mitigate attacks against the financial and critical infrastructures. CIS also has an operational unit that investigates international cyber-criminals involved in cyber-intrusions, identity theft, credit card fraud, bank fraud, and other computer-related crimes. The information and coordination provided by CIS is a crucial element to successfully investigating, prosecuting, and dismantling international criminal organizations.

---

[9] *See* Public Law 107-56 Section 105 (appears as note following 18 U.S.C. § 3056).

Electronic Crimes Special Agent Program

A central component of the Secret Service's cyber-crime investigations is its Electronic Crimes Special Agent Program (ECSAP), which is comprised of nearly 1,400 Secret Service special agents who have received at least one of three levels of computer crimes-related training.

Level I – Basic Investigation of Computers and Electronic Crimes (BICEP): The BICEP training program focuses on the investigation of electronic crimes and provides a brief overview of several aspects involved with electronic crimes investigations. This program provides Secret Service agents and our state and local law enforcement partners with a basic understanding of computers and electronic crime investigations and is now part of our core curriculum for newly hired special agents.

Level II – Network Intrusion Responder (ECSAP-NI): ECSAP-NI training provides special agents with specialized training and equipment that allows them to respond to and investigate network intrusions. These may include intrusions into financial sector computer systems, corporate storage servers, or various other targeted platforms. The Level II trained agent will be able to identify critical artifacts that will allow for effective investigation of identity theft, malicious hacking, unauthorized access, and various other related electronic crimes.

Level III – Computer Forensics (ECSAP-CF): ECSAP-CF training provides special agents with specialized training and equipment that allows them to investigate and forensically obtain digital evidence to be utilized in the prosecution of various electronic crimes cases, as well as criminally-focused protective intelligence cases.

These agents are deployed in Secret Service field offices throughout the world and have received extensive training in forensic identification, as well as the preservation and retrieval of electronically stored evidence. ECSAP-trained agents are computer investigative specialists, qualified to conduct examinations on all types of electronic evidence. These special agents are equipped to investigate the continually evolving arena of electronic crimes and have proven invaluable in the successful prosecution of criminal groups involved in computer fraud, bank fraud, identity theft, access device fraud and various other electronic crimes targeting our financial institutions and private sector.

National Computer Forensics Institute

The National Computer Forensics Institute (NCFI) initiative is the result of a partnership between the Secret Service, NPPD, the State of Alabama, and the Alabama District Attorney's Association. The goal of this facility is to provide a national standard of training for a variety of electronic crimes investigations. The program offers state and local law enforcement officers, prosecutors, and judges the training necessary to conduct computer forensics examinations. Investigators are trained to respond to network intrusion incidents and to conduct electronic crimes investigations. Since opening in 2008, the institute has held over 110 cyber and digital forensics courses in 13 separate subjects and trained and equipped more than 2,500 state and local officials, including more than 1,600 police investigators, 570 prosecutors and 180 judges from all 50 states and three U.S. territories. These NCFI graduates represent more than 1,000 agencies nationwide.

Partnerships with Academia

In August 2000, the Secret Service and Carnegie Mellon University Software Engineering Institute (SEI) established the Secret Service CERT[10] Liaison Program to provide technical support, opportunities for research and development, as well as public outreach and education to more than 150 scientists and researchers in the fields of computer and network security, malware analysis, forensic development, training and education. Supplementing this effort is research into emerging technologies being used by cyber-criminals and development of technologies and techniques to combat them.

The primary goals of the program are: to broaden the Secret Service's knowledge of software engineering and networked systems security; to expand and strengthen partnerships and relationships with the technical and academic communities; partner with CERT-SEI and Carnegie Mellon University to support research and development to improve the security of cyberspace and improve the ability of law enforcement to investigate crimes in a digital age; and to present the results of this partnership at the quarterly meetings of our ECTFs.

In August 2004, the Secret Service partnered with CERT-SEI to publish the first "Insider Threat Study" examining the illicit cyber activity and insider fraud in the banking and finance sector. Due to the overwhelming response to this initial study, the Secret Service and CERT-SEI, in partnership with DHS Science & Technology (S&T), updated the study and released the most recent version just last year, which is published at http://www.ccrt.org/insider_threat/.

To improve law enforcement's ability to investigate crimes involving mobile devices, the Secret Service opened the Cell Phone Forensic Facility at the University of Tulsa in 2008. This facility has a three-pronged mission: (1) training federal, state and local law enforcement agents in embedded device forensics; (2) developing novel hardware and software solutions for extracting and analyzing digital evidence from embedded devices; and (3) applying the hardware and software solutions to support criminal investigations conducted by the Secret Service and its partner agencies. To date, investigators trained at the Cell Phone Forensic Facility have completed more than 6,500 examinations on cell phone and embedded devices nationwide. Secret Service agents assigned to the Tulsa facility have contributed to over 300 complex cases that have required the development of sophisticated techniques and tools to extract critical evidence.

These collaborations with academia, among others, have produced valuable innovations that have helped strengthen the cyber ecosystem and improved law enforcement's ability to investigate cyber crime. The Secret Service will continue to partner closely with academia and DHS S&T, particularly the Cyber Forensics Working Group, to support research and development of innovate tools and methods to support criminal investigations.

Legislative Action to Combat Data Breaches

While there is no single solution to prevent data breaches of U.S. customer information, legislative action could help to improve the Nation's cybersecurity, reduce regulatory costs on

---

[10] CERT—not an acronym—conducts empirical research and analysis to develop and transition socio-technical solutions to combat insider cyber threats.

U.S. companies, and strengthen law enforcement's ability to conduct effective investigations. The Administration previously proposed law enforcement provisions related to computer security through a letter from OMB Director Lew to Congress on May 12, 2011, highlighting the importance of additional tools to combat emerging criminal practices. We continue to support changes like these that will keep up with rapidly-evolving technologies and uses.

Conclusion

The Secret Service is committed to safeguarding the Nation's financial payment systems by investigating and dismantling criminal organizations involved in cyber crime. Responding to the growth in these types of crimes and the level of sophistication these criminals employ requires significant resources and greater collaboration among law enforcement and its public and private sector partners. Accordingly, the Secret Service dedicates significant resources to improving investigative techniques, providing training for law enforcement partners, and raising public awareness. The Secret Service will continue to be innovative in its approach to cyber crime and cyber security and is pleased that the Committee recognizes the magnitude of these issues and the evolving nature of these crimes.

Department of Justice

STATEMENT OF

MYTHILI RAMAN
ACTING ASSISTANT ATTORNEY GENERAL
DEPARTMENT OF JUSTICE

BEFORE THE

COMMITTEE ON THE JUDICIARY
UNITED STATES SENATE

AT A HEARING ENTITLED

"PRIVACY IN THE DIGITAL AGE:
PREVENTING DATA BREACHES AND COMBATING CYBERCRIME"

PRESENTED
FEBRUARY 4, 2014

Statement of

Mythili Raman

Acting Assistant Attorney General

Department of Justice

Before the

Committee on the Judiciary

United States Senate

At a Hearing Entitled

"Privacy in the Digital Age: Preventing Data Breaches and Combating Cybercrime"

Presented

February 4, 2014

Good afternoon, Chairman Leahy, Ranking Member Grassley, and Members of the Committee. Thank you for the opportunity to appear before the Committee today to discuss the Department of Justice's fight against cybercrime. I also particularly want to thank the Chair for holding this hearing and for his continued leadership on these important issues.

At the Department of Justice, we are devoting significant resources and energy to fighting computer hacking and other types of cybercrime. The recent revelations about the massive thefts of financial information from large retail stores have served as a stark reminder to all of us about how vulnerable we are to cyber criminals who are determined to steal our personal information. The Justice Department is more committed than ever to ensuring that the full range of government enforcement tools is brought to bear in the fight against cybercrime.

Cybercrime has increased dramatically over the last decade, and our financial infrastructure has suffered repeated cyber intrusions. As we all know, it is becoming far too commonplace an occurrence that our email accounts are hijacked, our financial information siphoned away, and our personal information compromised. The technology revolution – which has brought enormous benefits to individuals, U.S. companies and our economy as a whole – has also facilitated these criminal activities, making available a wide array of new methods that identity thieves can use to access and exploit the personal information of others. Skilled criminal hackers are now able to perpetrate large-scale data breaches that leave, in some cases, tens of millions of individuals at risk of identity theft. Today's criminals, who often sit on the other side of the world, can hack into computer systems of universities, merchants, financial institutions, credit card processing companies, and data processors to steal large volumes of sensitive and valuable information. They then peddle the stolen information to other criminals, use the information for their own financial gain, or sometimes even terrorize and extort their victims.

Last December, Target, the second-largest U.S. discount chain, announced that credit and debit card data for as many as 40 million consumers who shopped in its stores between November 27 and December 15 may have been compromised. Target then disclosed on January 10 that thieves had also accessed the personal information, including names, phone numbers, home addresses, and/or email addresses, of as many as 70 million people – information that is valued by criminals because it can be used to lure victims with fake emails or hack into other accounts. The U.S. Secret Service, within the Department of Homeland Security, and the Department of Justice are investigating this massive data breach.

A few days later, retailer Neiman Marcus Inc. reported that it also was the victim of a suspected cyberattack over the holidays in which some of its customers' credit card information may have been stolen. Target and Neiman Marcus are just two of the latest known victims.

The Justice Department is vigorously responding to hacking and other cybercrimes through the tenacious work of the Criminal Division's Computer Crime and Intellectual Property Section, also known as CCIPS, which partners with Computer Hacking and Intellectual Property Coordinators in U.S. Attorney's Offices across the country as part of a network of almost 300 Justice Department cybercrime prosecutors. In addition, the Federal Bureau of Investigation has made combating cyber threats one of its top national priorities, working through Cyber Task Forces in each of its 56 field offices and continuing to strengthen the National Cyber Investigative Joint Task Force. Every day, these prosecutors and agents strive to hold to account cyber criminals who victimize Americans.

Consider, for instance, the case of Vladislav Horohorin, which was prosecuted here in the District of Columbia by CCIPS and the United States Attorney's Office, based on an investigation by the FBI and U.S. Secret Service. Horohorin, known by the online nickname

"BadB," used online criminal forums to sell stolen credit and debit card information to individuals around the world to enable fraudulent transactions by other cyber criminals. At the time of his arrest, he possessed more than 2.5 million stolen credit and debit card numbers. In one instance, he participated in a criminal group that, in a single 12-hour crime spree, stole over $9.4 million through fraudulent transactions at over 2,100 ATMs in 280 cities around the world. As a result of a massive investigation spanning several years – and several countries – we located and charged him, and he was arrested after leaving Russia for France. In April 2013, Horohorin was sentenced to serve 88 months in prison.

Our investigation of the Coreflood botnet is another example of our commitment to stopping massive computer crimes by using the most innovative law enforcement techniques. A botnet is a network of secretly hacked computers, sometimes numbering in the millions, which are located in homes, schools, and offices. The computers are infected with sophisticated malicious software, or "malware," and once the malware is installed, hackers can put these bots to countless illegal uses. The Coreflood botnet, for example, hijacked hundreds of thousands of computers for the purpose of stealing private personal and financial information – including usernames and passwords – from unsuspecting computer users. In one example, the Coreflood botnet software illegally monitored Internet communications between a computer user and her bank, took over an online banking session, and then emptied the user's bank account. Overall losses from the scheme were staggering, estimated to be in the tens of millions of dollars.

Although the individuals controlling the Coreflood network resided overseas and were largely outside the direct reach of U.S. law enforcement, in 2011, CCIPS, the United States Attorney's Office for the District of Connecticut, and the FBI used a combination of civil and criminal legal authorities to seize key control servers, shut down the network, and work with private sector partners to help disinfect victims' computer systems. Among other things, as part of this ground-breaking law enforcement operation, the Justice Department obtained a court order authorizing the government to respond to signals sent from infected computers in the United States to stop the Coreflood software from running, and thus to prevent further harm to hundreds of thousands of Americans whose computers were under the control of the botnet. And, in a relatively short period of time, the Coreflood botnet was dismantled.

The Department has continued to place a high priority on arresting and deterring those who create botnets. CCIPS and the U.S. Attorney's Office in Atlanta just last week announced the guilty plea of a Russian citizen named Aleksandr Panin for developing and distributing malware called "SpyEye." The SpyEye malware created botnets that stole personal and financial information such as credit card information, banking credentials, usernames, passwords, and personal identification numbers. Panin sold his software to at least 154 criminal "clients," who in turn used it to infect an estimated 1.4 million computers around the world. The FBI arrested Panin on July 1, 2013, while he was flying through Hartsfield-Jackson Atlanta International Airport.

Hacking can have terrifying consequences even when conducted on a smaller scale, and we have vigorously pursued hackers who have used the Internet to invade Americans' privacy. In 2011, for example, in a case investigated by the FBI, the United States Attorney's Office in Los Angeles successfully prosecuted a hacker named Luis Mijangos. Mijangos hacked for sexual thrill. He infected the computers of victims with malicious software that gave him complete control over their computers. He deliberately targeted teens and young women, reading their emails, turning on their computer microphones and listening to conversations taking place in their homes, and, most importantly for him, watching them through their webcams as they undressed. Even more frightening, Mijangos then extorted certain victims by threatening to post intimate pictures on the Internet unless the victims provided him with even more salacious images or videos of themselves. When one victim shared Mijangos's threats with a friend, Mijangos retaliated by posting nude pictures of the victim on her friend's social networking page. In another instance, Mijangos had infected the computers of a college student, her boyfriend, and her roommate. When the victim called her boyfriend, and they discussed calling the police, Mijangos reportedly sent the boyfriend an anonymous instant message that said: "I know you're talking to each other right now!" The victim then decided to call the police. But when she did, she got a message, too. "I know you just called the police," he wrote. His message was unmistakable: he was in control; he knew everything; and he had the power to hurt the victim further if she reported the crime. At the time of his arrest, FBI computer forensics experts had determined that Mijangos had infected more than 100 computers that were used by approximately 230 individuals, at least 44 of them minors. The Court sentenced Mijangos to 72 months in federal prison.

The Department has continued to place a high priority on arresting and deterring those who create botnets. CCIPS and the U.S. Attorney's Office in Atlanta just last week announced the guilty plea of a Russian citizen named Aleksandr Panin for developing and distributing malware called "SpyEye." The SpyEye malware created botnets that stole personal and financial information such as credit card information, banking credentials, usernames, passwords, and personal identification numbers. Panin sold his software to at least 154 criminal "clients," who in turn used it to infect an estimated 1.4 million computers around the world. The FBI arrested Panin on July 1, 2013, while he was flying through Hartsfield-Jackson Atlanta International Airport.

Hacking can have terrifying consequences even when conducted on a smaller scale, and we have vigorously pursued hackers who have used the Internet to invade Americans' privacy. In 2011, for example, in a case investigated by the FBI, the United States Attorney's Office in Los Angeles successfully prosecuted a hacker named Luis Mijangos. Mijangos hacked for sexual thrill. He infected the computers of victims with malicious software that gave him complete control over their computers. He deliberately targeted teens and young women, reading their emails, turning on their computer microphones and listening to conversations taking place in their homes, and, most importantly for him, watching them through their webcams as they undressed. Even more frightening, Mijangos then extorted certain victims by threatening to post intimate pictures on the Internet unless the victims provided him with even more salacious images or videos of themselves. When one victim shared Mijangos's threats with a friend, Mijangos retaliated by posting nude pictures of the victim on her friend's social networking page. In another instance, Mijangos had infected the computers of a college student, her boyfriend, and her roommate. When the victim called her boyfriend, and they discussed calling the police, Mijangos reportedly sent the boyfriend an anonymous instant message that said: "I know you're talking to each other right now!" The victim then decided to call the police. But when she did, she got a message, too. "I know you just called the police," he wrote. His message was unmistakable: he was in control; he knew everything; and he had the power to hurt the victim further if she reported the crime. At the time of his arrest, FBI computer forensics experts had determined that Mijangos had infected more than 100 computers that were used by approximately 230 individuals, at least 44 of them minors. The Court sentenced Mijangos to 72 months in federal prison.

up with technology so that we can keep pace with the cyber criminals, who are constantly developing new tactics and methods.

Computer Fraud and Abuse Act

In addition to the important law enforcement techniques that we must use to successfully investigate cyber criminals, our prosecutors also rely on substantive criminal statutes to bring cyber criminals to justice. One of the most important of these laws is the Computer Fraud and Abuse Act, also called the "CFAA." The CFAA is the primary Federal law against hacking. It protects the public against criminals who hack into computers to steal information, install malicious software, and delete files. The CFAA, in short, reflects our baseline expectation that people are entitled to have control over their own computers and are entitled to trust that information they store in their computers remains safe.

The CFAA was first enacted in 1986, at a time when the problem of cybercrime was still in its infancy. Over the years, a series of measured, modest changes have been made to the CFAA to reflect new technologies and means of committing crimes and to equip law enforcement with tools to respond to changing threats. The CFAA has not been amended since 2008, and the intervening years have again created the need for the enactment of modest, incremental changes. The Administration's May 2011 legislative proposal proposed revisions to keep Federal criminal law up-to-date. We continue to support changes like these that will keep up with rapidly-evolving technologies and uses.

Deterring Insider Threats

Another portion of the CFAA that has received considerable attention is the way that the law addresses the threat posed by insiders – those who have some right to access a system but who abuse that right, such as employees of a business who unlawfully make off with their employers' intellectual property. The CFAA addresses this problem by criminalizing conduct by those who "exceed authorized access" to a protected computer.

Some commentators have contended that the CFAA's provision criminalizing exceeding authorized access should be limited or abolished because the provision is subject to misuse or overuse. Some have worried, for example, that the statute permits prosecution of people who merely lie about their age when going to a dating site, or harmlessly violate the terms of service of an email provider. To that end, we are open to addressing these concerns by working with Congress to develop appropriate statutory amendments, such as new statutory thresholds regarding the value or sensitivity of the information improperly accessed under 1030(a)(2), or new language making more explicit that the statute does not permit prosecution based on access restrictions that are not clearly understood.

At the same time, insider hackers pose a serious threat to American businesses and citizens. Examples of insiders include employees at a credit card company or stock broker who regularly deal with sensitive information. There is generally no way to encrypt and password-protect every piece of data on a system to eliminate the insider threat, because employees need to be able access the data to do their jobs. Thus, written policies between employers and employees – which are simply a contractual means of ensuring trust – are an important way to secure information. Violating these written restrictions harms businesses. Just as businesses justifiably rely on the criminal law to deter thefts of physical property, so they also should be able to rely on it to deter misappropriation of their private, sensitive data – data that is often far more valuable than equipment or supplies.

In recent years, two courts of appeals have interpreted the CFAA to bar certain "insider" cases, creating a circuit split. Compare *United States v. Nosal*, 676 F.3d 854 (9th Cir. 2012) *(en banc)* and *WEC Carolina Energy Solutions LLC v. Miller*, 687 F.3d 199 (4th Cir. 2012), with *United States v. John*, 597 F.3d 263 (5th Cir. 2010); *United States v. Rodriguez*, 628 F.3d 1258 (11th Cir. 2010); and *Int'l Airport Ctrs., LLC v. Citrin*, 440 F.3d 418 (7th Cir. 2006). Specifically, the Fourth and Ninth Circuits have interpreted the statute not to permit prosecution as long as an insider was authorized to access the database or information in question for any purpose. Under this interpretation, the CFAA would not apply where a police officer accessed an arrest record for the purpose of harassing a romantic rival, because the officer was authorized to access the records to assist in criminal investigations. Similarly, under this interpretation, the CFAA would not apply where a bank employee accessed customer records for the purpose of selling them to organized crime members, because the employee was authorized to access the records to resolve customer complaints. This interpretation makes it substantially more challenging for DOJ to protect American companies from the misappropriation of their intellectual property and sensitive data – misappropriation that may also directly harm American citizens when that data includes their personal or financial information.

We look forward to working with Congress to address these important issues.

Data Breach Notification

While the Justice Department continues to use all of the tools at its disposal to combat cybercrime, the Administration recommends the establishment of a strong, uniform Federal standard requiring certain types of businesses to report data breaches and thefts of electronic personally identifiable information. Businesses should be required to provide prompt notice to consumers in the wake of a breach. We should balance the need to safeguard consumers and hold compromised entities accountable, while setting clear standards that avoid undue burdens on industry. We should include a safe harbor for breaches with no reasonable risk of harm or fraud. This approach would protect the privacy of individuals while holding firms accountable for failure to safeguard personal data.

In 2011, the Administration put forth a package of recommended cybersecurity amendments that included a data breach notification proposal.[2] The 2011 proposal is based upon the belief that American consumers should know when they are at risk of identity theft or other harms because of a data security breach. In addition, to strengthen the tools available to law enforcement to investigate data security breaches and to combat identity theft, the proposal would require that business entities notify the Federal government of a data security breach in a timely fashion so that law enforcement can promptly pursue the perpetrators of cyber intrusions and identity theft. The proposal has several sections of particular note.

First, under this proposal, following the discovery of a security breach, business entities must notify any individual whose sensitive, personally identifiable information has been, or is reasonably believed to have been, accessed or acquired, unless there is no reasonable risk of harm. Business entities covered under this requirement are those that use, access, transmit, store, dispose of, or collect sensitive, personally identifiable information about more than 10,000 people during any 12-month period. But the Administration believes that business entities which have demonstrated that they have effective data breach prevention programs should be exempt from notice to individuals if a risk assessment concludes that there is no reasonable risk that a security breach has harmed, or will harm, the individuals whose information was compromised.

---

[2] The Administration's Privacy and Innovation Blueprint, released in February 2012, also called for a data breach notification law.

The proposal would also recognize that such harm may be avoided where the stolen data has been rendered unusable by criminals; for example, through encryption, or through programs that block unauthorized financial transactions and provide effective notice to affected victims. The proposal also includes certain exceptions for notice that would impair law enforcement investigations or national security.

Because of the importance of bringing the perpetrators of data breaches to justice, the Administration's proposal would also require business entities to notify law enforcement agencies if the security breach involves (1) the sensitive information of more than 5,000 people; (2) a database or other data system containing sensitive information of more than 500,000 people nationwide; (3) databases owned by the Federal government; or (4) primarily the sensitive information of Federal employees and contractors involved in national security or law enforcement. Businesses would report to a single entity that would then promptly disseminate the reported information to key Federal law enforcement agencies. In recognition of the time-sensitivity of data breach investigations, the notice required under this section would be provided as promptly as possible, but no later than 72 hours before notification to an individual or 10 days after discovery of the events requiring notice, whichever comes first.

Millions of Americans every year are faced with the potential for fraud and identity theft from online breaches of their sensitive, personally identifiable information. The nation clearly needs strong protections for consumers' rights and privacy, and accountability for businesses that do not safeguard credit card and social security numbers, names and addresses, medical records, and other sensitive information. The Administration's proposal creates a strong national standard to notify consumers with clear, actionable information when their personal information is compromised. Responsible entities will be held accountable through these disclosures. At the same time, a consistent national standard and reasonable exemptions for harmless breaches will reduce unnecessary compliance costs. This proposal meets the dual challenge of ensuring privacy, security, and safety without burdening economic prosperity and innovation.

Access Device Fraud

To ensure that we can take action when cyber criminals acting overseas steal data from U.S. financial institutions, we also recommend a modification to what is known as the access device fraud statute, 18 U.S.C. § 1029. One of the most common motivations for hacking crime is to obtain financial information. The access device fraud statute proscribes the unlawful possession and use of "access devices," such as credit card numbers and devices such as credit card embossing machines. Not only do lone individuals commit this crime, but, more and more, organized criminal enterprises have formed to commit such intrusions and to exploit the stolen data through fraud.

The Department of Justice recommends that the statute be expanded to prosecute offenders in foreign countries who directly and significantly harm United States financial institutions and citizens. Currently, a criminal who trades in credit card information issued by a U.S. financial institution, but who otherwise does not take one of certain enumerated actions within the jurisdiction of the United States, cannot be prosecuted under section 1029(a)(3). Such scenarios are not merely hypothetical. United States law enforcement agencies have identified foreign-based individuals selling vast quantities of credit card numbers issued by U.S. financial institutions where there is no evidence that those criminals took a specific step within the United States to traffic in the data. The United States has a compelling interest in prosecuting such individuals given the harm to U.S. financial institutions and American citizens, and the statute should be revised to cover this sort of criminal conduct.

Deterring the Spread of Cell Phone Spying

The Department of Justice further recommends a legislative change to enable law enforcement to seize the profits of those who use cell phone spyware. The spread of computers and cellular phones in recent years has created a new market in malicious software that allows perpetrators to intercept victims' communications without their knowledge or consent. This is illegal under current law, and current law also provides that law enforcement can forfeit the surreptitious interception devices themselves. It does not, however, enable forfeiture of the proceeds of the sale or use of those devices, or the forfeiture of any property used to facilitate their manufacture, advertising, or distribution. Further, the surreptitious interception of communications is currently not listed as a predicate offense in the money laundering statute, 18 U.S.C. § 1956. Because perpetrators of these crimes often act from abroad, making it more difficult to prosecute them, it is particularly important that law enforcement be able to seize the money that the criminals make from engaging in this criminal surveillance, and seize the equipment they use.

Selling Access to Botnets

We also recommend amending current law to address the proliferation of botnets, such as the Coreflood botnet I discussed earlier. Botnets can be used for various nefarious purposes, including theft of personal or financial information, the dissemination of spam, and cyberattacks, such as Distributed Denial of Service attacks. But creators and operators of botnets do not always commit those crimes themselves – frequently they sell, or even rent, access to the infected computers to others. The CFAA does not clearly cover such trafficking in botnets, even though trafficking in infected computers is clearly illegitimate, and can be essential to furthering other criminal activity. We thus propose that the CFAA be amended to cover trafficking in access to botnets.

In addition, section 1030(a)(6) presently requires proof of intent to defraud. Such intent is often difficult to prove because the traffickers of unauthorized access to computers often have a wrongful purpose other than the commission of fraud, or do not know or care why their customers are seeking unauthorized access to other people's computers. This has made it more challenging in many cases for prosecutors to identify a provable offense even when they can establish beyond a reasonable doubt that individuals are selling access to thousands of infected computers. We therefore recommend that Congress consider amending the CFAA to address this shortcoming.

Conclusion

I very much appreciate the opportunity to discuss with you the ways in which the Department protects American citizens and businesses by aggressively investigating and prosecuting hackers – both outsiders and insiders. We understand how devastating it is to victims of cybercrime who have their personal and financial information siphoned away, whether by hackers on the other side of the world or by insiders at a company that might hold their personal information. The Justice Department is committed to using the full range of investigative tools and laws available to us to fight these crimes and protect Americans. And, we will continue to use these tools responsibly.

Thank you for the opportunity to discuss the Department's work in this area, and I look forward to answering any questions you might have.

133

**Written Questions for the Record of Chairman Leahy
for John J. Mulligan
Executive Vice President and Chief Financial Officer
Target Corporation
February 11, 2014**

1. At the February 4, 2014 hearing, you testified that Target suffered two data breaches: The first affected the payment information of approximately 40 million customers. A second data breach affected the sensitive personal information of approximately 70 million customers.

    a. Did both of these data breaches involve the same malware and the same perpetrator(s)? Please explain.

    b. Vast amounts of stored consumer data can become an attractive target for cyber thieves. Does Target store its customers' personally identifiable information on its computer systems? If so, what steps does Target take to protect this sensitive data from data breaches or other cyber attacks?

    c. Does Target notify its customers about the company's policy on the collection and retention of customer data?

    d. Do Target customers have the ability to opt out of any program involving the collection or retention of their personal information?

2. During the hearing, you discussed your support for so-called "Chip and Pin" technology for point of sale transactions.

    a. When do you anticipate that Target will adopt Chip and Pin technology at its stores?

    b. Do you have any concerns about this technology?

    c. Has Target explored any other payment processing methods to help protect the privacy of sensitive financial and consumer data during the payment process?

3. Has the investigation into the data breach at Target prompted any changes in Target's security of online transactions or stored customer data? If so, please explain.

QUESTIONS SUBMITTED BY SENATOR GRASSLEY FOR JOHN J. MULLIGAN AND MICHAEL R. KINGSTON

"Privacy in the Digital Age: Preventing Data Breaches and Combating Cybercrime."
Questions for the Record Submitted by
Ranking Member Charles E. Grassley of Iowa,
February 11, 2014.

Questions for Mr. John Mulligan and Mr. Michael Kingston

1. The recent attack your company suffered highlights the problem with the current patchwork of state notification laws. There are differing views whether a federal breach notification standard should serve as a "floor" or preempt the current breach notification laws. Given your recent experience with issuing notification, please discuss the following:

   a. How would a federal notification standard that permits states to include additional requirements have affected the company during the wake of the breach? .

   b. What would the approach have been if a federal uniform notification standard was in place that fully preempted current notification laws?

   c. What impact would the two different approaches have on a company's resources as compared to the other, i.e., full preemption versus a federal standard that serves as a "floor"?

   d. Is current law preferable to either of the approaches discussed above?

2. In the Congress there are several data breach notification proposals, all of which differ from the other. One important consideration is that of timing for issuing notification. Some legislation requires notice of a breach be issued as soon as possible; another says within 48 hours of discovery. Please describe the general process involved in issuing notice to consumers, including a consideration whether statutory time frames for issuing notifications would be helpful or harmful.

3. Another significant issue concerns the penalties associated with a company's failure to comply with any notification requirements. Do you believe that providing criminal – as opposed to civil – penalties for failing to notify consumers would be helpful or harmful? Why?

4. Please provide any additional thoughts that you might have on the issues raised by the hearing, including but not limited to expanding on your testimony, responding to the testimony of the other witnesses and/or anything else that came up at the hearing, which you did not have a chance to respond to.

**Written Questions for the Record of Chairman Leahy
for Michael R. Kingston
Senior Vice President and Chief Information Officer
The Neiman Marcus Group
February 11, 2014**

1. At the February 4, 2014 hearing, you testified that Neiman Marcus did not currently use so-called "Chip and PIN" technology to process payments. But, you also testified that Neiman Marcus would explore this technology for payment processing at its stores.

    a. When do you anticipate that Neiman Marcus would adopt Chip and Pin technology?

    b. Do you have any concerns about this technology? If so, please explain.

    c. Has Neiman Marcus explored any other payment processing methods to help protect the privacy of sensitive financial and consumer data?

Written Questions for the Record of Chairman Leahy
For Delara Derakhshani
Policy Counsel, Consumers Union
February 11, 2014

1. During the Committee's February 4, 2014 hearing, there was a great deal of discussion about how American retailers, and other industries, can better protect sensitive financial and personal data from data breaches and cyber attacks.

    a. What can consumers do to better protect their sensitive personal information and financial data when making purchases in a store or online?

    b. What steps should consumers take after being notified that their personal or financial information has been compromised due to a data breach or other cyberthreat?

2. Do online purchases and transactions pose any additional privacy risks for consumers? Please explain.

**Written Questions for the Record of Chairman Leahy
for Fran Rosch
Senior Vice President
Security Product and Services, Endpoint and Mobility
Symantec Corporation
February 11, 2014**

1. During the February 4, 2014 hearing, you testified about steps that American retailers could take to better protect customer data from data breaches and cyber attacks.

    a. In your view, what are the key steps that retailers should take to safeguard consumer data during the payment process for point of sale transactions?

    b. What about during the payment process for online purchases?

2. In your experience, where are data breaches involving payment card data most likely to occur today -- during "point of sale" transactions, or during online transactions?

3.   Do you anticipate the trend of data breaches involving point of sale transactions will continue, given the recent data breaches involving American retailers?

"Privacy in the Digital Age: Preventing Data Breaches and Combating Cybercrime."
Questions for the Record Submitted by
Ranking Member Charles E. Grassley of Iowa,
February 11, 2014.

Questions for Mr. Fran Rosch

1. In your written testimony, you stated that it is important for a federal breach notification law to minimize "false positives," i.e., issuing notice to individuals who are later shown not to have been impacted by a breach. I share this concern because over-notification can also be harmful as it might lead to consumer apathy. Could you please share your thoughts and advice for the following:

   a. Discuss what we should consider when drafting legislation that minimizes the risk of "false positives"?

   b. How can we strike the right balance for notification so that companies understand when to issue notice, and consumers are armed with the information they need to monitor the potential for harm?

2. In your written testimony, you noted that data breach notification legislation should apply equally to all. Do you also support the position that a federal breach notification standard should preempt the current patchwork of state breach notification laws? If so, explain why preemption is so important?

3. Please provide any additional thoughts that you might have on the issues raised by the hearing, including but not limited to expanding on your testimony, responding to the testimony of the other witnesses and/or anything else that came up at the hearing, which you did not have a chance to respond to.

**Written Questions for the Record of Chairman Leahy
for the Honorable Edith Ramirez
Chairwoman
Federal Trade Commission
February 11, 2014**

1. During the Committee's February 4, 2014 hearing, you testified about how American retailers can better protect consumers' sensitive financial and personal data from data breaches and cyber attacks.

    a. What can consumers do to better protect their sensitive personal information and financial data when making point of sale purchases? What about during online transactions?

    b. What steps should consumers take after being notified that their personal or financial information has been compromised due to a data breach or other cyber attacks?

2. Has the Federal Trade Commission issued any best practices or guidance regarding how American businesses can help safeguard the privacy and security of consumers' sensitive personally identifiable information? If so, please briefly explain.

3. The collection and retention of consumer data is also a significant privacy issue for many American consumers and businesses.

    a. What are the FTC's views on whether consumers should be notified about commercial data collection and retention practices?

    b. In your view, should businesses that collect and retain consumer data allow their customers to "opt out" of these data collection and retention activities?

4. In your experience, are "point of sale" or online commercial transactions most likely to result in a data breach involving consumer data?

5. Do you anticipate that we will witness an increase in "point of sale" data breaches given the recent trend of data breaches involving American retailers?

**Written Questions for the Record of Chairman Leahy
for William Noonan
Deputy Special Agent in Charge
Criminal Investigative Division, United States Secret Service
February 11, 2014**

1. Are there additional legal tools and/or resources that would help the United States Secret Service to investigate and prevent data breaches and other cybercrimes?

2. Given the recent trend of "point of sale" data breaches involving United States retailers and the use of so-called "scraping" malware in some of those data breaches, do you anticipate that there will be an increase in this kind of cybercrime involving payment cards in the future?

3. Do you anticipate that we will witness an increase in "point of sale" data breaches, given the recent trend of data breaches involving major American retailers?

**Written Questions for the Record of Chairman Leahy
for Mythili Raman
Acting Assistant Attorney General
Criminal Division, United States Department of Justice
February 11, 2014**

1. During the February 4, 2014, hearing, you testified about the Department's important work in combating and prosecuting cybercrime. Are there any changes to existing law that would assist the Department in that effort?

2. Given the recent trend of "point of sale" data breaches involving United States retailers and the use of so-called "scraping" malware in some of those data breaches, do you anticipate that there will be an increase in this kind of cybercrime involving payment cards in the future?

3. During the hearing, you also testified that many of the perpetrators of cyber attacks on United States computers are located outside of the country.

    a. How successful has the Department been at extraditing foreign perpetrators of cybercrime?

    b. Are there any new legal tools that would assist the Department in addressing any obstacles to extradition in cybercrime matters?

Written Questions for the Record of Chairman Leahy
for John J. Mulligan
Executive Vice President and Chief Financial Officer
Target Corporation
February 11, 2014

1. At the February 4, 2014 hearing, you testified that Target suffered two data breaches: The first affected the payment information of approximately 40 million customers. A second data breach affected the sensitive personal information of approximately 70 million customers.

   a. Did both of these data breaches involve the same malware and the same perpetrator(s)? Please explain.

Chairman Leahy, I appreciate the opportunity to clarify the details surrounding the breach and the impacted data. We have consistently stated that the breach affected two types of data: payment card data which affected approximately 40 million guests and partial personal data which affected up to 70 million guests. The theft of the payment card data affected guests who shopped at our U.S. stores from November 27 through December 18. The theft of partial personal data included name, mailing address, phone number or email address.

We now know that the intruder stole a vendor's credentials to access our system and place malware on our point-of-sale registers. The malware was designed to capture payment card data from the magnetic strip of credit and debit cards prior to encryption within our system. The intruder also accessed partial personal data for up to 70 million guests. This partial personal data included name, address, email address and telephone number.

While the investigation is still active and ongoing, we believe the same attacker is responsible for the theft of both sets of data.

   b. Vast amounts of stored consumer data can become an attractive target for cyber thieves. Does Target store its customers' personally identifiable information on its computer systems? If so, what steps does Target take to protect this sensitive data from data breaches or other cyber attacks?

Target stores its guests' data on its computer systems. For many years, Target has invested significant capital and resources in security technology, personnel and processes, including firewalls, malware detection software, intrusion detection and prevention capabilities and data loss prevention tools. We perform internal and external validation and benchmarking assessments. Target's last assessment for compliance with the Payment Card Industry Data Security Standards ("PCI DSS") was completed on

September 20, 2013 by Trustwave. On that date, Trustwave certified Target as compliant with PCI DSS.

    c.   Does Target notify its customers about the company's policy on the collection and retention of customer data?

At Target, we want our guests to know how we collect, use, share, and protect information about them. By interacting with Target, our guests consent to use of information that is collected or submitted as described in our privacy policy (link to our privacy policy included below).

http://www.target.com/spot/privacy-policy#?lnk=fnav_t_spc_2_2&intc=28074|null

    d.   Do Target customers have the ability to opt out of any program involving the collection or retention of their personal information?

We provide our guests with choices about receiving marketing from Target and sharing of personal information with other companies for their marketing purposes. Our privacy policy provides our guests with information related to the collection, use, sharing and protection of information about them.

http://www.target.com/spot/privacy-policy#?lnk=fnav_t_spc_2_2&intc=28074|null

2. During the hearing, you discussed your support for so-called "Chip and Pin" technology for point of sale transactions.

    a.   When do you anticipate that Target will adopt Chip and Pin technology at its stores?

At Target, we've been working for years towards adoption of this technology. Since the breach, we are accelerating our own $100 million investment to put chip-enabled technology in place. Our goal is to implement this technology in our stores and on our proprietary REDcards by early 2015, more than six months ahead of our previous plan.

    b.   Do you have any concerns about this technology?

For consumers, this technology differs in important ways from what is widely used in the United States today. The standard credit and debit cards we use now have a magnetic stripe containing account information. When first introduced, that stripe was an innovation. But in today's world, more is needed. The latest "smart cards" have tiny microprocessor chips that encrypt the personal data shared with the sales terminals used by merchants. This change is important because even if a thief manages to steal a smart card number, it's useless without the chip.

In addition, requiring the use of a four-digit personal identification number (PIN) to complete a sales transaction would provide even greater safety. While there is no consensus across the business community on the use of PINs in conjunction with chip-enabled cards, Target supports the goal and will work toward adoption of the practice in our own stores and more widely.

In the United Kingdom, where smart card technology is widely used, financial losses associated with lost or stolen cards are at their lowest levels since 1999 and have fallen by 67 percent since 2004, according to industry estimates. In Canada, where Target and others have adopted smart cards, losses from card skimming were reduced by 72 percent from 2008 to 2012, according to industry estimates.

    c.   Has Target explored any other payment processing methods to help protect the privacy of sensitive financial and consumer data during the payment process?

Target is investing in solutions that will make mobile transactions more secure. We know work is needed to strengthen protections for e-commerce, an important long-term goal. In the meantime, adopting chip-enabled cards would be a clear step in the right direction.

3. Has the investigation into the data breach at Target prompted any changes in Target's security of online transactions or stored customer data? If so, please explain.

In addition to the active and ongoing criminal investigation, we are in the midst of a comprehensive, end-to-end review of our entire network. It is our expectation that the findings from the internal review will provide us with opportunities to make security enhancements as appropriate.

"Privacy in the Digital Age: Preventing Data Breaches and Combating Cybercrime."
Questions for the Record Submitted by
Ranking Member Charles E. Grassley of Iowa,
February 11, 2014.

Questions for Mr. John Mulligan and Mr. Michael Kingston

1. The recent attack your company suffered highlights the problem with the current patchwork of state notification laws. There are differing views whether a federal breach notification standard should serve as a "floor" or preempt the current breach notification laws. Given your recent experience with issuing notification, please discuss the following:

    a. How would a federal notification standard that permits states to include additional requirements have affected the company during the wake of the breach?

    There is much debate surrounding a federal breach notification standard and while I do not want to speculate about the appropriate path Congress should take, I can speak to our actions. We provided substitute notice, including by (1) posting notice on our website; (2) providing notice by e-mail to each relevant guest for whom we had an e-mail address; and (3) providing notice to nationwide and state media. Of the various aspects of our substitute notice, only e-mail was provided directly to specific guests. In this regard, we provided notice by e-mail to each relevant guest for whom we had an e-mail address.

    In general, Target's efforts to provide substitute notice were the same with respect to guests residing in all States. For example, Target posted notice on its website for all guests, not just guests residing in certain States. In addition, Target sent information to news media in every State. In Massachusetts and Texas, however, Target took out paid notices in statewide newspapers, as provided for by relevant State law.

    On December 15, we confirmed that criminals had infiltrated our system, had installed malware on our point-of-sale network, and had potentially stolen guest payment card data. That same day, we removed the malware from virtually all registers in our U.S. stores. Over the next two days, we began notifying the payment processors and card networks, preparing to publicly notify our guests and equipping our call centers and stores with the necessary information and resources to address the concerns of our guests.

    On December 18 we disabled malware on about 25 additional registers which were disconnected from our system when we completed the initial malware removal on December 15. Our actions leading up to our public announcement on December 19 – and since – have been guided by the principle of serving our guests, and we have been moving as quickly as possible to share accurate and actionable information with the public. When we announced the intrusion on December 19 we used multiple forms of communication, including email, prominent notices on our website, and social media channels.

    b. What would the approach have been if a federal uniform notification standard was in place that fully preempted current notification laws?

Target's priority was to provide accurate and actionable notification to our guests.

    c.   What impact would the two different approaches have on a company's resources as compared to the other, i.e., full preemption versus a federal standard that serves as a "floor"?

We have not determined the impact on our resources if a federal standard were in place.

    d.   Is current law preferable to either of the approaches discussed above?

There is much debate surrounding a federal breach notification standard, and I would defer to Congress on the appropriate policy in this area.

2.   In the Congress there are several data breach notification proposals, all of which differ from the other. One important consideration is that of timing for issuing notification. Some legislation requires notice of a breach be issued as soon as possible; another says within 48 hours of discovery. Please describe the general process involved in issuing notice to consumers, including a consideration whether statutory time frames for issuing notifications would be helpful or harmful.

I understand that Congress is considering various legislative proposals. Regardless of the outcome, Target will continue to comply with applicable notification laws. As for the process involved as we prepared to notify our guests, I can share the following:

On December 15, we confirmed that criminals had infiltrated our system, had installed malware on our point-of-sale network and had potentially stolen guest payment card data. That same day, we removed the malware from virtually all registers in our U.S. stores. Over the next two days, we began notifying the payment processors and card networks, preparing to publicly notify our guests and equipping our call centers and stores with the necessary information and resources to address the concerns of our guests. On December 18 we disabled malware on about 25 additional registers which were disconnected from our system when we completed the initial malware removal on December 15.

Our actions leading up to our public announcement on December 19 – and since – have been guided by the principle of serving our guests, and we have been moving as quickly as possible to share accurate and actionable information with the public. When we announced the intrusion on December 19 we used multiple forms of communication, including email, prominent notices on our website, and social media channels.

3.   Another significant issue concerns the penalties associated with a company's failure to comply with any notification requirements. Do you believe that providing criminal – as opposed to civil – penalties for failing to notify consumers would be helpful or harmful? Why?

Target's priority was on providing accurate and actionable information to our guests. We are not in a position to speculate on the impact of criminal penalties for failing to notify consumers.

4. Please provide any additional thoughts that you might have on the issues raised by the hearing, including but not limited to expanding on your testimony, responding to the testimony of the other witnesses and/or anything else that came up at the hearing, which you did not have a chance to respond to.

Thank you for the opportunity to appear before your Committee.

Neiman Marcus | Group

February 26, 2014

Honorable Patrick Leahy
Chairman, Senate Committee on the Judiciary
224 Dirksen Senate Office Building
Washington, DC 20510

Dear Chairman Leahy:

The Neiman Marcus Group appreciated the opportunity to testify before the Senate Committee on the Judiciary during the Hearing entitled "Privacy in the Digital Age: Preventing Data Breaches and Combating Cybercrime" on February 4, 2014. In response to questions posed during and after the hearing, we have attached a response that has three parts.

First, after the hearing, you and Senator Grassley sent us additional questions. Our responses are included in Parts A and B of the Attachment.

Second, during the hearing, Senator Blumenthal requested that we provide a more detailed description of how our security practices align with the recommendations issued by Symantec Corp. in its February 3, 2014 report entitled "A Special Report on Attacks on Point of Sales Systems" (the "Symantec Report"). Our response, including information regarding our security architecture, is included in Part C of the Attachment. Given that this information will become part of the public record, we hope you will appreciate our need to provide our response in a way that will not compromise the security of our systems.

Third, we have provided some updated information relating to the forensic investigations of the cybersecurity attack on our system, which is included in Part D of the Attachment.

The Neiman Marcus Group appreciates your interest and concern regarding this urgent matter, and we support the efforts of the Senate, House, consumer groups and the retail and financial services industries to ensure that consumers are able to shop in a secure and trusted environment.

Sincerely,

Michael R. Kingston
Senior Vice President and Chief Information Officer
The Neiman Marcus Group

cc: Honorable Chuck Grassley
        Ranking Member
        Senate Committee on the Judiciary
        152 Dirksen Senate Office Building
        Washington, DC 20510

        Honorable Richard Blumenthal
        United States Senate
        724 Hart Senate Office Bldg.
        Washington, DC 20510

Attachment to February 26, 2014 letter from
Neiman Marcus Group Chief Information Officer Michael R. Kingston to Chairman Leahy

A.   <u>Response to questions from Chairman Leahy:</u>

      1.   *At the February 4, 2014 hearing, you testified that Neiman Marcus did not currently use so-called "Chip and PIN" technology to process payments. But, you also testified that Neiman Marcus would explore this technology for payment processing at its stores.*

           a.   *When do you anticipate that Neiman Marcus would adopt Chip and Pin technology?*
           b.   *Do you have any concerns about this technology? If so, please explain.*
           c.   *Has Neiman Marcus explored any other payment processing methods to help protect the privacy of sensitive financial and consumer data?*

As part of our ongoing evaluations of new technologies, the Neiman Marcus Group is actively evaluating Chip and PIN technologies. The National Retail Federation has pointed out that retailers like Neiman Marcus need the card brands, merchant banks, issuing banks and consumers to adopt cards with chips (EMV) in coordination with one another before retailers can take meaningful steps in this area.

We agree that "Chip and PIN" is worthy of discussion and has been a focus of the current conversation about payment card data security. We note that Chip and PIN is an older technology at this point, and also has well-documented security gaps, including its limited impact on card-not-present (CNP) fraud (such as online payments). Like many retailers, the Neiman Marcus Group has a growing online business presence. The prevention of CNP fraud is an important consideration for the U.S. economy. In the face of rapidly-changing technologies, we want to make sure that any significant investment we make in payment-card data security is clearly considered a strong and effective best practice that will keep all our customers' payment information safe over the long term.

In the meantime, we continue to evaluate practical improvements we can make in our own payment card environment to increase our robust consumer protections. In particular, we are currently exploring point-to-point encryption capabilities, as well as progressive payment technologies, including mobile payment technologies and platforms that may not require that consumers disclose certain financial information to Neiman Marcus as part of retail transactions.

The Neiman Marcus Group is committed to working with Congress, law enforcement, industry-leading cybersecurity providers, consumer groups, merchant banks, payment card brands, Payment Card Industry (PCI) stakeholders and others in order to enhance the already robust protections that it uses to protect our customers' personal data. We look forward to continuing this important work.

B.   *Response to questions from Senator Grassley:*

1.   *The recent attack your company suffered highlights the problem with the current patchwork of state notification laws. There are differing views whether a federal breach notification standard should serve as a "floor" or preempt the current breach notification laws. Given your recent experience with issuing notification, please discuss the following:*
   a. *How would a federal notification standard that permits states to include additional requirements have affected the company during the wake of the breach?*
   b. *What would the approach have been if a federal uniform notification standard was in place that fully preempted current notification laws?*
   c. *What impact would the two different approaches have on a company's resources as compared to the other, i.e., full preemption versus a federal standard that serves as a "floor"?*
   d. *Is current law preferable to either of the approaches discussed above?*

The Neiman Marcus Group took swift action to notify its customers as soon as reasonably possible. A federal notification standard, whether with full preemption or serving as a "floor", would not likely have affected the timing or approach of the Neiman Marcus Group's response, unless it included substantially different considerations. The timing of our customer notifications was driven not only by our intention to comply with the law, but also by our commitment to providing the highest level of security and service to our customers.

Companies targeted by sophisticated cyber criminal organizations do face significant compliance costs in responding to these attacks because of the current patchwork of state laws. U.S. data breach notification obligations include all but a handful of states, plus the District of Columbia, Puerto Rico and the U.S. Virgin Islands each with their own, varying, data breach notification laws. A federal standard that serves as a floor would not have changed the compliance burdens in any meaningful way. A uniform federal standard, however, would have eliminated some of the complexity involved with the notice process.

2.   *In the Congress there are several data breach notification proposals, all of which differ from the other. One important consideration is that of timing for issuing notification. Some legislation requires notice of a breach be issued as soon as possible; another says within 48 hours of discovery. Please describe the general process involved in issuing notice to consumers, including a consideration whether statutory time frames for issuing notifications would be helpful or harmful.*

As detailed in our written statement and further explained at the hearing, the Neiman Marcus Group notified customers as soon as reasonably possible after identifying the malware; disassembling and decrypting it to determine how it operated (including determining whether any consumer information could have been affected); and disabling it in a way that would not draw the attention of cybercriminals intent on harming our customers. The time period from which the Neiman Marcus Group confirmed the malware had the capability to capture payment card information to the date of containment and customer notification was *four days*. The Neiman Marcus Group began notifying customers the *same day* the malware was contained.

Further, within two weeks, the Neiman Marcus Group took steps to directly notify *all* customers that had shopped at Neiman Marcus Group stores or online between January 1, 2013 and January 22, 2014, for which it had contact information, in addition to the broad public notice from our website and media coverage. The Neiman Marcus Group has no indication that online activity was affected, and we have now confirmed that the malware was in operation only between July 16 and October 30, 2013, and only at certain stores on differing dates within this time period. Nevertheless, out of an abundance of caution, the Neiman Marcus Group chose to make this significantly broader and direct notification, which included one year of free credit monitoring and identity-theft insurance. Fundamentally, our goal is to communicate directly to all our customers that taking care of them is and has always been our top concern.

In our view, any statutory time frame must consider the practical needs of ongoing investigations (including cooperating with law enforcement investigations), the need to restore integrity to compromised systems, the logistics of printing and mailing notices, the need to train customer service representatives with current and accurate information, and the importance of not alerting the criminals responsible for such attacks that they have been discovered at a time when they can inflict additional damage on the merchant and its customers.

> 3. *Another significant issue concerns the penalties associated with a company's failure to comply with any notification requirements. Do you believe that providing criminal – as opposed to civil – penalties for failing to notify consumers would be helpful or harmful? Why?*

The Neiman Marcus Group promptly provided customers broad and direct notice of its data security incident. The question asks about an entirely different situation, in which a company actually fails to provide any notification to customers whose information was compromised by an incident that falls within a future data-breach-notification statute. In such cases, civil liability would seem a more than adequate incentive to ensure notification is provided. Indeed, to impose criminal penalties on a company that itself has been subjected to a criminal attack seems inappropriate.

> 4. *Please provide any additional thoughts that you might have on the issues raised by the hearing, including but not limited to expanding on your testimony, responding to the testimony of the other witnesses and/or anything else that came up at the hearing, which you did not have a chance to respond to.*

The Neiman Marcus Group is committed to working with Congress, law enforcement, industry-leading cybersecurity providers, consumer groups, merchant banks, payment card brands, Payment Card Industry (PCI) stakeholders and others in order to enhance the already robust protections that it uses to protect our customers' personal data. We look forward to continuing this important work.

C. *Response to question from Senator Blumenthal:*

"... I would like to ask ... you to provide perhaps some detailed answer in writing to the question about whether you were going beyond your present practices and procedures to adopt these steps that Symantec has recommended. Not saying they're the only solutions, but just a kind of benchmark. And if you could provide that in writing, I would appreciate it."

The Neiman Marcus Group applauds Symantec's efforts to increase awareness on these persistent, stealthy, and sophisticated criminals. As the report notes, "[d]espite improvements in card security technologies and the requirements of the Payment Card Industry Data Security Standard (PCI DSS), there are still gaps in the security of POS systems." The Neiman Marcus Group is currently working with and committed to continue working with industry-leading cybersecurity providers, consumer groups, its merchant bank, the major payment card brands, and the other Payment Card Industry (PCI) stakeholders in order to enhance the already robust protections that it uses to protect our customers' personal data.

We view the Symantec Report as an important and respected voice in that dialogue, and we understand that the Symantec Report recommends the following "practical steps to take" in regards to security infrastructure:

1. Implementation of PCI Security Standard
    *   Install and maintain a firewall to facilitate network segmentation
    *   Change default system passwords and other security parameters
    *   Encrypt transmission of cardholder data across open, public networks
    *   Encrypt stored primary account number (PAN) and do not store sensitive authentication data
    *   Use and regularly update security software
    *   Use intrusion protection system (IPS) at critical points and the perimeter of the [Cardholder Data Environment, or] CDE
    *   Use file integrity and monitoring software
    *   Use strong authentication including two-factor authentication for remote systems
    *   Monitor all network and data access [Security Information and Event Management] (SIEM)
2. Test security systems, perform pen-testing, and implement a vulnerability management program.
3. Maintain security policies and implement regular training for all personnel
4. Implement multi-layered protections including outside the CDE. Typically, the attacker will need traverse multiple networks and layers of security before reaching a POS system. Any single layer that the attacker is unable to bypass prevents successful data exfiltration.
5. Implement [Point to Point Encryption, or] P2PE or EMV ("Chip and PIN")
6. Increase network segmentation and reduce pathways between the CDE and other networks.

7. Maintain strict auditing on connections to between the CDE and other networks. Reduce the number of personnel who have access to systems that have access to both the CDE and other networks.

8. Employ two-factor authentication at all entry points to the CDE and for any personnel with access rights to the CDE

9. Employ two-factor authentication for all system configuration changes within the CDE environment

10. Implement system integrity and monitoring software to leverage features such as system lockdown, application control, or whitelisting

As I stressed in my written and oral testimony to the Committee, the security of our customers' data is our top priority. We have built, implemented, and maintained a comprehensive, multi-layered array of tools to protect our networks and systems. Our security design provides strong protection to our systems and customer data by any industry standard, including the Symantec Report recommendations. With this orientation, we provide specific responses to each of Symantec's recommendations.

1. The Neiman Marcus Group's security protocols adhere to, and in many cases exceed, those required by the Payment Card Industry ("PCI") Standards. Indeed, although the Neiman Marcus Group is a Level 2 merchant, we voluntarily apply Level 1 assessment practices to our compliance processes by employing a PCI approved annual external assessor. Our level of compliance with the PCI-DSS has just been assessed by a forensic investigative firm with respect to the very systems that were the subject of the incident. That forensic investigative report has now found that the Neiman Marcus Group was fully compliant for all systems relevant to the data security incident and that no recognized deficiency in the security architecture contributed to the incident. (We provide further information about the report in our update below, the last section of this attachment.)

We are not surprised by this result because the Neiman Marcus Group uses numerous firewalls at the corporate and store level, network segmentation, a customized tokenization tool, numerous encryption methods, regular software updating, file integrity monitoring, network access monitoring, and an intrusion detection system. We also require two-factor authentication for external access to user accounts and for various other parts of our networks. We not only require default system password changes, but require users change network login credentials more frequently than the 90 day requirement. And our encryption methods exceed those PCI-DSS requirements which do not require encrypting network traffic within the retailer environment.

2. In addition to the PCI Security Standards, and as recommended in the Symantec report, the Neiman Marcus Group routinely tests its security systems, performs pen-testing, and uses industry-standard and centrally-managed enterprise anti-virus software that is regularly updated.

3. All Neiman Marcus Group personnel who have access to customer data receive regular training on our security policies, including our strict access control policy, which allows only those employees with a legitimate business purpose to access customer data.

4.   The Neiman Marcus Group employs a multi-layered defense-in-depth approach to security across the environment by leveraging technology and people to keep our customer data secure. We create multiple roadblocks to intrusions by segmenting our network and applying restrictions to limit traffic for legitimate business purposes only in each segment.

5.   The Neiman Marcus Group is committed to working with all relevant industry stakeholders – including, most importantly, our customers – to assess new technologies that can improve the security of our customer's data, including the use of P2PE, EMV ("Chip and PIN") technology, as well as next-generation mobile payment mechanisms with even further security protections.

6.   We use multiple pairs of firewalls to segment our network and inhibit an intruder's lateral movement.

7.   We maintain significant monitoring and segregation of the connections between the CDE and other networks, and strive to minimize the number of personnel who have access to systems that have access to both the CDE and other networks.

8.   The Neiman Marcus Group uses two-factor authentication for all external access to the servers and workstations on the network. Access to the CDE is controlled via policy-based routing, so that a user must be on a host in the network. If the user is not local, then they have to VPN into the correct network, pass two-factor authentication checks, and then be in the right active directory group to be able to remotely access a host in the CDE.

9.   The Neiman Marcus Group uses two-factor authentication for all external access to the servers and workstations on the network as described above, but not specifically for system configuration changes within the CDE.

10.   The Neiman Marcus Group employs advanced system integrity and monitoring software features including strong system lockdown and application control.

Despite these significant protections, no system – no matter how sophisticated – is completely immune from cyber attack. A recent report prepared by the Secret Service and others in federal law enforcement confirmed this unfortunate reality when they concluded that comparable RAM-scraping malware (perhaps less sophisticated than the one in our case, according to our investigators) had a *zero percent* anti-virus detection rate. Through our ongoing forensic investigation, we have learned – and the Secret Service has confirmed – that the malware which penetrated our system included exceedingly sophisticated features, including some specifically customized to evade our multi-layered security architecture. Therefore, while the Neiman Marcus Group will continue to further improve our systems to better shield against cyber attacks, our recent incident demonstrates that attackers using sophisticated tools to gain access to company networks and systems remain a serious concern for all of corporate America, and we must confront these threats with continued vigilance in coordination with the federal law enforcement officials committed to protecting America's customers and companies from cybercriminals.

D.   *Update regarding forensic investigations:*

First, we have now completed the next phase in the more detailed review of the time period when the card-scraping malware was operating (July 16 to October 30, 2013), with assistance from our forensic investigators. We therefore have updated numbers to report regarding potentially affected cardholders.

I explained in my February 4 testimony to the Committee that, based upon the information we had at that time, approximately 1.1 million payment cards were potentially exposed during this period, because this was the number of cards used at all Neiman Marcus Group stores during the date range. But I also explained that the malware was not operating at all stores, and where it was operating, it was not operating on each day during the date range. Analysis has now been completed that calculates the number of unique payment cards used at the particular stores and on the particular days when the malware was operating.

This analysis shows that approximately *350,000* cardholders were potentially exposed to the malware, a significant reduction from the previously reported 1.1 million figure. This number may be reduced further in the future, since even on the days when the malware was operating at a particular store, the forensic evidence shows that the malware was not operating during the entire day. The company has now received reports from the card brands and issuing banks that approximately 9,200 cards used at any Neiman Marcus Group store during the July 16 – October 30 period were subsequently used fraudulently. We have updated our website to provide these updated numbers to our customers.

Second, the computer forensic investigative firm we initially hired in this matter – one of the firms approved by the PCI Security Standards Council to provide PCI Forensics Investigator services in the U.S – has now finished its work, and we recently received a final report from them ("the PFI report"). This report (which is highly confidential and contains very sensitive information about Neiman Marcus' internal security systems) is still under review by the card brands. Nonetheless, we wish to highlight a few points from the report.

The report finds Neiman Marcus to be in compliance with PCI DSS for the relevant systems – that is, all required PCI DSS controls are noted as "In Place," and the key question, "Potential Contribution to Breach?" is marked "No" for every set of controls.

The report also confirms the date range I previously provided to the Committee regarding the operation of the card-scraping malware. Specifically, the report finds that the first and last known dates that the card-scraping malware was operating in the POS environment were July 16 and October 30, 2013.

The report confirms that, as I testified, related malware that ultimately helped the card-scraping malware function and escape detection was present in Neiman Marcus' systems earlier in 2013 (March 2013 as set out in the report), and remained undetected in Neiman Marcus' systems during this time period. The report points out that because of the sophisticated customization of the card-scraping malware, the entries in Neiman Marcus' endpoint protection logs during the July 16 to October 30 period that showed activity by this malware only listed a program name that was almost identical to the name of the company's legitimate POS software. These entries on the endpoint protection logs, which occurred over a 3 ½ month period and numbered in aggregate about 60,000, would have been on average around 1% or less of the daily entries on these logs, which have tens of thousands of entries every day. These logs and numerous other protection logs gathered by the company to analyze information about potentially suspicious activities were regularly examined using various security tools, but because of the sophisticated anti-detection measures taken by the attacker, these well-concealed entries did not reveal the attack. Again, having said this, the report finds that the first and last known dates of card-scraping malware operating in the POS environment were July 16 and October 30, 2013.

Regarding exfiltration, the report states that it did not find any evidence of successful exfiltration of credit card information. According to the report, no known attacker is operating in the environment, and all known malware related to this attack has been mitigated by the containment plan. Moreover, the report confirms that the malware operated at 77 of 85 stores, and that the execution of the malware was not continuous at each store.

Third, we also continue to work closely with the U.S. Secret Service on its ongoing criminal investigation. On February 5, the day after this Committee's hearing, the House Committee on Energy & Commerce's Subcommittee on Commerce, Manufacturing, and Trade held a similar hearing. During that hearing, the Deputy Special Agent in Charge of the Cyber Operations Branch of the Secret Service's Criminal Investigations Division testified that the cyber attack on Neiman Marcus – and the malware that was inserted in Neiman Marcus' systems – was highly sophisticated and unprecedented in the manner in which it was customized to defeat Neiman Marcus' defenses and remain undetected. The Secret Service also testified that Neiman Marcus used a robust security plan to protect customer data, but that the attacker nevertheless succeeded in having malware operate in Neiman Marcus' systems because of the attack's level of sophistication.

The PFI report reaffirms the Secret Service's view that this was an extremely sophisticated attack, and confirms that the card-scraping malware was customized for the Neiman Marcus environment and included tools designed to help it escape detection, such as secure deletion, communication across surreptitious channels, and customized encryption.

****

158

Responses to Questions for the Record
Delara Derakhshani, Policy Counsel, Consumers Union
February 11, 2014

1. *During the Committee's February 4, 2014 hearing, there was a great deal of discussion about how American retailers, and other industries, can better protect sensitive financial and personal data from data breaches and cyber attacks.*

      a.   What can consumers do to better protect their sensitive personal information and financial data when making purchases in a store or online?

In our June 2013 issue of *Consumer Reports*, we identified several steps that consumers can take to help protect their personal information online, such as safeguarding the computers and mobile devices that they use to make online purchases. Smartphones, for example, may contain a great deal of personal information about you – including your contacts, e-mails, and bank account information – yet our research suggests that many Americans are not taking sufficient measures to adequately protect their smart phones. We've advised consumers to use screen locks and strong passcodes, back up their data, make sure their security software is up-to-date, and install apps to locate a missing phone and remotely erase data. Before selling or recycling a phone, consumers should also delete any sensitive data from the phone, remove any memory cards, and restore the phone's original factory settings. And the same thing applies to disposing of an old PC or laptop: consumers should make sure a hard drive is properly erased before recycling, donating, or disposing of a computer.

      b.   What steps should consumers take after being notified that their personal or financial information has been compromised due to a data breach or other cyberthreat?

Consumers should regularly review their bank accounts and credit and debit cards to be on the look out for fraudulent use. Consumers who spot any suspicious charges should report them immediately to their financial institutions. For additional protection, consumers can also replace their debit and credit cards, which will stop fraud on those accounts if the account number is what has been compromised. Consumers can also set up account alerts, so that their debit or credit card provider sends an e-mail or text if a transaction occurs over a specified limit.

In the event of a breach, some companies may offer free credit monitoring services. Credit monitoring will catch the opening of new accounts, but it is not designed to catch is fraudulent use of existing accounts. Consumers may want to take advantage of free credit monitoring service, so long as they understand its limitations. For example, credit monitoring won't immediately catch fraudulent transactions on your current credit, debit, and prepaid cards, so consumers affected by a breach still need to be vigilant in checking their existing accounts. Furthermore, we have advised consumers to be aware of when any free monitoring period ends, so that they aren't automatically charged for continuing such services. Finally, in order for credit monitoring to be most effective, consumers should obtain credit reports from all three credit bureaus, not just one, because the information from each of the three bureaus can be different.

Consumers may also want to place a fraud alert or security freeze on their credit reports. Setting up a fraud alert requires anyone who would be extending you new credit to take extra steps to verify your identity. A fraud alert is a less drastic step than a security freeze, which stops new creditors from accessing a credit report. If there is a chance that a data breach includes your Social Security number, then a freeze would be more effective than a fraud alert to protect yourself from this kind of scam.

It's also possible, however, that thieves might also use stolen data to help them obtain your Social Security number, which they could then use to open new accounts in your name. For this reason, consumers should not give out personal information unless they have independently verified the legitimacy of any messages they receive on behalf of a bank or other institution.

It's worth noting that in many states, there is a cost attached to security freezes. When you want to engage in a legitimate transaction, you may need to temporarily lift and then re-impose the security freeze, which can cost money. In some states, you have to provide a report from the police, motor vehicles department, or some other agency in order to obtain a freeze at no cost. Consumers should check credit bureaus' websites to find out what is required for freezes and temporary lifts.

2. *Do online purchases and transactions pose any additional privacy risks for consumers? Please explain.*

Online purchases and transactions can pose a number of privacy risks for consumers. Anything from weak passwords to shady websites to insecure wireless connections put consumers at risk. Consumer Reports and Consumers Union continues to seek to educate consumers about these risks through our various print and online publications.

We are also concerned about public Wi-Fi networks that many consumers use to make financial transactions. Our June 2013 issue of *Consumer Reports* estimated that thirteen million users engaged in financial transactions at wireless hotspots, but consumers are not always aware that this information can be intercepted. We have advised against conducting transactions over insecure Wi-Fi networks, as this can expose your credit card numbers, user information, passwords, and other information to anyone who has access to that network.

We have recommend a number of tips to consumers to protect themselves in these instances, including turning off Wi-Fi and switching their phone to 3G/4G mode before sending or receiving sensitive data. We have also suggested the use of virtual private networks, which encrypt data before sending. Finally, we have suggested that consumers who use an app to conduct a transaction check the app's privacy policy to see how it handles sensitive information being transmitted wirelessly.

**Written Questions for the Record of Chairman Leahy
for Fran Rosch
Senior Vice President
Security Products and Services, Endpoint and Mobility
Symantec Corporation
February 11, 2014**

1. During the February 4, 2014 hearing, you testified about steps that American retailers could take to better protect customer data from data breaches and cyber attacks.

   a. In your view, what are the key steps that retailers should take to safeguard consumer data during the payment process for point of sale transactions?

   There are a number of key steps that companies can take to secure consumer data during point of sale (PoS) transactions. First, it is critical that retailers implement Payment Card Industry (PCI) Data Security Standards (DSS). This includes installing a firewall to facilitate network segmentation, changing default system passwords, encrypting cardholder data as it passes through the company's systems, regularly updating security software, and using strong authentication including two-factor authentication for remote systems. We also recommend the use of file integrity and monitoring software to monitor all network and data access points. Finally, companies should lock down the PoS devices themselves by restricting their operations to only those required to perform their functions, and by restricting what software can be installed on them.

   Second, we recommend the adoption of point to point encryption (P2PE) technology which will protect consumer credit card data from "RAM scraping" attacks. Most systems today encrypt consumer data as that data move across the network; however sensitive information still sits in plain text within the memory banks of the PoS system making it highly vulnerable. By implementing P2PE, retailers can ensure that all consumer data is encrypted from the moment a customer swipes their card until the moment that information is received by the payment card processing company.

   Finally, good security is not just about the technology. Threats are always evolving, so it is important that companies view security as a continuing responsibility that integrates people, processes and technology.

   b. What about during the payment process for online purchases?

   Retailers need to ensure that they are using secure, encrypted communications channels, and should provide assurances to their customers that they are doing so. Encryption is enabled by "SSL digital certificates" which are issued by "Certificate Authorities," – a trusted third party that "vouches" for the identity of the business. There are different classes of certificates, however, and the most secure is called Extended Validation (EV) certificate. EV certificates are only issued to the website after the business has undergone an extensive validation process by the Certificate Authority. EV certificates cause the address bar in popular browsers to turn green, a visual cue to consumers that they are dealing with a trusted vendor.

Once a retailer has obtained payment information, it should be treated like any other highly sensitive personal information – kept on highly secure servers and encrypted whether the data is at rest or in transit.

2. In your experience, where are data breaches involving payment card data most likely to occur today -- during "point of sale" transactions, or during online transactions?

> Although many of the recent data breaches in the news involved point of sale systems that does not mean either environment is more or less susceptible to attack. Criminals will continue to adapt to our every move and will try to exploit all users and systems to get what they want – when PoS systems are made more secure, they will look to other avenues to steal information. The best we can do is to make it harder for them to access sensitive data by ensuring that it is protected and secured to the highest degree possible. This means using encryption, stronger passwords, employing company-wide cybersecurity policies, patching systems, and using the latest generation computer security software.

3. Do you anticipate the trend of data breaches involving point of sale transactions will continue, given the recent data breaches involving American retailers?

> Yes, for a time. Cyber criminals have a business model – that is, they are in it to make money. These criminals will continue to develop new and adaptive ways to breach systems and steal sensitive financial information from consumers. Right now, they've been effective at compromising some PoS systems, and they will continue to do that until we make it too difficult – and costly – to do so. Once that happens, they will shift their methods.

"Privacy in the Digital Age: Preventing Data Breaches and Combating Cybercrime."
Questions for the Record Submitted by
Ranking Member Charles E. Grassley of Iowa,
February 11, 2014.

Questions for Mr. Fran Rosch

1. In your written testimony, you stated that it is important for a federal breach notification law to minimize "false positives," i.e., issuing notice to individuals who are later shown not to have been impacted by a breach. I share this concern because over-notification can also be harmful as it might lead to consumer apathy. Could you please share your thoughts and advice for the following:

    a. Discuss what we should consider when drafting legislation that minimizes the risk of "false positives"?

    Data breaches are complex events, and it can take a significant amount of forensic work to determine what data was stolen. In determining whether an individual has indeed been meaningfully impacted, there are two essential considerations: first, what data was stolen, and second was that data encrypted or otherwise rendered unusable. As to the first point, companies hold a variety of information about people, and while all of it should be protected, only some of it can be used to commit financial crimes or identity theft. Notification may be necessary if the information that was taken can individually or in the aggregate lead to a financial loss, identity theft, or fraud. As to the second point, an organization must determine if the information stolen is in fact usable. If it was properly encrypted or otherwise rendered unusable it should not be necessary for a company to notify users because they are not at risk for fraud or identity theft.

    b. How can we strike the right balance for notification so that companies understand when to issue notice, and consumers are armed with the information they need to monitor the potential for harm?

    We believe that while companies should produce information about a breach in a timely manner, they should have time to engage law enforcement, investigate the breach and repair the vulnerability. Every breach is different and it is important that companies are given the time to analyze what happened so that they provide the public the most accurate information and minimize the risks of "false positives." Notification should be made as expeditiously as possible, but as long as companies are acting in good faith to assess the extent of the data breach and determine how to repair the vulnerability, a company should not be required to notify individual customers until it verifies that those customers were impacted and that the vulnerability has been patched, so as not to further expose other data or systems.

2. In your written testimony, you noted that data breach notification legislation should apply equally to all. Do you also support the position that a federal breach notification standard should preempt the current patchwork of state breach notification laws? If so, explain why preemption is so important?

    Today there are at least 48 state-specific data breach notification laws. This creates an enormous compliance burden, particularly for smaller companies that have to try to comply with myriad and often conflicting standards. This current situation does nothing to offer additional protection to consumers, and in fact can create confusion when residents of different states receive different information about the same breach. A federal standard should create uniformity for consumers and businesses alike, and avoid confusing, even contradictory consumer notices.

3. Please provide any additional thoughts that you might have on the issues raised by the hearing, including but not limited to expanding on your testimony, responding to the testimony of the other witnesses and/or anything else that came up at the hearing, which you did not have a chance to respond to.

> Symantec appreciates the opportunity to testify on this important issue, and looks forward to assisting the Committee in any way possible in the future.

**Written Questions for the Record of Chairman Leahy
for the Honorable Edith Ramirez
Chairwoman
Federal Trade Commission
February 11, 2014**

1. **During the Committee's February 4, 2014 hearing, you testified about how American retailers can better protect consumers' sensitive financial and personal data from data breaches and cyber attacks.**

   a. **What can consumers do to better protect their sensitive personal information and financial data when making point of sale purchases? What about during online transactions?**

   The FTC provides information to consumers about steps they can take to protect their personal information, both online and offline.[1] As to point of sale transactions, there is little consumers can do while shopping to detect and prevent breaches. However, they should make sure to review their billing statements afterwards and report unauthorized transactions immediately. They should also check their credit reports regularly by going to annualcreditreport.com. For online transactions, we recommend that consumers do the following: (1) keep up with security updates on browsers and operating systems; (2) make sure any website that they use to transmit financial information is encrypted, which they can tell by making sure the URL starts with https (the "s" stands for secure); and (3) create strong passwords and keep them safe. While consumers should take these measures, it is also incumbent on businesses to take reasonable steps to protect consumer information from access or use by hackers or identity thieves.

   b. **What steps should consumers take after being notified that their personal or financial information has been compromised due to a data breach or other cyber attacks?**

   The FTC has long published a victim recovery guide and other resources to explain the immediate steps identity theft victims should take to address the crime; how to obtain a free credit report and correct fraudulent information in credit reports; how to file a police report; and how to protect their personal information.[2] Also, for consumers who may have been affected by the recent Target and other breaches, the FTC has posted information online about steps they should take to help protect themselves.[3] This guidance recommends that consumers review their credit card and bank statements; check their credit reports every few months; and delete phishing emails or text messages that ask consumers to confirm or provide account information.

---

[1] *See* http://www.consumer.ftc.gov/articles/0272-how-keep-your-personal-information-secure.

[2] *See* http://www.consumer.ftc.gov/features/feature-0014-identity-theft.

[3] *See* Nicole Vincent Fleming, *An Unfortunate Fact About Shopping*, FTC Consumer Blog, http://www.consumer.ftc.gov/blog/unfortunate-fact-about-shopping (Jan. 27, 2014); Nicole Vincent Fleming, *Are you affected by the recent Target hack?*, FTC Consumer Blog, https://www.consumer.ftc.gov/blog/are-you-affected-recent-target-hack (Dec. 19, 2013).

2. Has the Federal Trade Commission issued any best practices or guidance regarding how American businesses can help safeguard the privacy and security of consumers' sensitive personally identifiable information? If so, please briefly explain.

The FTC widely disseminates its business guide on data security,[4] along with an online tutorial based on the guide.[5] These resources are designed to provide a variety of businesses – and especially small businesses – with practical, concrete advice to be used as they develop data security programs and plans for their companies. The Commission has also released guidance directed towards a non-legal audience regarding basic data security issues for businesses.[6] For example, because mobile applications ("apps") and devices often rely on consumer data, the FTC has developed specific security guidance for mobile app developers as they create, release, and monitor their apps.[7] The FTC also publishes business educational materials on specific topics – such as the risks associated with peer-to-peer ("P2P") file-sharing programs and companies' obligations to protect consumer and employee information from these risks[8] and how to properly secure and dispose of information on digital copiers.[9]

3. The collection and retention of consumer data is also a significant privacy issue for many American consumers and businesses.

a. What are the FTC's views on whether consumers should be notified about commercial data collection and retention practices?

Companies should be transparent about their data practices and should provide simplified notice to consumers of their data practices – where possible on a just-in-time basis – to the extent such practices are inconsistent with the context of an interaction. More comprehensive notices of privacy practices should also be provided and are important, both for consumers who are interested in comparing companies' practices and for regulators, consumer advocates, and other watchdog organizations who can hold companies accountable. It is important for these comprehensive privacy notices to provide a clear and concise description of the company's data collection and use practices. Notice aside, companies should also follow principles of privacy by design, such as limiting their collection of consumers' information to the extent they need it in order to fulfill a legitimate business purpose. They should assess how long they need to store consumers' information in order to meet these purposes, and dispose of the information when it

---

[4] *See Protecting Personal Information: A Guide for Business, available at* http://business.ftc.gov/documents/bus69-protecting-personal-information-guide-business.
[5] *See Protecting Personal Information: A Guide for Business (Interactive Tutorial), available at* http://business.ftc.gov/multimedia/videos/protecting-personal-information.
[6] *See generally* http://www.business.ftc.gov/privacy-and-security/data-security.
[7] *See Mobile App Developers: Start with Security* (Feb. 2013), *available at* http://business.ftc.gov/documents/bus83-mobile-app-developers-start-security.
[8] *See Peer-to-Peer File Sharing: A Guide for Business* (Jan. 2010), *available at* http://business.ftc.gov/documents/bus46-peer-peer-file-sharing-guide-business.
[9] *See Copier Data Security: A Guide for Business* (Nov. 2010), *available at* http://business.ftc.gov/documents/bus43-copier-data-security.

is no longer needed. All of these best practices are described in greater detail in the Commission's Privacy Report.[10]

> **b. In your view, should businesses that collect and retain consumer data allow their customers to "opt out" of these data collection and retention activities?**

The FTC has encouraged companies to provide simpler and more streamlined choices to consumers about their data practices. In the Commission's Privacy Report, we stated that companies need to provide choice before collecting and using consumers' data for practices that are inconsistent with the context of the consumer's interaction with the business. In these instances, consumers should have the ability to make informed and meaningful choices at a "just-in-time" point.[11] Choice is not necessary for data practices that are consistent with the context of the transaction, the company's relationship with the consumer, or as required or specifically authorized by law. For example, companies need not give consumers choices about collecting their address in order to deliver a product.

4. In your experience, are "point of sale" or online commercial transactions most likely to result in a data breach involving consumer data?

We have seen no clear trend as to the source or type of data breach. Reported breaches range from lost laptops to hacking, to inadequate website security, to corrupt insiders, to misplaced shipments.

This is precisely why we have encouraged companies to implement reasonable information security practices to protect consumers' sensitive information. The Commission's Gramm-Leach-Bliley Safeguards Rule provides a good roadmap as to the procedures and basic elements necessary to develop a sound security program. Although it applies only to non-bank financial institutions, we believe it provides valuable guidance to other companies as well.

5. Do you anticipate that we will witness an increase in "point of sale" data breaches given the recent trend of data breaches involving American retailers?

I am not in a position to predict whether we will witness an increase in point of sale data breaches given recently announced breaches involving American retailers. However, reports of data breaches affecting American consumers continue to rise. This is precisely why the Commission has unanimously called for federal legislation that would (1) strengthen existing authority governing data security standards on companies and (2) require companies, in appropriate circumstances, to provide notification to consumers when there is a security breach.

---

[10] *See Protecting Consumer Privacy in an Era of Rapid Change* (Mar. 2012), *available at* http://www.ftc.gov/sites/default/files/documents/reports/federal-trade-commission-report-protecting-consumer-privacy-era-rapid-change-recommendations/120326privacyreport.pdf.

[11] *Id.* at 48-50.

Mr. Noonan's Answers to the Questions for the Record

Committee on the Judiciary
Privacy in the Digital Age: Preventing Data Breaches and Combating Cybercrime

Answers to the Questions for the Record from Chairman Leahy

William Noonan
Deputy Special Agent in Charge
United States Secret Service
Criminal Investigative Division
Cyber Operations Branch

Committee on the Judiciary
United States Senate

"Privacy in the Digital Age: Preventing Data Breaches and Combating Cybercrime"
February 4, 2014

1. **Are there additional legal tools and/or resources that would help the United States Secret Service to investigate and prevent data breaches and other cybercrimes?**

On May 12, 2011, the Administration sent Congress a cybersecurity legislative proposal. This proposal includes various provisions that would aid in the investigation and prevention of data breaches. Significantly, the proposal includes a national data breach notification standard that requires victim companies to report to a law enforcement agency with investigative jurisdiction, and allows law enforcement to delay any required public disclosure if this notification would impede an ongoing criminal investigation. It also includes Law Enforcement Provisions Related to Computer Security, which proposes changes to the scope and penalties of violations under 18 USC § 1030, including making these violations RICO predicate offenses, enhancing criminal and civil forfeiture, and providing for stronger penalties.

Given the growing sophistication and transnational nature of cyber crime, the Secret Service recommends amending 18 USC § 1030(a)(6) to criminalize the selling of unauthorized access to computers, including access to botnets, regardless of intent to defraud. The Secret Service also recommends amending 18 USC § 1029 to include criminals who traffic in the payment card data of U.S. financial institutions outside of the United States.

Investigating and preventing cyber crime requires skilled criminal investigators and effective partnerships with federal, state, local and international law enforcement. A constrained budget environment coupled with sequestration has limited the ability of the Secret Service to hire special agents to backfill positions lost through attrition, and to conduct training on cyber crime investigations. With additional resources, the Secret Service could strengthen its capacity to

Mr. Noonan's Answers to the Questions for the Record

Committee on the Judiciary
Privacy in the Digital Age: Preventing Data Breaches and Combating Cybercrime

combat cyber crime by providing special agents with recurring computer forensics and network intrusion training. In addition, increased training for the Secret Service's law enforcement partners through the National Computer Forensics Institute would serve as a force multiplier in defeating transnational organized cyber crime.

2. **Given the recent trend of "point of sale" data breaches involving United States retailers and the use of so-called "scraping" malware in some of those data breaches, do you anticipate that there will be an increase in this kind of cybercrime involving payment cards in the future?**

Since it was first published in 2008, the annual Verizon Data Breach Investigations Report (DBIR) has identified payment card data as the type of data most often stolen. Of the 621 confirmed data breaches analyzed in the 2013 DBIR, 28% involved the compromise of a "point of sale" (POS) terminal or server. Similarly, the 2013 Trustwave Global Security Report analyzed over 450 cyber incident response investigations conducted by Trustwave in 2012, in response to reports of suspected or confirmed data breaches. Of these, 47% involved the compromise of POS or payment processing systems. Both of these reports also show the substantial role of memory scraping malware to obtain financial information as part of cyber crime activity. The Secret Service contributes to both of these reports.

Over the past decade, cyber criminals have become highly adept at stealing large quantities of payment card data, and have established sophisticated online marketplaces for trafficking in the stolen data. Total annual financial losses to U.S. companies, due to cyber crime involving the fraudulent use of payment card data, are estimated by the Nilson Report to exceed $5 billion in 2012, and to have grown every year since at least 2003. Similarly, the Secret Service has observed an increase in the scale of cyber crime activity that we investigate, with total fraud losses associated with Secret Service cyber crime cases exceeding $200 million each year since 2010. The Secret Service will continue to prioritize its investigative efforts to most effectively suppress this sort of criminal activity, by focusing on the transnational, organized cyber criminals that have demonstrated the greatest ability and desire to inflict substantial financial losses to U.S. merchants and the financial services industry.

Mr. Noonan's Answers to the Questions for the Record

Committee on the Judiciary
Privacy in the Digital Age: Preventing Data Breaches and Combating Cybercrime

3.   **Do you anticipate that we will witness an increase in "point of sale" data breaches, given the recent trend of data breaches involving major American retailers?**

Data breaches, like the recently reported events, are a frequent occurrence. The 2013 Verizon Data Breach Investigations Report (DBIR) analyzes 621 confirmed data breaches, of which 28% involved the compromise of a "point of sale" (POS) terminal or server, while the 2013 Trustwave Global Security Report found that, of the over 450 cyber incident response investigations that Trustwave conducted in 2012, 47% involved the compromise of POS or payment processing systems. These reports also demonstrate that cyber criminals continue to primarily target retailers and other points of collection and processors of large quantities of payment card data like food and beverage, hospitality, and financial services companies. The Secret Service anticipates that this trend will likely continue.

Increased public awareness through news coverage of major data breaches, like the recently reported events, may result in enhanced scrutiny by companies and the uncovering of additional network intrusions and associated breaches, thereby increasing the number of reported incidents in the near future. The Secret Service is committed to proactively investigating this type of criminal activity, and to preventing and minimizing the financial losses to U.S. companies and the financial services industry from cyber crime.

Hearing Before the
Committee on the Judiciary
United States Senate

Entitled
"Privacy in the Digital Age: Preventing Data Breaches and Combating Cybercrime"

February 4, 2014

Questions for the Record
Submitted to
The Department of Justice

1. During the February 4, 2014, hearing, you testified about the Department's important work in combating and prosecuting cybercrime. Are there any changes to existing law that would assist the Department in that effort?

Yes, there are several changes to existing laws that would assist the Department in our efforts to combat cybercrime. As an initial matter, we believe that data breach notification legislation, as described further below and in then Acting Assistant Attorney General Raman's written statement at the hearing, is critical to our efforts to protect Americans whose personal information is compromised by cybercriminals. We also have suggested a number of improvements to the criminal laws on which the Department relies in combating cybercrime. One of the most important of those laws is the Computer Fraud and Abuse Act ("CFAA"). It was first enacted in 1986, when the problem of cybercrime was still in its infancy. Over the years, a series of modest changes have been made to the CFAA to reflect new technologies and means of committing crimes, and to equip law enforcement with tools to respond to changing threats. The CFAA has not been amended since 2008, and the intervening years have again created the need for the enactment of modest, incremental changes. The Administration is proposing several such revisions to keep Federal criminal law up-to-date with rapidly-evolving technologies. Many of these proposals are reflected in a bill you recently introduced. For the record, we recap some of these proposals, which are also further described in Ms. Raman's written statement. Finally, we discuss an additional proposal, currently before the Rules Committee for the Federal Rules of Criminal Procedure (Rules Committee), which would improve the process for obtaining warrants to search computers.

Data Breach Notification

Millions of Americans every year are faced with the potential for fraud and identity theft from online breaches of their sensitive, personally identifiable information. The nation clearly needs strong protections for consumers' rights and privacy for sensitive data such as credit card and social security numbers, names and addresses, and medical records. The Administration recommends, as it did in its 2011 proposal, the establishment of a strong, uniform Federal standard requiring businesses to provide prompt notice to consumers and to law enforcement in the wake of a breach of electronic personally identifiable information. Such a law should also provide for appropriate periods of delay of consumer notification where it would impair a criminal investigation

Deterring Insider Threats

The CFAA addresses the threat posed by insiders – such as employees of a business or of a government agency – by criminalizing conduct by those who "exceed authorized access" to a protected computer. Some have contended that this provision should be limited or abolished because it potentially could be subject to misuse or overuse, such as through the prosecution of people who merely lie about their age when going to a dating site, or harmlessly violate the terms of service of an email provider. In a recent case, an appellate court barred an otherwise meritorious prosecution under the CFAA because of this worry. We are open to working with Congress to assist in developing appropriate statutory amendments, such as new statutory thresholds regarding the value or sensitivity of the information improperly accessed (which would assure that criminal prosecutions could not be brought on the basis of trivial conduct, such as lying about one's age on a dating website), or new language making more explicit that the statute does not permit prosecution based on access restrictions that are not clearly understood.

Access Device Fraud

To ensure that we can prosecute cyber criminals acting overseas who steal data concerning customers of U.S. financial institutions, we also recommend a modification to the access device fraud statute, 18 U.S.C. § 1029. One of the most common motivations for hacking crimes is to obtain financial information. The access device fraud statute proscribes the unlawful possession and use of "access devices," such as credit card numbers. Organized criminal enterprises – often located abroad – have committed such intrusions and exploited the stolen data through fraud that directly affects Americans and United States financial institutions. Yet, under current law, a criminal who possesses or traffics in stolen credit card information issued by a U.S. financial institution, but who otherwise does not take one of certain enumerated actions within the jurisdiction of the United States, cannot be prosecuted under section 1029. The Department recommends that the statute be expanded to allow for the prosecution of offenders in foreign countries who directly and significantly harm United States citizens and financial institutions.

Deterring the Spread of Cell Phone Spying

The Department of Justice recommends the enactment of legislation that would enable law enforcement to seize the profits of those who market and use cell phone spyware. The spread of computers and smartphones in recent years has created a new market in malicious software that allows users to pay a small fee to download sophisticated tools to intercept the communications of unsuspecting victims, such as estranged spouses and business competitors. Selling or using such software is illegal under current law, and current law also provides that courts can order the forfeiture of the surreptitious interception devices themselves. It does not, however, allow for the forfeiture of the proceeds of the sale or use of those devices, or the forfeiture of any property used to facilitate their manufacture, advertising, or distribution. Further, the surreptitious interception of communications is currently not listed as a predicate offense in the money laundering statute, 18 U.S.C. § 1956. Because perpetrators of these crimes often act from abroad, making it more difficult to prosecute them in the United States, it is particularly important that law enforcement be able to seize the money that the criminals make from engaging in this criminal surveillance and to seize the equipment they use.

Selling Access to Botnets

We also recommend amending current law to better enable the Department of Justice to combat the proliferation of botnets. A botnet is a network of secretly hacked computers, sometimes numbering in the millions, which are located in homes, schools, and offices. Botnets can be used for various nefarious purposes, including the theft of personal or financial information, the dissemination of spam, and cyber attacks, such as Distributed Denial of Service attacks. Federal criminal law already criminalizes the creation of botnets, as well as the use of botnets to hack into other computers or to commit fraud. But those who merely control an existing botnet are not necessarily covered by these laws, nor are those who sell, or even rent, access to the infected computers to others. The Department of Justice recommends that the CFAA be amended to clearly cover such trafficking in access to botnets.

Ensuring Proper Judicial Review of Warrants for Computers

The Department of Justice has previously recommended to the Rules Committee an amendment to Rule 41 of the Federal Rules of Criminal Procedure to update the territorial limits for warrants to search electronic storage media. Currently, Rule 41 does not directly address the special circumstances that arise when officers execute search warrants, via remote access, over modern communications networks such as the Internet. The need for such warrants has increased significantly for at least two reasons.

First, criminals are increasingly using sophisticated anonymizing technologies like proxy services when they commit crimes over the Internet. There are techniques that law enforcement can use to identify a criminal's computer by conducting a remote search of the computer. Yet even when investigators can demonstrate probable cause to believe that the evidence sought via a remote search will aid in the apprehension or conviction of an individual for committing a particular criminal offense, Rule 41 does not explicitly authorize a judge to issue a warrant where law enforcement is unable to identify the district in which the targeted device is located.

Second, criminals are using multiple computers in many districts simultaneously as part of complex criminal schemes, and effective investigation and disruption of these schemes often requires remote access to Internet-connected computers in many different districts. For example, a large botnet investigation is likely to require action in all 94 districts. In some circumstances, search warrants could be used to take action against botnets, but coordinating 94 simultaneous warrants in the 94 districts is impossible as a practical matter.

The Department proposed to the Rules Committee that Rule 41 be amended to authorize a court in a district where activities related to a crime have occurred to issue a warrant for electronic storage media within or outside the district. While the Department continues to work with the Rules Committee to make this important change to clearly empower courts to review and authorize such warrants, the rules process is a lengthy one. Given the pace of technological change and the urgent need to address this issue, we would welcome Congressional action that could implement this proposal expeditiously.

2. Given the recent trend of "point of sale" data breaches involving United States retailers and the use of so-called "scraping" malware in some of those data breaches, do you anticipate that there will be an increase in this kind of cybercrime involving payment cards in the future?

Yes, the Department has seen and expects to continue to see an increase in cyber attacks on point of sale terminals. The Department's experience with cybercrime has shown two things: (1) cyber criminals will target systems or data that allow them to profit, and (2) cyber criminals have been highly adaptive to changes in cybersecurity practices. Payment card information has long been of interest to financially motivated cyber criminals for the simple reason that the data is valuable. Cyber criminals either use such data in fraud schemes or sell it to others for such use, causing tremendous fraud losses every year. When such data is collected in large databases on retailers' or others' computers, cyber criminals target those databases in order to gain access to the data. As a result of such attacks, many companies have adapted and increased protections for such databases. Today, most stored data containing payment card information is encrypted. As a result, attackers have moved to systems from which useable data may still be collected, most often the point of sale terminals of retailers, where the data valuable to cyber criminals is available in an unencrypted form. As long as valuable data can be gathered from those systems, we expect cyber criminals to continue to try to breach them.

3. During the hearing, you also testified that many of the perpetrators of cyber attacks on United States computers are located outside of the country.

a. How successful has the Department been at extraditing foreign perpetrators of cybercrime?

Extraditing foreign perpetrators of cybercrime, or any other crime, presents significant challenges. Some countries have laws that prevent the extradition of their nationals. In addition, extradition treaties generally require that both the U.S. and the foreign country have made the conduct a crime; thus, extradition can be very difficult if the foreign country from which we seek the extradition of a criminal has not passed laws that criminalize cyber activities to the same extent as the United States. To deal with these challenges, the Department of Justice, in partnership with the Department of State, develops and provides training to countries to improve their capacity to investigate and prosecute cybercrime and to develop criminal laws harmonized with the laws of the United States and other developed countries. Additionally, the Departments of Justice and State promote worldwide adoption of the Council of Europe Convention on Cybercrime – to which the United States and 40 other countries are parties – which sets up a regime for the criminalization of malicious cyber activities. By establishing a common baseline of criminal laws, the Convention helps to assure that gaps in foreign countries' laws will not prevent extradition.

Despite these challenges, the Department has worked exceptionally hard to address international cybercrime and, as a result, we have had many successes. Listed below are just some of these successes from quite literally around the world:

- Romania has been an excellent partner in extraditing cyber criminals to the United States. For example, on May 25, 2012, Romania extradited Romanian national Adrian Tiberiu Oprea to stand trial in the District of New Hampshire, where he was charged for his participation in an international, multi-million-dollar, online scheme to hack into U.S. merchants' point of sale computer systems in order to steal their customers' credit, debit, and gift card data. From 2008, members of the conspiracy hacked into point of sale systems at more than 200 point of sale systems throughout the country, compromised over 100,000 credit card accounts, and made unauthorized charges in excess of $17.5 million. Oprea was convicted following his extradition and, in September 2013, was sentenced to serve 15 years' imprisonment.

- In another case, in December 2012, law enforcement officers in Romania, the Czech Republic, the UK, and Canada arrested six Romanians in a coordinated takedown targeting a widespread cyber fraud, passport fraud, and money laundering ring. The suspects were extradited from Romania in March 2013; from the U.K. in July 2013; and from the Czech Republic in the autumn of 2013. All have since pled guilty in Federal court. Extradition proceedings in Canada are pending.

- The Department also successfully extradited defendants from Estonia, South Africa, and France in another major cybercrime prosecution. The case involved the infiltration of the computer system of a credit card processor in Atlanta in which three hackers obtained debit card numbers and decrypted the associated PIN codes. In a 12-hour period, criminals fraudulently withdrew approximately $9.4 million from ATMs around the world.

- In February 2014, the Republic of Georgia, despite the absence of an extradition treaty, used its domestic law to extradite a Turkish national to stand trial in the Middle District of Florida. The fugitive is charged with acquiring stolen credit card numbers obtained from U.S.-based companies by computer hacking. The investigation of this criminal conspiracy has already resulted in 17 convictions in the United States.

- In 2012, a defendant was extradited from Paraguay after his arrest at a hotel, where he was found in possession of counterfeit payment cards and electronic implements to re-encode cards. The defendant had been a fugitive for ten years. He was charged in the District of New Jersey in connection with participation in the "Shadowcrew" forum, an online marketplace for hacking and identity theft. Paraguay extradited him to the United States after he completed a sentence for offenses he committed in Paraguay.

- In 2012, a Russian citizen waived extradition from the Netherlands and was surrendered to stand trial in the District of New Jersey on offenses related to hacking into bank computer networks and subsequently selling stolen debit and credit cards and other personal information.

- In 2012, a Pakistani national waived extradition from the Netherlands and was convicted in the Eastern District of New York of access device charges in connection with orchestrating "unlimited operations" involving intrusions into payment processors and financial institutions, including fraudulent withdrawals of $14 million made within the span of 48 hours in 2011 that targeted the largest payment processor in the world at the time. He was sentenced in 2013.

- In 2013, a Bulgarian national was extradited from Bulgaria to stand trial in a hacking case charged in the District of New Jersey. The case is pending.

- In 2013, a UK national was extradited from the Netherlands, and in 2012, another was temporarily surrendered to face charges that they operated an illicit business in Europe in which they stole point of sale access card reader devices used in commercial establishments and replaced them with non-functional dummy devices and installed "skimmers" in the stolen card readers that intercepted the data from cards swiped through the device and PIN codes entered by the consumer.

- In 2013, Germany extradited a Ukrainian hacker to stand trial in the Eastern District of Virginia.

- In 2013, an alleged hacker was extradited from Thailand to stand trial in the Northern District of Georgia in connection with his role in developing the malicious software SpyEye and also operating a SpyEye botnet.

- In 2012, a Kosovo national was extradited from Germany for his alleged role in a large-scale series of intrusions into payment processors and financial institutions. He is currently being prosecuted in the Eastern District of New York.

- Between 2007 and 2012, thirteen defendants were extradited to stand trial in the District of Connecticut for a "phishing" scheme, which uses the Internet to target individuals and obtain private personal and financial information. Ten were extradited from Romania; one from Bulgaria; one from Canada; and one from Sweden.

- In 2011, a U.S. citizen was extradited from Japan on passport fraud charges to stand trial in the Southern District of California. The defendant was a San Diego IT contractor who stole the personal information of approximately 90 employees and used it to enrich himself. He also made fraudulent statements in order to obtain two different passports.

- In 2011, at the request of the United States, six Estonian nationals were arrested in Estonia on charges of wire fraud and computer intrusion. The arrests were part of a coordinated takedown that included requests for the seizure of financial accounts in several countries. The six are wanted in the Southern District of New York to stand trial for their involvement in a criminal enterprise that infected millions of computers worldwide with malicious software. Two defendants were extradited from Estonia to the United States in 2012.

- In 2009, an Israeli hacker was extradited from Canada to stand trial in the Eastern District of New York on charges involving the orchestration of several intrusions into payment processors and financial institutions. He was ultimately convicted and sentenced in 2011.

- In 2009, a U.S. citizen who fled to Mexico was successfully extradited to stand trial in the District of New Jersey on computer hacking charges.

- In May 2007, an Indian national living in Malaysia was extradited from Hong Kong to stand trial in the District of Nebraska and a second Indian national was extradited from Hong Kong in June 2009. The defendants, while in Thailand and Hong Kong in 2006, had hacked into online brokerage accounts in the United States and operated a "pump and dump" stock fraud scheme that artificially inflated the value of securities. Both defendants pleaded guilty.

While prosecution in the United States for crimes committed here is often our primary goal, we also have worked extensively to encourage prosecutions in those foreign countries where a perpetrator's extradition is not viable and the respective jurisdiction can impose appropriate consequences for cybercrime. We will continue to work with international partners to ensure that justice is done in whatever manner is most appropriate in a given case.

       b. Are there any new legal tools that would assist the Department in addressing any obstacles to extradition in cybercrime matters?

The legal tools that Congress has provided to the Department have allowed us to bring prosecutions and, when necessary, successfully extradite defendants in cybercrime matters. Although we are not currently seeking any new legal tools from Congress relating to the extradition of defendants, we continuously evaluate the effectiveness of existing authorities. In addition, we note that in order to secure the cooperation of foreign law enforcement agencies, we need to ensure that the U.S. government can appropriately respond to foreign requests for electronic evidence. The Department's funding for such activities has not kept pace with the dramatic rise in foreign requests, resulting in a backlog. As the President has laid out in his Fiscal Year 2015 budget, substantial additional resources are needed for the Department of Justice to devote to satisfying foreign requests for evidence in cybercrime and electronic evidence cases.

**CONFIDENTIALITY
COALITION**

Statement of the Confidentiality Coalition

The Confidentiality Coalition respectfully submits this Statement to the Senate Judiciary Committee in connection with its February 4, 2014, hearing on "Privacy in the Digital Age: Preventing Data Breaches and Combating Cybercrime."

The Confidentiality Coalition is composed of a broad group of hospitals, medical teaching colleges, health plans, pharmaceutical companies, medical device manufacturers, vendors of electronic health records, biotech firms, employers, health product distributors, pharmacies, pharmacy benefit managers, health information and research organizations, patient groups, and others founded to advance effective patient confidentiality protections.

The Coalition's mission is to advocate policies and practices that safeguard the privacy of patients and healthcare consumers while, at the same time, enabling the essential flow of patient information that is critical to the timely and effective delivery of healthcare, improvements in quality and safety, and the development of new lifesaving and life-enhancing medical interventions. The Confidentiality Coalition is committed to ensuring that consumers and thought leaders are aware of the privacy protections that are currently in place. As healthcare providers make the transition to a nationwide, interoperable system of electronic health information, the Confidentiality Coalition members believe it is essential to replace the current mosaic of sometimes conflicting state healthcare privacy laws, rules, and guidelines with a strong, comprehensive national confidentiality standard for healthcare information.

Our Coalition members strongly support appropriate activities to protect the confidentiality of personal information. The current privacy and security rules for the healthcare industry and its business associates stem from the regulations implemented following the passage of the Health Insurance Portability and Accountability Act (HIPAA) in 1996. These rules – which have been in effect for more than a decade for health care companies and now apply directly to business associates as well – provide specific and detailed requirements for the protection of personal health information.

We support the approach the Committee takes regarding healthcare in the proposed language in sections 201 and 211 of the Personal Data Privacy and Security Act of 2014 (S.1897). This legislation provides important new consumer protections, while providing an exemption from the bill's new data security and breach notification provisions for entities subject to the HIPAA rules, including both covered entities and business associates. We believe that the current HIPAA Rules provide appropriate protections for the confidentiality of personal health information. Imposing additional, duplicative and potentially inconsistent regulation on these companies would create unnecessary and inappropriate burdens and costs. Therefore, we strongly support the Committee's efforts to exempt HIPAA covered entities and business associates from the provisions of this bill.

Bill Cheney
President & CEO

February 4, 2014

The Honorable Patrick Leahy
Chairman
Committee on the Judiciary
United State Senate
Washington, DC 20510

The Honorable Chuck Grassley
Ranking Member
Committee on the Judiciary
United State Senate
Washington, DC 20510

Dear Chairman Leahy and Ranking Member Grassley:

On behalf of the Credit Union National Association (CUNA) and America's credit unions, I am writing today to thank you for holding today's hearing entitled "Privacy in the Digital Age: Preventing Data Breaches and Combating Cybercrime." CUNA is the largest credit union advocacy organization in the United States, representing America's 6,700 state and federally chartered credit unions and their 99 million members.

This hearing is an important and timely response to recent merchant data breaches affecting millions of Americans and their financial institutions. We appreciate the Committee's focus on safeguarding consumer data, and we look forward to today's testimony and discussion of what should be done to ensure an appropriate response to not only these data breaches, but data breaches that may occur next week, next month, or next year.

We encourage Congress to take a holistic approach to this issue. In the years to come, consumers will use many payment methods, including magnetic (mag) stripe cards, chip and PIN cards (EMV), cloud-based mobile payments, tokenization, and other methods we can only imagine at this point in time. Focusing on one payment method as the absolute answer to solving data security breaches is both shortsighted and distracts from the greater need of a federal data security framework for all entities. Instead, Congress should take a broad look at how consumer data is secured and the improvements that are necessary to prevent future breaches from taking place.

Data breaches occur, in part, because merchants are not required to adhere to the same statutory data security standards that credit unions and other financial institutions must follow, and merchants are rarely held accountable for the costs others incur as a result of the breaches. All participants in the payment process have a shared responsibility to protect consumer data, but the law and the incentive structure today allows merchants to abdicate that responsibility, making consumers vulnerable.

Since the initial reporting of the Target data breach, credit unions have focused on protecting their members from harm, to the extent they can. They have taken many steps including, but not limited to, notifying their members that a breach had occurred, reissuing new debit and credit cards to affected members, and increasing staff at call centers to account for additional member inquiries.

The impact of merchant data breach related costs is far reaching; for not-for-profit credit unions operating on already thin margins, these costs make a significant difference in their ability to offer services to their members. CUNA recently conducted a survey of credit unions regarding the costs they are incurring to help their members respond and recover from the recent breach at Target. Preliminary data indicates that credit unions are incurring a cost of approximately $5.10 per affected card and that the system has incurred a total estimated cost of between $25-30 million as a result of this breach. This figure will continue to increase because this data does not include fraud costs which may develop in the near future.

In addition to the actual costs credit unions must bear as result of the breach, they also face reputational damage because they have an obligation to notify their members that their account has been compromised but are often limited in their ability to disclose the name of the merchant where the breach occurred. So, when members are notified that their account has been compromised, the credit union is unable to tell them where the compromise occurred and some members assume the problem was with the credit union.

As Congress considers legislative remedies, credit unions support three basic principles:

1. All participants in the payments system should be responsible and be held to comparable levels of data security requirements.

Under current federal law, credit unions and other financial institutions are held to high standards of data security for consumer information under the *Gramm-Leach-Bliley Act*. There is no comparable federal data security responsibility for a national merchant holding consumer data. This represents a weak link in the chain and it needs to be addressed. We support legislation, such as S. 1927, the *Data Security Act of 2014*, introduced by Senators Carper and Blunt, that would provide a national standard for businesses to protect sensitive consumer information, rather than a myriad of differing state laws and regulations.

2. Those responsible for the data breach should be responsible for the costs of helping consumers.

It has been said by merchants that consumers will not be responsible for any financial loss in their accounts. That is true, but not because the merchant will reimburse affected consumers. It happens because the consumer's financial institution pays for the costs related to a merchant data breach involving accounts held at that institution. Under current law, the merchant is not obligated to reimburse financial institutions for any costs incurred as a result of the breach. In other words, even though the breach happened on the merchant's watch, retailers have no responsibility for the costs of the breach because financial institutions take care of their members and customers.

When a merchant data breach occurs, credit unions are there to help their members. Whether it is increased staffing to handle additional member questions, notifying members, reissuing cards, tracking possible fraudulent activity, or reimbursing a member for fraudulent charges caused by a third party, credit unions bear the costs even though the merchant was responsible for the breach. We support legislation to address this problem and make it easier for credit unions to recoup the costs they incur. We believe that if Congress sets strong merchant data security standards and those standards are not met by a merchant whose data is breached, the merchant should be held responsible for the credit union's costs associated with that breach.

3. Consumers should know where their information was breached.
Credit unions also support legislation that requires merchants to provide notice to those consumers affected by a data breach, and permits credit unions to disclose where a breach occurs when notifying members that their account has been compromised.

When it comes to bad news like a data breach, it is easy to "blame the messenger." In today's world, the credit union is the messenger and, depending on the state, may not be permitted to identify the breach source to the consumer member. Consumers need transparency and knowledge to understand where their data has been put at risk. S. 1927 addresses this priority as well.

In conclusion, we look forward to the Committee's dialogue regarding data security. It is a complicated and dynamic issue. As these latest merchant breaches have demonstrated, millions of consumers, and their respective credit unions, are affected. We believe the best answer is a federal comprehensive approach to data security.

On behalf of America's credit unions and their 99 million members, thank you for your attention to this very critical matter and your consideration of our views.

Best regards,

Bill Cheney
President & CEO

February 3, 2014

The Honorable Patrick Leahy   The Honorable Charles Grassley
Chairman   Ranking Member
Committee on the Judiciary   Committee on the Judiciary
U.S. Senate   U.S. Senate
Washington, D.C. 20510   Washington, D.C. 20510

Re: Hearing Titled "Privacy in the Digital Age: Preventing Data Breaches and Combating
    Cybercrime"

Dear Chairman Leahy and Senator Grassley:

The undersigned organizations representing the financial services industry are writing to
commend you for holding this hearing on the recent breaches of sensitive consumer financial and
personal information at several major retailers across the country. The financial services
industry stands ready to assist policymakers in ensuring that robust security requirements apply
to all participants in the payments system, and we respectfully request that this letter be made
part of the record for your hearing.

In all data breaches, including the recent retailer breaches, the financial services industry's first
priority is to protect consumers from fraud caused by the breach. Banks and credit unions do this
by providing consumers "zero liability" from fraudulent transactions in the event of a breach.
Although financial institutions bear no responsibility for the loss of the data from a retailer's
system, they assume the liability for a majority of the resulting card-present fraud. In most
instances, financial institutions have historically received very little reimbursement from the
breached entities – literally pennies on the dollar.

For example, virtually every bank and credit union in the country is impacted by the Target
breach. Our understanding is that the breach affects up to 40 million credit and debit card
accounts nationwide, and also has exposed the personally identifiable information (name,
address, email, telephone number) of potentially 70 million people. To put the scope of the
breach in perspective, on average, the breach has affected 10 percent of the credit and debit card
customers of every bank and credit union in the country.

The Target breach alone is estimated to cost financial institutions millions of dollars to reissue
cards and increase customer outreach, with substantial longer-term costs associated with fraud
and mitigation efforts to limit the damage to customers. Although a variety of factors can go into
the calculation, for banks and credit unions the cost of reissuing cards can range from $5 up to
$15 per card, and a preliminary survey of banks impacted by the Target breach conducted by the
Consumer Bankers Association indicated that more than 15.3 million debit and credit cards have
been replaced to date. The numbers of cards issued, along with the total costs, are nearly certain
to rise, especially as the extent to which other retailers have been breached becomes more
certain.

For consumers, the critical issue is the security of their personal information. Banks, credit unions, and other financial companies dedicate hundreds of millions of dollars annually to data security and adhere to strict regulatory and network requirements at both the federal and state levels for compliance with security standards. However, criminal elements are growing increasingly sophisticated in their efforts to breach vulnerable links in the payments system where our retailer partners have not yet been able to align with the financial sector's higher standards of practice in security. In fact, according to the Identity Theft Resource Center, there were more than 600 reported data breaches in 2013 – a 30 percent increase over 2012. The two sectors reporting the highest number of breaches were healthcare (43 percent) and business, including merchants (34 percent). Because of the Target breach, the business sector accounted for almost 82 percent of the breached records in 2013. In contrast, the financial sector accounted for only 4 percent of all breaches and less than 2 percent of all breached records.

Our payments system is made up of a wide variety of players: financial institutions, card networks, retailers, processors, and new entrants. Protecting this eco-system is a shared responsibility of all parties involved and all must invest the necessary resources to combat increasingly sophisticated breach threats to the payments system.

Indeed, extensive efforts are under way to improve card security, including implementation of EMV (chip-based technology) standards by encouraging investment in point-of-sale terminal upgrades and card reissuance to accommodate EMV transactions, and investing in additional security innovations. The major card networks started the EMV migration domestically in 2011, and in 2015 at the retail point-of-sale the party that is not EMV capable (either the issuer or merchant) will be responsible for counterfeit fraud. EMV migration will be fully implemented by October 2017. This liability shift incentivizes both retailers and financial institutions to implement chip-based technology.

EMV technology improves current security by generating a one-time code for each transaction, so that if the card number is stolen it cannot be used at an EMV card-present environment. However, while EMV addresses card-present fraud, it does not increase the security of on-line transactions, which is an increased target in countries that have implemented EMV.

Threats to data security are ever changing and unpredictable. Therefore, policymakers should not mandate or embrace any one solution or technology, such as EMV, as the answer to all concerns. As the threat evolves, so too must coordinated efforts to combat fraud and data theft that harm consumers. To address the emerging risks posed by mobile payments, for example, industry-driven solutions, such as the TCH Secure Cloud, are already underway employing "tokenization" technology.

Tokenization adds additional security by generating a random limited-used number for e-commerce or mobile transactions, rather than using the actual account number. If stolen and attempted to be used as a legitimate account number, it would be of limited or no use. It also takes merchants out of harm's way by eliminating the need for them to even store sensitive account numbers. As threats continue to evolve, so to must our efforts to combat fraud and data theft that harm consumers, financial institutions, and the economy.

As you and your colleagues consider next steps for dealing with this important issue, we have several recommendations that would help to strengthen the payments system and better protect consumers in the event of a breach.

1) **Establish a national data security breach and notification standard.** We believe that legislation should be enacted to better protect consumers by replacing the current patchwork of state laws with a national standard for data protection and notice. A good example of this is the Data Security Act of 2014 (S. 1927) introduced by Senators Tom Carper (D-DE) and Roy Blunt (R-MO).

2) **Make those responsible for data breaches responsible for their costs.** Financial institutions bear the brunt of fraud costs. An entity that is responsible for a breach that compromises sensitive customer information should be responsible for the costs associated with that breach to the extent the entity has not met necessary security requirements.

3) **Better Sharing of Threat Information.** Unnecessary legal and other barriers to effective threat information sharing between law enforcement and the financial and retail sectors should be removed through private sector efforts and enactment of legislation. For example, one such private sector effort is the expansion of membership in the Financial Services Information Sharing and Analysis Center to include the merchant community. No one organization or sector alone can meet the challenges of sophisticated cyber-crime syndicates, so robust communities of trust and collective protection must constantly be developed.

Our organizations and the thousands of banks, credit unions, and financial services companies we represent are aggressively investing in a safe and secure payments system for our nation. Protecting this system is a shared responsibility of all parties involved and we need to work together to combat the ever-present threat of criminal activity. The financial services industry stands ready to assist policymakers in ensuring that robust security requirements apply to all facets of the payments system.

Sincerely,

American Bankers Association
The Clearing House
Consumer Bankers Association
Credit Union National Association
Financial Services Information Sharing and Analysis Center
The Financial Services Roundtable
Independent Community Bankers of America
National Association of Federal Credit Unions

Cc: Members of the Senate Judiciary Committee

Where Creativity Happens·

MICHAEL J. VEITENHEIMER
SVP, Secretary & General Counsel
Direct Dial: 972-409-1655
Telecopier: 972-409-1965
veitenhm@michaels.com

January 31, 2014

The Honorable Patrick Leahy
Chairman
Senate Committee on the Judiciary
221 Hart Senate Office Building
Washington, DC 20510

Dear Chairman Leahy:

Thank you for your invitation to Michaels Stores, Inc. to testify on February 4, 2014 at the Senate Judiciary Committee hearing on "Privacy in the Digital Age: Preventing Data Breaches and Combating Cybercrime." I am writing to respectfully decline your invitation.

As you are aware, on January 25, 2014, Michaels issued a press release and posted a letter on our corporate website from our CEO Chuck Rubin to Michaels customers. In this letter, we noted that Michaels recently learned of possible fraudulent activity on some U.S. payment cards that had been used at our stores, suggesting that we may have experienced a data security attack. We took this action in the interest of consumer protection and in the context of great public attention to data security attacks against other retailers. Immediately, upon knowledge of this possible fraudulent activity, we began working closely with federal law enforcement officials, and we continue to do so. Additionally, we are conducting an investigation with the assistance of third-party data security experts to establish all of the facts. At this time, the investigation of this matter is ongoing and will not be completed by the date of your Committee hearing. Therefore, we are unable to testify about this matter.

Our first priority is our customers, and we are committed to protecting the safety and integrity of their privacy and data. The topic of your hearing is one we take very seriously at Michaels, and for that reason it is imperative that a full and fair investigation of this matter be completed before further comment. Additionally, we appreciate that your constituents in Vermont are also our customers. Their privacy and security is of critical importance to us, and we will continue to address this issue with vigilance. When a full investigation of this matter is concluded, we will appropriately inform you of relevant information in our findings.

Thank you again for your invitation, and I look forward to working with you in the future.

Sincerely,

Michael J. Veitenheimer

8000 BENT BRANCH DRIVE
IRVING, TEXAS 75063
972.409.1300

STATEMENT OF THOMAS M. BOYD
COUNSEL
NATIONAL BUSINESS COALITION ON E-COMMERCE AND PRIVACY
BEFORE THE SENATE JUDICIARY COMMITTEE
ON S.1897
FEBRUARY 4, 2014

Chairman Leahy, Senator Grassley, Members of the Committee, thank you for allowing me to submit a statement for the record at this hearing. My name is Thomas M. Boyd, and I am a partner in the Washington, D.C. office of DLA Piper LLP. I am submitting this statement on behalf of the National Business Coalition on E-Commerce and Privacy (the "Coalition"), to which I serve as Counsel; the Coalition's Chairman is Tony Hadley, of Experian, and its Vice-Chair is Tamara Salmon, of the Investment Company Institute ("ICI"). Created at the behest of former GE CEO Jack Welsh following the adoption of Title V of the Gramm-Leach-Bliley ("GLB") Act in 1999, the Coalition opened for business in February, 2000, and it has been an active participant in the public policy and regulatory debate affecting privacy ever since.

The Coalition represents brand name American companies, many of which have global operations, and each of which wish to see reasonable, workable, and commercially sustainable public policy put in place where privacy is concerned, both at the Federal and state level. Its members include, among others, Acxiom, JP MorganChase, Bank of America, VISA, The Vanguard Group, Charles Schwab & Co., Fidelity Investments, Ally Financial, The Principal Financial Group, Fiserv, Inc., Deere and Co., and the ICI. While its membership is disproportionately financial, the Coalition is not solely a financial services entity. Through the years its membership has included, in addition to its current non-financial members, several other brand name non-financial companies.

I.

With respect to data security and breach notification, the Coalition has long and consistently supported enactment of a national, preemptive Federal law. We specifically endorsed S. 1212, legislation introduced in April, 2007, by Sen. Jeff Sessions (R-AL), and ever since we have actively encouraged policymakers in the Congress, as well as the Executive Branch, to focus on passing uniform data security and breach notification legislation in a stand-alone bill.

Until now, each time it has been considered, legislation that should have narrowly focused on data security and breach notification has been broadened to include a number of privacy-related provisions. This has inevitably resulted in consistently and repeatedly forestalling the adoption of any legislation whatsoever, thereby sacrificing the enactment into Federal law of necessary provisions governing data security and breach notification. This sequence of events has been the same, now, for nearly eight years.

We believe it's time to try a new approach.

In the wake of Edward Snowden's decision to leak critical information from the National Security Agency and the recent, highly publicized consumer data breaches, we feel that the time has now come for the Senate and the House, in coordination with the business community, consumers, and the White House, to make enacting uniform data security and breach notification legislation a public policy priority. We firmly believe that this effort can start with this Committee. Indeed, if there were bipartisan support on this Committee for a clean data security and breach notification bill – and there should be – we are confident that it would have the enthusiastic and active support of both consumers and the business community, leading, in relatively short order, to a Federally-preemptive final result.

As the Committee well knows, since 2005, the absence of Federal action on data security and breach notification has not resulted in a landscape devoid of compliance obligations for custodians of sensitive personally identifiable data. Instead, some 46 states and the District of Columbia have attempted to fill the void at the Federal level by enacting statutes designed to address this issue. The patchwork and inconsistency of these various laws have proved challenging for Coalition members and others subject to them. Moreover, states are constantly revising these laws, which only adds to the complexity of the compliance challenge for firms, such as members of the Coalition, that operate in all 50 states. A single set of national standards would adequately protect individuals throughout our country, without requiring companies to ensure compliance with myriad different and ever-changing laws, with the unfortunate result that resources would be unnecessarily diverted that should otherwise be focused on privacy and data security protection efforts. Already in 2014, there are six such bills pending in five states.

The time is ripe, therefore, for this Committee to act and quickly report a clean data security and breach notification bill. The Coalition is happy to provide whatever assistance it can to help the Committee achieve this critically important goal.

II.

As it considers legislation in this area, we believe it is very important that the Committee and the Senate segregate the facts and circumstances surrounding the recent and ongoing NSA debate from data privacy and data security generally. They are very different from one another and they should be considered and addressed separately. Unfortunately, this is not always the case. For example, in his January 17th speech outlining steps he planned to take to address issues surrounding the NSA leaks, President Obama unfortunately conflated the intelligence community's collection and use of national security data with "[c]orporations of all shapes and sizes [that] track what you buy, store and analyze our data and use it for commercial purposes". That is a link that was as unfortunate as it was inapplicable. America's companies collect data to improve the products they offer and sell and to provide consumers with a more relevant shopping experience. Companies make their data collection and use practices transparent through readily-accessible privacy policies, and many provide consumers choices about how information pertaining to them is used.

While the essential legal obligation to secure sensitive personally identifiable data is already required by Federal law, currently it applies only to HIPAA-regulated entities and "financial institutions", as defined by GLB, as well as to certain other narrow industry sectors (such as consumer reporting agencies under the Fair Credit Reporting Act) and types of information (such as personal information about children under the age of 13). In section 501(b) of Title V of GLB, functional regulators were required to, and have adopted rules to insure the "security and confidentiality of customer records and information", protect against any "anticipated threats or hazards to the security or integrity of such records", and protect against "unauthorized access to or use of such records or information which could result in substantial harm or inconvenience to any customer". Entities outside the scope of these functional regulators are currently not subject to similar requirements. We believe they should be and such obligations should be extended nationally to any custodian that maintains sensitive personally identifiable data on 10,000 or more United States persons.

Once the obligation to secure the confidentiality of sensitive personally identifiable data is in place, there are a number of other important provisions that the Coalition believes ought to be incorporated into any final data security and breach notification legislation. In summary, these provisions are as follows:

1. **Encryption.** As a practical matter, eliminating breaches is virtually impossible. What can happen, however, is that stored data can be rendered unusable, without a cryptographic "key" to convert it into readable, or usable, form. It is therefore imperative that all sensitive personally identifiable data be unusable if accessed by a person without appropriate authorization. This could be achieved through means such as the use of encryption technology, as long as other necessary measures, such as securing the cryptographic key and implementing appropriate system access controls, are in place. Since such technology is expensive and not always technologically feasible to install (such as on legacy mainframe systems and applications where the cryptographic conversions unreasonably slow transaction speeds) , custodians can be incentivized to employ it if a discretionary "safe harbor" from prosecution is available and applied with respect to data that is stored using commercially reasonable encryption technology and processes.

2. **Breach.** Since a breach sets in motion an often complicated and costly notification and remediation process, it is similarly critical that the term "breach" be properly and reasonably defined to protect appropriately any individuals to whom sensitive personally identifiable data pertains. Toward this end, the standard for notification should be a reasonable basis on the part of the custodian to conclude that a significant risk of identity theft exists as a result of the unauthorized access to protected data. In other words, the trigger that initiates the breach notification process should be consistent with that set forth in section 212(b)(1)(A) of Chairman Leahy's bill, S. 1897.

3. **Notificotion.** Once the breach notification process has been triggered, all affected persons should be notified by the custodian and informed of what steps need to be taken to protect themselves from the risk of identity theft. The timing of such notification should be swift and expeditious, without unreasonable delay. Specific timelines, however, such as the 48-hour timeline referenced in some proposals, are too short and do not take into consideration the often difficult practical process of performing necessary systems analysis and data forensics, including assessing the damage, identifying those who may be at risk, protecting against the risk of additional data exposure, and ensuring that proper persons are effectively notified. Moreover, there may also be circumstances in which federal law enforcement agencies such as the Federal Bureau of Investigation or the Secret Service may wish to delay notification, and that option needs to be available as well.

4. **Preemption.** In the absence of effective preemption, there is no practical public policy reason to have a Federal law; there are already 46 state laws on the subject. In our view, language such as that in sections 219 and 204(a) of S.1897, are examples of generally effective preemption language. To be effective, such preemptive language *must totally* supersede State law on the same subject; merely setting a floor does not achieve the significant benefits of having a uniform national standard. This result can best be achieved by using language, as S. 1897 does, that covers any State law that "relates to" the subject of the Federal law (*i.e.*, data security and breach notification). Some proposals have sought to exclude from preemption undefined State "consumer laws,", thereby resulting in such generalized exclusions becoming loopholes that can be used to defeat the purpose of the preemption clause altogether. The language in section 214(b) of S. 1897 could similarly be read to create a loophole in an otherwise sound preemption section.

5. *Enforcement.* The general rule with respect to preemptive statutes is that if State law is superseded, then Federal law enforcement takes priority. Thus, either a Federal functional regulator or, for those persons without a functional Federal regulator, the United States Attorney General or the Federal Trade Commission ("FTC"), are charged with enforcing the Federal law. That does not mean, however, that State Attorneys General should be excluded from the enforcement process. On the contrary, they -- and only they -- should serve to augment Federal enforcement because they collectively have greater resources and are closer in proximity to the consumer. However, contrary to language contained in section 203(c)(1) of S. 1897, no other state offices or agencies should be authorized to enforce the Federal statute. It is similarly important, once a Federal enforcement action is undertaken, that all State enforcement options are superseded, as it serves no public purpose to subject the target of such Federal action to the prospect of 51 separate actions based on the same alleged violation and the same facts. Section 218(c) of S. 1897 takes the position that such State enforcement action should be superseded, and we agree with it.

6. *Private Right of Action.* Given the range of enforcement options available at the Federal and State level, and the importance ensuring that a safe harbor that provides strong incentives with respect to data security are effective, there is no public policy justification for the existence of a private right of action in the event of a data breach. Like section 218(f) of S. 1897, any bill on this subject should therefore bar any such action.

7. *Criminal/Civil Action.* Only the United States Attorney General and State Attorneys General should have jurisdiction to bring *criminal* actions against violators of this statute, and those actions should be limited to cases of egregious violations. By contrast, both Federal and State Attorneys General, as well as the FTC, should have jurisdiction to bring *civil* actions, subject to a publicly available memorandum of understanding ("MOU") with the United States Department of Justice. That said, we also do not believe that there should be unplugged multipliers for civil damages or that the FTC should have rulemaking authority such as that envisioned in proposed sections 216(c) and 217(f) of S. 1897.

Again, Mr. Chairman and Members of the Committee, the Coalition urges the Committee and the Leadership of the Senate to seize upon this opportunity to craft a bipartisan bill that would, once and for all, establish a nationally uniform standard for data security and breach notification, one that, in concert with the states, would provide consumers with a high degree of confidence that their sensitive personally identifiable data that is held by private sector custodians is secure and, in the event of a breach that creates a significant risk of identity theft, affected consumer can be assured that they would be promptly notified and able to take appropriate steps to protect themselves against the risk of identity theft. We stand available to work with you and the Committee staff every step of the way, and we welcome the opportunity.

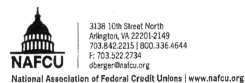

3138 10th Street North
Arlington, VA 22201-2149
703.842.2215 | 800.336.4644
F: 703.522.2734
dberger@nafcu.org

B. Dan Berger
President & Chief Executive Officer

National Association of Federal Credit Unions | www.nafcu.org

February 3, 2014

The Honorable Patrick Leahy
Chairman
Committee on the Judiciary
United States Senate
Washington, D.C. 20510

The Honorable Chuck Grassley
Ranking Member
Committee on the Judiciary
United States Senate
Washington, D.C. 20510

Re: The Importance of Data Security to Our Nation's Credit Unions

On behalf of the National Association of Federal Credit Unions (NAFCU), the only trade association exclusively representing the interests of our nation's federally chartered credit unions, I write in advance of tomorrow's important hearing, "Privacy in the Digital Age: Preventing Data Breaches and Combating Cybercrime." As you know from previous correspondence, data security is a chief priority of NAFCU member credit unions and the 97 million credit union members they serve. We appreciate the opportunity to share our concerns with you and look forward to the hearing exploring the impact of ongoing data breaches on consumers as well as the community based financial institutions that serve them. As the number of data breaches at U.S. retailers continues to climb, so does the emotional toll and financial burden on tens of millions of consumers across the country.

Unfortunately, large national data breaches are becoming all too common. Consumers and credit unions have not only been hit with the recent Target Corporation breach, but also with additional national breaches recently coming to light at Neiman Marcus, Michaels and the White Lodging hotel management company. Tens of millions of Americans have been adversely impacted by these breaches. While these breaches draw national attention, the reality is that data breaches are also happening all the time, often on a smaller scale that doesn't garner the national headlines but still, when taken together, impact just as many American consumers.

A January 2014, survey of NAFCU-member credit unions found that, on average, credit unions were notified over 100 times in 2013 of possible breaches of their members' financial information. That same survey found that nearly 80% of the time those notifications led to the credit union issuing a new plastic card to the member at their request because of the security breach, at an average cost of $5.00 to $15.00 per card.

The recent Target breach has been especially onerous on credit unions. Our member credit unions report that, on average, they have received hundreds of inquiries from their members seeking assistance due to the recent Target breach. NAFCU estimates that this particular breach could end up costing the credit union community nearly $30 million. This cost comes from the monitoring, reissuance of cards and fraud investigations and losses from this breach, and does not count the intangible cost of the staff time needed to handle all of the member service issues that stem from the breach. Unfortunately, credit unions will likely never recoup much of this cost, as there is no statutory requirement on merchants to be accountable for costs associated with breaches that result on their end.

As we first wrote to Congress last February as part of NAFCU's five-point plan on regulatory relief, these incidents must be addressed by lawmakers. Every time consumers choose to use plastic cards for payments at a register or make online payments from their accounts, they unwittingly put themselves at risk. Many are not aware that their financial and personal identities could be stolen or that fraudulent charges could appear on their accounts, in turn damaging their credit scores and reputations. Consumers trust that entities collecting this type of information will, at the very least, make a minimal effort to protect them from such risks. Unfortunately, this is not always true.

Financial institutions, including credit unions, have been subject to standards on data security since the passage of *Gramm-Leach-Bliley*. However, retailers and many other entities that handle sensitive personal financial data are not subject to these same standards, and they become victims of data breaches and data theft all too often. While these entities still get paid, financial institutions bear a significant burden as the issuers of payment cards used by millions of consumers. Credit unions suffer steep losses in re-establishing member safety after a data breach occurs. They are often forced to charge off fraud-related losses, many of which stem from a negligent entity's failure to protect sensitive financial and personal information or the illegal maintenance of such information in their systems. Moreover, as many cases of identity theft have been attributed to data breaches, and as identity theft continues to rise, any entity that stores financial or personally identifiable information should be held to minimum standards for protecting such data.

While some argue for financial institutions to expedite a switch to a "chip and pin" card, the reality is that it is no panacea for data security and preventing merchant data breaches. Many financial institutions that issue "chip and pin" cards had those cards stolen in the Target data breach as the retailer only accepted magnetic stripe technology at the point of sale where the breach occurred. Furthermore, "chip and pin" cards can be compromised and used in online purchase fraud, as the technology is designed to hinder card duplication and card information can still be compromised. This fact highlights the need for greater national data security standards as the way to truly help protect consumer financial information.

Again, recent breaches are just the latest in a string of large-scale data breaches impacting millions of American consumers. The aftermath of these and previous breaches demonstrate what we have been communicating to Congress all along: credit unions and other financial institutions – not retailers and other entities – are out in front protecting consumers, picking up the pieces after a data breach occurs. It is the credit union or other financial institution that must notify its account holders, issue new cards, replenish stolen funds, change account numbers and accommodate increased customer service demands that inevitably follow a major data breach. Unfortunately, too often the negligent entity that caused these expenses by failing to protect consumer data loses nothing and is often undisclosed to the consumer.

NAFCU specifically recommends that Congress make it a priority to craft legislation and act on the following issues related to data security:

- **Payment of Breach Costs by Breached Entities:** NAFCU asks that credit union expenditures for breaches resulting from card use be reduced. A reasonable and equitable way of addressing this concern would be to require entities to be accountable for costs of data breaches that result on their end, especially when their own negligence is to blame.

- **National Standards for Safekeeping Information:** It is critical that sensitive personal information be safeguarded at all stages of transmission. Under Gramm-Leach-Bliley, credit unions and other financial institutions are required to meet certain criteria for safekeeping consumers' personal information. Unfortunately, there is no comprehensive regulatory structure akin to Gramm-Leach-Bliley that covers retailers, merchants and others who collect and hold sensitive information. NAFCU strongly supports the passage of legislation requiring any entity responsible for the storage of consumer data to meet standards similar to those imposed on financial institutions under the Gramm-Leach-Bliley Act.

- **Data Security Policy Disclosure:** Many consumers are unaware of the risks they are exposed to when they provide their personal information. NAFCU believes this problem can be alleviated by simply requiring merchants to post their data security policies at the point of sale if they take sensitive financial data. Such a disclosure requirement would come at little or no cost to the merchant but would provide an important benefit to the public at large.

- **Notification of the Account Servicer:** The account servicer or owner is in the unique position of being able to monitor for suspicious activity and prevent fraudulent transactions before they occur. NAFCU believes that it would make sense to include entities such as financial institutions on the list of those to be informed of any compromised personally identifiable information when associated accounts are involved.

- **Disclosure of Breached Entity:** NAFCU believes that consumers should have the right to know which business entities have been breached. We urge Congress to mandate the disclosure of identities of companies and merchants whose data systems have been violated so consumers are aware of the ones that place their personal information at risk.

- **Enforcement of Prohibition on Data Retention:** NAFCU believes it is imperative to address the violation of existing agreements and law by merchants and retailers who retain payment card information electronically. Many entities do not respect this prohibition and store sensitive personal data in their systems, which can be breached easily in many cases.

- **Burden of Proof in Data Breach Cases:** In line with the responsibility for making consumers whole after they are harmed by a data breach, NAFCU believes that the evidentiary burden of proving a lack of fault should rest with the merchant or retailer who incurred the breach. These parties should have the duty to demonstrate that they took all necessary precautions to guard consumers' personal information but sustained a violation nonetheless. The law is currently vague on this issue, and NAFCU asks that this burden of proof be clarified in statute.

We applaud you and the Committee for your leadership on this issue. NAFCU would welcome the opportunity to work with you on legislation to strengthen data security standards for those who do not have such requirements now.

On behalf of our nation's credit unions and their 97 million members we thank you for your attention to this important matter. If my staff or I can be of assistance to you, or if you have any questions regarding this issue, please feel free to contact myself, or NAFCU's Vice President of Legislative Affairs, Brad Thaler, at (703) 842-2204.

Sincerely,

B. Dan Berger
President and CEO

cc: Members of the Senate Judiciary Committee

National Retail Federation®

The Voice of Retail Worldwide

Statement
On Behalf of

The National Retail Federation,
The National Council of Chain Restaurants,
and Shop.org

For

The Senate Judiciary Committee's

Hearing on

**"Privacy in the Digital Age:
Preventing Data Breaches and Combating Cybercrime"**

February 4, 2014

Prepared by
Mallory Duncan
General Counsel and
Senior Vice President

National Retail Federation
325 7th Street, N.W., Suite 1100
Washington, D.C. 20004
(202) 783 –7971
www.nrf.com

Chairman Leahy, Ranking Member Grassley and members of the Committee, thank you for holding a hearing examining data breaches and cyber crime. The National Retail Federation (NRF) is the world's largest retail trade association, representing discount and department stores, home goods and specialty stores, Main Street merchants, grocers, wholesalers, chain restaurants and Internet retailers from the United States and more than 45 countries. Retail is the nation's largest private sector employer, supporting one in four U.S. jobs – 42 million working Americans. Contributing $2.5 trillion to annual GDP, retail is a daily barometer for the nation's economy.

Collectively, retailers spend billions of dollars safeguarding consumers' data and fighting fraud. Data security is something that our members strive to improve every day. Virtually all of the data breaches we've seen in the United States during the past couple of months – from those at retailers that have been prominent in the news to those at banks and card network companies that have received less attention – have been perpetrated by criminals that are breaking the law. All of these companies are victims of these crimes and we should keep that in mind as we explore this topic and public policy initiatives relating to it.

This issue is one that we urge the Committee to examine in a holistic fashion: we need to reduce fraud. That is, we should not be satisfied with deciding what to do after a data breach occurs – who to notify and how to assign liability. Instead, it's important to look at why such breaches occur and what the perpetrators get out of them so that we can find ways to reduce and prevent not only the breaches themselves, but the fraudulent activity that is often the goal of these events. If breaches become less profitable to criminals then they will dedicate fewer resources to committing them and our goals will become more achievable.

With that in mind, this testimony is designed to provide some background on data breaches and on fraud, explain how these events interact with our payments system, discuss some of the technological advancements that could improve the current situation, raise some ways to achieve those improvements, and then discuss the aftermath of data breaches and some ways to approach things when problems do occur.

Data Breaches in the United States

Unfortunately, data breaches are a fact of life in the United States. In its 2013 data breach investigations report, Verizon analyzed more than 47,000 security incidents and 621 confirmed data breaches that took place during the prior year. Virtually every part of the economy was hit in some way: 37% of breaches happened at financial institutions; 24% happened at retail; 20% happened at manufacturing, transportation and utility companies; and 20% happened at information and professional services firms.

It may be surprising to some given recent media coverage that more data breaches occur at financial institutions than at retailers. And, it should be noted, even these figures obscure the fact that there are far more merchants that are potential targets of criminals in this area. There are hundreds of times as many merchants accepting card payments in the United States than there are financial institutions issuing and processing those payments. So, proportionally, and not surprisingly, the thieves focus far more often on banks which have our most sensitive financial information – including not just card account numbers but bank account numbers, social security numbers and other identifying data that can be used to steal identities beyond completing some fraudulent transactions.

Who are the victims?

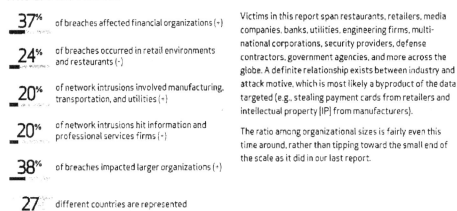

37% of breaches affected financial organizations (+)

24% of breaches occurred in retail environments and restaurants (-)

20% of network intrusions involved manufacturing, transportation, and utilities (+)

20% of network intrusions hit information and professional services firms (-)

38% of breaches impacted larger organizations (+)

27 different countries are represented

Victims in this report span restaurants, retailers, media companies, banks, utilities, engineering firms, multi-national corporations, security providers, defense contractors, government agencies, and more across the globe. A definite relationship exists between industry and attack motive, which is most likely a byproduct of the data targeted (e.g., stealing payment cards from retailers and intellectual property [IP] from manufacturers).

The ratio among organizational sizes is fairly even this time around, rather than tipping toward the small end of the scale as it did in our last report.

Source: 2013 Data Breach Investigations Report, Verizon

Nearly one-fifth of all of these breaches were perpetrated by state-affiliated actors connected to China. Three in four breaches were driven by financial motives. Two-thirds of the breaches took months or more to discover and 69% of all breaches were discovered by someone outside the affected organization.[1]

These figures are sobering. There are far too many breaches. And, breaches are often difficult to detect and carried out in many cases by criminals with real resources behind them. Financially focused crime seems to most often come from organized groups in Eastern Europe rather than state-affiliated actors in China, but the resources are there in both cases. The pressure on our financial system due to the overriding goal of many criminals intent on financial fraud is acute. We need to recognize that this is a continuous battle against determined fraudsters and be guided by that reality.

Background on Fraud

Fraud numbers raise similar concerns. Just a year ago, Forbes found that Mexico and the United States were at the top of the charts worldwide in credit and debit card fraud.[2] And fraud losses in the United States have been going up in recent years while some other countries have had success reducing their fraud rates. The United States in 2012 accounted for nearly 30

---

[1] 2013 Data Breach Investigations Report, Verizon.

[2] "Countries with the most card fraud: U.S. and Mexico," *Forbes* by Halah Touryalai, Oct. 22, 2012.

percent of credit and debit card charges but 47 percent of all fraud losses.[3] Credit and debit card fraud losses totaled $11.27 billion in 2012.[4] And retailers spend $6.47 billion trying to prevent card fraud each year.[5]

Fraud is particularly devastating for retailers in the United States. LexisNexis and Javelin Strategy & Research have published an annual report on the "True Cost of Fraud" each year for the last several years. The 2009 report found, for example, that retailers suffer fraud losses that are 10 times higher than financial institutions and 20 times the cost incurred by consumers. This study covered more than just card fraud and looked at fraudulent refunds/returns, bounced checks, and stolen merchandise as well. Of the total, however, more than half of what merchants lost came from unauthorized transactions and card chargebacks.[6] The founder and President of Javelin Strategy, James Van Dyke, said at the time, "We weren't completely surprised that merchants are paying more than half of the share of the cost of unauthorized transactions as compared to financial institutions. But we were very surprised that it was 90-10."[7] Similarly, Consumer Reports wrote in June 2011, "The Mercator report estimates U.S. card issuers' total losses from credit- and debit-card fraud at $2.4 billion. That figure does not include losses that are borne by merchants, which probably run into tens of billions of dollars a year."[8]

Online fraud is a significant problem. It has jumped 36 percent from 2012 to 2013.[9] In fact, estimates are that online and other fraud in which there is no physical card present accounts for 90 percent of all card fraud in the United States.[10] And, not surprisingly, fraud correlates closely with data breaches among consumers. More than 22 percent of breach victims suffered fraud while less than 3 percent of consumers who didn't have their data breached experienced fraud.[11]

---

[3] "U.S. credit cards, chipless and magnetized, lure global fraudsters," by Howard Schneider, Hayley Tsukayama and Amrita Jayakumar, *Washington Post*, January 21, 2014.

[4] "Credit Card and Debit Card Fraud Statistics," CardHub 2013, available at http://www.cardhub.com/edu/credit-debit-card-fraud-statistics/.

[5] *Id.*

[6] A fraud chargeback is when the card-issuing bank and card network take the money for a transaction away from the retailer so that the retailer pays for the fraud.

[7] "Retailers are bearing the brunt: New report suggests what they can do to fight back," by M.V. Greene, NRF Stores, Jan. 2010.

[8] "House of Cards: Why your accounts are vulnerable to thieves," Consumer Reports, June 2011.

[9] 2013 True Cost of Fraud, LexisNexis at 6.

[10] "What you should know about the Target case," by Penny Crosman, *American Banker*, Jan. 23, 2014.

[11] 2013 True Cost of Fraud, LexisNexis at 20.

Figure 11. Fraud Incidence Rate Among All Consumers, Data
Breach Victims, And Non Data Breach Victims (2010 -2012)

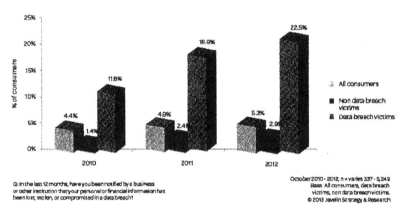

Source: 2013 True Cost of Fraud, LexisNexis

These numbers provide insights as to how to get to the right solutions of better safeguarding consumer and cardholder data and the need to improve authentication of transactions to protect against fraud. But before delving into those areas, some background on our payments system could be helpful.

The Payments System

Payments data is sought in breaches more often than any other type of data.[12] Now, every party in the payment system, financial institutions, networks, processors, retailers and consumers, has a role to play in reducing fraud. However, although all parties have a responsibility, some of those parties are integral to the system's design and promulgation while others, such as retailers and consumers, must work with the system as it is delivered to them.

As the following chart shows, while the banks are intimately connected to Visa and MasterCard, merchants and consumers have virtually no role in designing the payment system. Rather, they are bound to it by separate agreements issued by financial intermediaries.

---

[12] 2013 Data Breach Investigations Report, Verizon at 445, figure 35.

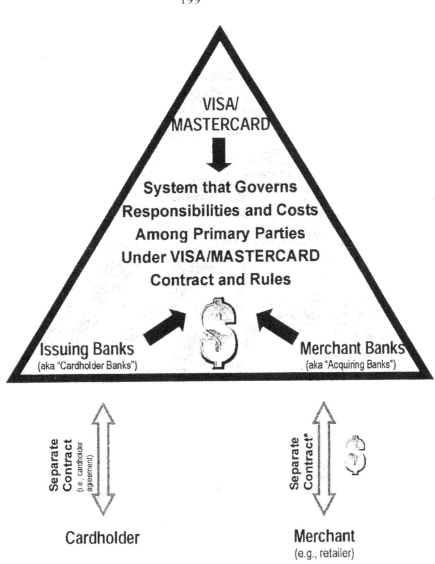

VISA/
MASTERCARD

**System that Governs
Responsibilities and Costs
Among Primary Parties
Under VISA/MASTERCARD
Contract and Rules**

Issuing Banks
(aka "Cardholder Banks")

Merchant Banks
(aka "Acquiring Banks")

**Separate
Contract**
(i.e., cardholder
agreement)

**Separate
Contract***

Cardholder

Merchant
(e.g., retailer)

* Typically contract between merchant bank and its retailers requires retailers to reimburse merchant bank for any costs, penalties, or fees imposed by the system on the merchant bank (including chargebacks – i.e., disputed charges – and costs of data breaches)

Thus consumers are obligated to keep their cards safe and secure in their wallets and avoid misuse, but must necessarily turn their card data over to others in order to effectuate a transaction. Retailers are likewise obligated to collect and protect the card data they receive, but are obligated to deliver it to processors in order to complete a transaction, resolve a dispute or process a refund. In contrast, those inside the triangle have much more systemic control.

For example, retailers are essentially at the mercy of the dominant credit card companies when it comes to protecting payment card data. The credit card networks – Visa, MasterCard, American Express, Discover and JCB – are responsible for an organization known as the PCI (which stands for Payment Card Industry) data security council. PCI establishes data security standards (PCI-DSS) for payment cards. While well intentioned in concept, these standards have not worked quite as well in practice. They have been inconsistently applied, and their avowed purpose has been significantly altered.

PCI has in critical respects over time pushed card security costs onto merchants even when other decisions might have more effectively reduced fraud – or done so at lower cost. For example, retailers have long been required by PCI to encrypt the payment card information that they have. While that is appropriate, PCI has not required financial institutions to be able to accept that data in encrypted form. That means the data often has to be de-encrypted at some point in the process in order for transactions to be processed.

Similarly, merchants are expected to annually demonstrate PCI compliance to the card networks, often at considerable expense, in order to benefit from a promise that the merchants would be relieved of certain fraud inherent in the payment system, which PCI is supposed to prevent. However, certification by the networks as PCI Compliant apparently has not been able to adequately contain the growing fraud and retailers report that the "promise" increasingly has been abrogated or ignored. Unfortunately, as card security expert Avivah Litan of Gartner Research wrote recently, "The PCI (Payment Card Industry) security standard has largely been a failure when you consider its initial purpose and history."[13]

PCI has not addressed many obvious deficiencies in cards themselves. There has been much attention to the fact that the United States is one of the last places on earth to put card information onto magnetic stripes on the backs of cards that can easily be read and can easily be counterfeited (in part because that data is static and unchanging). We need to move past magstripe technology.

But, before we even get to that question, we need to recognize that sensitive card data is right on the front of the card, embossed with prominent characters. Simply seeing the front of a card is enough for some fraudsters and there have been fraud schemes devised to trick consumers into merely showing someone their cards. While having the embossed card number on the front of the card might have made sense in the days of knuckle-buster machines and carbon copies, those days are long passed.

In fact, cards include the cardholder's name, card number, expiration date, signature and card verification value (CVV) code. Everything a fraudster needs is right there on the card. The

---

[13] "How PCI Failed Target and U.S. Consumers," by Avivah Litan, Gartner Blog Network, Jan. 20, 2014, available at http://blogs.gartner.com/avivah-litan/2014/01/20/how-pci-failed-target-and-u-s-consumers/.

bottom line is that cards are poorly designed and fraud-prone products that the system has allowed to continue to proliferate.

PCI has also failed to require that the identity of the cardholder is actually verified or authenticated at the time of the transaction. Signatures don't do this. Not only is it easy to fake a signature, but merchants are not allowed by the major card networks to reject a transaction based on a deficient signature. So, the card networks clearly know a signature is a useless gesture which proves nothing more than that someone was there purporting to be the cardholder.

The use of personal identification numbers (PINs) has actually proven to be an effective way to authenticate the identity of the cardholder. PIN numbers are personal to each cardholder and do not appear on the cards themselves. While they are certainly not perfect, their use is effective at reducing fraud. On debit transactions, for example, PIN transactions have one-sixth the amount of fraud losses that signature transactions have.[14] But PINs are not required on credit card transactions. Why? From a fraud prevention perspective, there is no good answer except that the card networks which set the issuance standards have failed to protect people in a very basic way.

As noted by LexisNexis, merchant fraud costs are much higher than banks' fraud costs. When credit or debit card fraud occurs, Visa and MasterCard have pages of rules providing ways that banks may be able to charge back the transaction to the retailer (which is commonly referred to as a "chargeback"). That is, the bank will not pay the retailer the money for the fraudulent transaction even though the retailer provided the consumer with the goods in question. When this happens, and it happens a lot, the merchant loses the goods *and* the money on the sale. According to the Federal Reserve, this occurs more than 40 percent of the time when there is fraud on a signature debit transaction,[15] and our members tell us that the percentage is even higher on credit transactions. In fact, for online transactions, which as noted account for 90 percent of fraud, merchants pay for the vast majority of fraudulent transactions.[16]

Retailers have spent billions of dollars on card security measures and upgrades to comply with PCI card security requirements, but it hasn't made them immune to data breaches and fraud. The card networks have made those decisions for merchants and the increases in fraud demonstrate that their decisions have not been as effective as they should have been.

Improved Technology Solutions

There are technologies available that could reduce fraud. An overhaul of the fraud-prone cards that are currently used in the U.S. market is long overdue. As I noted, requiring the use of a PIN is one way to reduce fraud. Doing so takes a vulnerable piece of data (the card number) and makes it so that it cannot be used on its own. This ought to happen not only in the brick-

---

[14] *See* 77 Fed. Reg. 46261 (Aug. 3, 2012) reporting $1.11 billion in signature debit fraud losses and $181 million in PIN debit fraud losses.

[15] *Id.* at 46262.

[16] Merchants assume 74 percent of fraud losses for online and other card-not-present signature debit transactions. 77 Fed. Reg. 46262.

and-mortar environment in which a physical card is used but also in the online environment in which the physical card does not have to be used. Canada, for example, is exploring the use of a PIN for online purchases. The same should be true here. Doing so would help directly with the 90 percent of U.S. fraud which occurs online. It is not happenstance that automated teller machines (ATMs) require the entry of a PIN before dispensing cash. Using the same payment cards for purchases should be just as secure as using them at ATMs.

Cards should also be smarter and use dynamic data rather than magnetic stripes. In much of the world this is done using computer chips that are integrated into physical credit and debit cards. That is a good next step for the United States. It is important to note, however, that there are many types of technologies that may be employed to make this upgrade. EMV, which is an acronym for Europay, MasterCard and Visa, is merely one particular proprietary technology. As the name indicates, EMV was established by Europay, MasterCard and Visa. A proprietary standard could be a detriment to the other potentially competitive networks.[17] Adopting a closed system, such as EMV, means we are locking out the synergistic benefits of competition.

But even within that closed framework, it should also be noted that everywhere in the world that EMV has been deployed to date the card networks have required that the cards be used with a PIN. That makes sense. But here, the dominant card networks are proposing to force chips (or even EMV) on the U.S. market without requiring PIN authentication. Doing that makes no sense and loses a significant part of the fraud prevention benefits of chip technology. To do otherwise would mean that merchants would spend billions to install new card readers without they or their customers obtaining PINs' fraud-reducing benefits. We would essentially be spending billions to combine a 1990's technology (chips) with a 1960's relic (signature) in the face of 21st century threats.

Another technological solution that could help deter and prevent data breaches and fraud is encryption. Merchants are already required by PCI standards to encrypt cardholder data but, as noted earlier, not everyone in the payments chain is required to be able to accept data in encrypted form. That means that data may need to be de-encrypted at some points in the process. Experts have called for a change to require "end-to-end" (or point-to-point) encryption which is simply a way to describe requiring everyone in the payment-handling chain to accept, hold and transmit the data in encrypted form.

---

[17] There are issues with EMV because the technology is just one privately owned solution. For example, EMV includes specifications for near field communications that would form the technological basis of Visa and MasterCard's mobile payments solutions. That raises serious antitrust concerns for retailers because we are just starting to get some competitors exploring mobile payments. If the currently dominant card networks are able to lock-in their proprietary technology in a way that locks-out competition in mobile payments, that would be a bad result for merchants and consumers who might be on the verge of enjoying the benefits of some new innovations and competition.

So, while chip cards would be a step forward in terms of improving card products, if EMV is forced as the chip card technology that must be used – rather than an open-source chip technology which would facilitate competition and not predetermine mobile payment market-share – it could be a classic case of one step forward and two steps backward.

According to the September 2009 issue of the Nilson Report "most recent cyberattacks have involved intercepting data in transit from the point of sale to the merchant or acquirer's host, or from that host to the payments network." The reason this often occurs is that "data must be decrypted before being forwarded to a processor or acquirer because Visa, MasterCard, American Express, and Discover networks can't accept encrypted data at this time."[18]

Keeping sensitive data encrypted throughout the payments chain would go a long way to convincing fraudsters that the data is not worth stealing in the first place – at least, not unless they were prepared to go through the arduous task of trying to de-encrypt the data which would be necessary in order to make use of it. Likewise, using PIN-authentication of cardholders now would offer some additional protection against fraud should this decrypted payment data be intercepted by a criminal during its transmission "in the clear."

Tokenization is another variant that could be helpful. Tokenization is a system in which sensitive payment card information (such as the account number) is replaced with another piece of data (the "token"). Sensitive payment data could be replaced with a token to represent each specific transaction. Then, if a data breach occurred and the token data were stolen, it could not be used in any other transactions because it was unique to the transaction in question. This technology has been available in the payment card space since at least 2005.[19]

And, mobile payments offer the promise of greater security as well. In the mobile setting, consumers won't need to have a physical card – and they certainly won't replicate the security problem of physical cards by embossing their account numbers on the outside of their mobile phones. It should be easy for consumers to enter a PIN or password to use payment technology with their smart phones. Consumers are already used to accessing their phones and a variety of services on them through passwords. Indeed, if we are looking to leapfrog the already aging current technologies, mobile-driven payments may be the answer.

Indeed, as much improved as they are, chips are essentially dumb computers. Their dynamism makes them significantly more advanced than magstripes, but their sophistication pales in comparison with the common smartphone. Smartphones contain computing powers that could easily enable comparatively state-of-the-art fraud protection technologies. The phones soon may be nearly ubiquitous, and if their payment platforms are open and competitive, they will only get better.

The dominant card networks have not made all of the technological improvements suggested above to make the cards issued in the United States more resistant to fraud, despite the availability of the technology and their adoption of it in many other developed countries of the world, including Canada, the United Kingdom, and most countries of Western Europe.

In this section, I have merely described some of the solutions available, but the United States isn't using any of them the way that it should be. While everyone in the payments space has a responsibility to do what they can to protect against fraud and data theft, the card networks

[18] The Nilson Report, Issue 934, Sept. 2009 at 7.
[19] For information on Shift4's 2005 launch of tokenization in the payment card space see http://www.internetretailer.com/2005/10/13/shift4-launches-security-tool-that-lets-merchants-re-use-credit.

have arranged the establishment of the data security requirements and yet, in light of the threats, there is much left to be desired.

A Better System

How can we make progress toward the types of solutions that would reduce the crimes of data theft and fraud? One thing seems clear at this point: we won't get there by doing more of the same. We need PIN-authentication of card holders, regardless of the chip technology used on newly issued cards. We also need chip cards that use open standards and allow for competition among payment networks as we move into a world of growing mobile commerce. Finally, we need companies throughout the payment system to work together on achieving end-to-end encryption so that there are no weak links in the system where sensitive card payment information may be acquired more easily than in other parts of the system.

Steps Taken by Retailers After Discovery of a Breach of Security

In our view, it is after a fulsome evaluation of data breaches, fraud, the payments system and how to improve each of those areas in order to deter and prevent problems that we should turn to the issue of what to do when breaches occur. Casting blame and trying to assign liability is, at best, putting the cart before the horse and, at worst, an excuse for some actors to ignore their own responsibility for trying to prevent these crimes.

One cannot reasonably demand greater security of a system than the system is reasonably capable of providing. Some participants act as if the system is more robust than it is. Currently, when the existing card products are hit in a criminal breach, that company is threatened from many sides. The threats come from entities seeking to exact fines and taking other penalizing action even before the victimized company can secure its network from further breaches and determine through a forensic analysis what has happened in order to notify potentially affected customers. For example, retailers that have suffered a breach are threatened with fines for the breach based on allegations of non-compliance with PCI rules (even when the company has been certified as PCI-compliant). Other actors may expect the breached party to pay for all of the fraudulent transactions that take place on card accounts that were misused, even though the design of the cards facilitated their subsequent counterfeiting. Indeed, some have seriously suggested that retailers reimburse financial institutions for the cost of reissuing more fraud-prone cards. And, as a consequence of the breach, some retailers must then pay higher fees on its card transactions going forward. Retailers pay for these breaches over and over again, despite often times being victims of sophisticated criminal methods not reasonably anticipated prior to the attack.

Breaches require retailers to devote significant resources to remedy the breach, help inform customers and take preventative steps to ward off future attacks and any other potential vulnerabilities discovered in the course of the breach investigation. Weeks or months of forensic analysis may be necessary to definitively discover the cause and scope of the breach. Any discovered weaknesses must be shored up. Quiet and cooperative law enforcement efforts may be necessary in an effort to identify and capture the criminals. Indeed, law enforcement may temporarily discourage publication of the breach so as to not alert the perpetrators that their efforts have been detected.

It is worth noting that in some of these cases involving payment card data, retailers discover that they actually were not the source of the breach and that someone else in the payments chain was victimized or the network intrusion and theft occurred during the transmission of the payment card data between various participants in the system. For this reason, early attempts to assign blame and shift costs are often misguided and policy makers should take heed of the fact that often the earliest reports are the least accurate. Additionally, policy makers should consider that there is no independent organization devoted to determining where a breach occurred, and who is to blame – these questions are often raised in litigation that can last for years. This is another reason why it is best to at least wait until the forensic analysis has been completed to determine what happened. Even then, there may be questions unanswered if the attack and technology used was sophisticated enough to cover the criminals' digital tracks.

The reality is that when a criminal breach occurs, particularly in the payments system, all of the businesses that participate in that system and their shared customers are victimized. Rather than resort to blame and shame, parties should work together to ensure that the breach is remedied and steps are taken to prevent future breaches of the same type and kind.

Legislative Solutions

In addition to the marketplace and technological solutions suggested above, NRF also supports a range of legislative solutions that we believe would help improve the security of our networked systems, ensure better law enforcement tools to address criminal intrusions, and standardize and streamline the notification process so that consumers may be treated equally across the nation when it comes to notification of data security breaches.

NRF supports the passage by Congress of the bipartisan "Cyber Intelligence Sharing and Protection Act" (H.R. 624) so that the commercial sector can lawfully share information about cyber-threats in real-time and enable companies to defend their own networks as quickly as possible from cyber-attacks as soon as they are detected elsewhere by other business.

We also support legislation that provides more tools to law enforcement to ensure that unauthorized network intrusions and other criminal data security breaches are thoroughly investigated and prosecuted, and that the criminals that breach our systems to commit fraud with our customers' information are swiftly brought to justice.

Finally, and for nearly a decade, NRF has supported passage of legislation that would establish one, uniform federal breach notification law that would be modeled on, and preempt, the varying breach notification laws currently in operation in 46 states, the District of Columbia and federal territories. A federal law could ensure that all entities handling the same type of sensitive consumer information, such as payment card data, are subject to the same statutory rules and penalties with respect to notifying consumers of a breach affecting that information. Further, a preemptive federal breach notification law would allow retailers and other businesses that have been victimized by a criminal breach to focus their resources on remedying the breach and notifying consumers rather than hiring outside legal assistance to help guide them through the myriad and sometimes conflicting set of 50 data breach notification standards in the state and federal jurisdictions. Additionally, the use of one set of standardized notice rules would permit the offering to consumers of the same notice and the same rights regardless of where they live.

Conclusion

In closing three points are uppermost.

First, retailers take the increasing incidence of payment card fraud very seriously. We do so as Main Street members of the community, because it affects our neighbors and our customers. We do so as businesses, because it affects the bottom line. Merchants already bear at least an equal, and often a greater, cost of fraud than any other participant in the payment card system. We have every reason to want to see fraud reduced, but we have only a portion of the ability to make that happen. We did not design the system; we do not configure the cards; we do not issue the cards. We will work to effectively upgrade the system, but we cannot do it alone.

Second, the vast majority of breaches are criminal activity. The hacked party, whether a financial institution, a card network, a processor, a merchant, a governmental institution, or a consumer is the victim of a crime. Traditionally, we don't blame the victim of violence for the resulting stains; we should be similarly cautious about penalizing the hackee for the hack. The payment system is complicated. Every party has a role to play; we need to play it together. No system is invulnerable to the most sophisticated and dedicated of thieves. Consequently, eliminating all fraud is likely to remain an aspiration. Nevertheless, we will do our part to help achieve that goal.

Third, it is long past time for the U.S. to adopt PIN and chip card technology. The PIN authenticates and protects the consumer and the merchant. The chip authenticates the card to the bank. If the goal is to reduce fraud we must, at a minimum, do both.

Payment Card Industry
Security Standards Council LLC

401 Edgewater Place, Suite 600
Wakefield, MA 0 1880
Phone: 781.876.8855

Statement for the Record

Bob Russo
General Manager
Payment Card Industry Security Standards Council

Senate Judiciary Committee
United States Senate

Privacy in the Digital Age: Preventing Data Breaches and Combating Cybercrime

February 4, 2014

Introduction

My name is Bob Russo and I am the General Manager of the <u>Payment Card Industry (PCI) Security Standards Council (SSC),</u> a global industry initiative and membership organization, focused on securing payment card data. Working with a global community of industry players, our organization has created data security standards—notably the PCI Data Security Standard (PCI DSS)—certification programs, training courses and best practice guidelines to help improve payment card security.

Together with our community of over one thousand of the world's leading businesses, we're tackling data security challenges from password complexity to proper protection of PIN entry devices on terminals. Our work is broad for a simple reason: there is no single answer to securing payment card data. No one technology is a panacea; security requires a multi-layered approach across the payment chain.

The PCI Security Standards Council is an excellent example of effective industry collaboration to develop private sector standards. Simply put, the PCI Standards are the best line of defense against the criminals seeking to steal payment card data. And while several recent high profile breaches have captured the nation's attention, great progress has been made over the past seven years in securing payment card data, through a collaborative cross-industry approach, and we continue to build upon the way we protect this data.

Consumers are understandably upset when their payment card data is put at risk of misuse and—while the PCI Security Standards Council is not a name most consumers know—we are sensitive to the impact that breaches cause for consumers. And consumers should take comfort from the fact that a great number of the organizations they do business with have joined the PCI SSC to collaborate in the effort to better protect their payment card data.

Payment card security: a dynamic environment

Since the threat landscape is constantly evolving, the PCI SSC expects its standards will do the same. Confidence that businesses are protecting payment card data is paramount to a healthy economy and payment process—both in person and online. That's why to date, more than one thousand of the world's leading retailers, airlines, banks, hotels, payment processors, government agencies, universities, and technology companies have joined the PCI Council as members and as part of our assessor community to develop security standards that apply across the spectrum of today's global multi-channel and online businesses.

Our community members are living on the front lines of this challenge and are therefore well placed, through the unique forum of the PCI Security Standards Council, to provide input on threats they are seeing and ideas for how to tackle these threats through the PCI Standards.

The Council develops standards through a defined, published three year lifecycle. Our Participating Organization members told us that three years was the appropriate timeframe to update and deploy security approaches in their organizations. In addition to the formal lifecycle, the Council and the PCI community have the resources to continually monitor and provide updates through standards, published FAQs, Special Interest Group work, and guidance papers on emerging threats and new ways to improve payment security. Examples include updated wireless guidance and security guidelines for merchants wishing to accept mobile payments.

This year, on January 1, 2014, our latest version of the PCI Data Security Standard (PCI DSS) became effective. This is our overarching data security standard, built on 12 principles that cover everything from implementing strong access control, monitoring and testing networks, to having an information security policy. During updates to this standard, we received hundreds of pieces of feedback from our community. This was almost evenly split between feedback from domestic and international organizations, highlighting the global nature of participation in the PCI SSC and the need to provide standards and resources that can be adopted globally to support the international nature of the payment system.

This feedback has enabled us to be directly responsive to challenges that organizations are facing every day in securing cardholder data. For example, in this latest round of PCI DSS revisions, community feedback indicated changes were needed to secure password recommendations. Password strength remains a challenge—as "password" is still among the most common password used by global businesses—and is highlighted in industry reports as a common failure leading to data compromise. Small merchants in particular often do not change passwords on point of sale (POS) applications and devices. With the help of the PCI community, the Council has updated requirements to make clear that default passwords should never be used, all passwords must be regularly changed and not continually repeated, should never be shared, and must always be of appropriate strength. Beyond promulgating appropriate standards, we have taken steps through training and public outreach to educate the merchant community on the importance of following proper password protocols.

Recognizing the need for a multi-layer approach, in addition to the PCI DSS, the Council and community have developed standards that cover payment applications and point of sale devices. In other areas, based on community feedback, we are working on standards and guidance on other technologies such as tokenization and point-to-point encryption. These technologies can dramatically increase data security at vulnerable points along the transactional chain. Tokenization and point-to-point encryption remove or render payment card information useless to cyber criminals, and work in concert with other PCI Standards to offer additional protection to payment card data.

In addition to developing and updating standards, every year the PCI community votes on which topics they would like to explore with the Council and provide guidance on. Over the last few years the working groups formed by the Council to address these concerns have drawn hundreds of organizations to collaborate together to produce resources on third party security assurance, cloud computing, best practices for maintaining compliance, e-commerce guidelines, virtualization, and wireless security. Other recent Council initiatives have addressed ATM security, PIN security, and mobile payment acceptance security for developers and merchants.

EMV Chip & PCI Standards—a strong combination

One technology that has garnered a great deal of attention in recent weeks is EMV chip—a technology that has widespread use in Europe and other markets. EMV chip is an extremely effective method of reducing counterfeit and lost/stolen card fraud in a face-to-face payments environment. That's why the PCI Security Standards Council supports the deployment of EMV chip technology.

Global adoption of EMV chip, including broad deployment in the U.S. market, does not preclude the need for a strong data security posture to prevent the loss of cardholder data from intrusions and data breaches. We must continue to strengthen data security protections that are designed to prevent the unauthorized access and exfiltration of cardholder data.

Payment cards are used in variety of remote channels—such as electronic commerce—where today's EMV chip technology is not typically an option for securing payment transactions. Security innovation continues to occur for online payments beyond existing fraud detection and prevention systems. Technologies such authentication, tokenization, and other frameworks are being developed, including some solutions that may involve EMV chip—yet broad adoption of these solutions is not on the short-term horizon. Consequently, the industry needs to continue to protect cardholder data across all payment channels to minimize the ongoing risks of data loss and resulting cross-channel fraud such as may be experienced in the online channel.

Nor does EMV chip negate the need for secure passwords, patching systems, monitoring for intrusions, using firewalls, managing access, developing secure software, educating employees, and having clear processes for the handling of sensitive payment card data. These processes are critical for all businesses—both large retailers and small businesses—who themselves have become a target for cyber criminals. At smaller businesses, EMV chip technology will have a strong positive impact. But if small businesses are not aware of the need to secure other parts of their systems, or if they purchase services and products that are not capable of doing that for them, then they will still be subject to the ongoing exposure of the compromise of cardholder data and resulting financial or reputational risk.

Similarly, protection from malware-based attacks requires more than just EMV chip technology. Reports in the press regarding recent breaches point to insertion of complex malware. EMV chip technology could not have prevented the unauthorized access, introduction of malware, and subsequent exfiltration of cardholder data. Failure of other security protocols required under Council standards is necessary for malware to be inserted.

Finally, EMV chip technology does not prevent memory scraping, a technique that has been highlighted in press reports of recent breaches. Other safeguards are needed to do so. In our latest versions of security standards for Point of Sale devices, (PCI PIN Transaction Security Requirements), the Council includes requirements to further counter this threat. These include improved tamper responsiveness so that devices will "self-destruct" if they are opened or tampered with and the creation of electronic signatures that prevent applications that have not been "whitelisted" from being installed. Our recently released update to the standard, PTS 4.0, requires a default reset every 24 hours that would remove malware from memory and reduce the risk of data being obtained in this way. By responding to the Council's PTS requirements, POS manufacturers are bringing more secure products to market that reflect a standards development process that incorporates feedback from a broad base of diverse stakeholders.

Used together, EMV chip, PCI Standards, along with many other tools can provide strong protections for payment card data. I want to take this opportunity to encourage all parties in the payment chain—whether they are EMV chip ready or not—to take a multi-layered approach to protect consumers' payment card data. There are no easy answers and no shortcuts to security.

Global adoption of EMV chip is necessary and important. Indeed, when EMV chip technology does become broadly deployed in the US marketplace and fraud migrates to less secure transaction environments, PCI Standards will remain critical.

Beyond Standards – building a support infrastructure

An effective security program through PCI is not focused on technology alone; it includes people and process as key parts of payment card data protection. PCI Standards highlight the need for secure software development processes, regularly updated security policies, clear access controls, and security awareness education for employees. Employees have to know not to click on suspicious links, why it is important to have secure passwords, and to question suspicious activity at the point of sale.

Most standards' organizations create standards, and no more. PCI Security Standards Council, however, recognizes that standards, without more, are only tools, and not solutions. And this does not address the critical challenges of training people and improving processes.

To help organizations improve payment data security, the Council takes a holistic approach to securing payment card data, and its work encompasses both PCI Standards development and maintenance of programs that support standards implementation across the payment chain. The Council believes that providing a full suite of tools to support implementation is the most effective way to ensure the protection of payment card data. To support successful implementation of PCI Standards, the Council maintains programs that certify and validate certain hardware and software products to support payment security. For example, the Council wants to make it easy for merchants and financial institutions to deploy the latest and most secure terminals and so maintains a public listing on its website for them to consult before purchasing products. We realize it takes time and money to upgrade POS terminals and we encourage businesses that are looking to upgrade for EMV chip to consider other necessary security measures by choosing a POS terminal from this list. Similarly, we are supporting the adoption of point-to-point encryption, and listing appropriate solutions on our website to take a solutions-oriented approach to helping retailers more readily implement security in line with the PCI standards.

Additionally, the Council runs a program that develops and maintains a pool of global assessment personnel to help work with organizations that deploy PCI Standards to assess their performance in using PCI Standards. The Council also focuses on creating education and training opportunities to build expertise in protecting payment card data in different environments and from the various viewpoints of stakeholders in the payment chain. Since our inception, we have trained tens of thousands of individuals, including staff from large merchants, leading technology companies and government agencies. Finally, we devote substantial resources to creating public campaigns to raise awareness of these resources and the issue of protecting payment card data.

The PCI community and large organizations that accept, store, or transmit payment card data worldwide have made important strides in adopting globally consistent security protocols. However, the Council recognizes that small organizations remain vulnerable. Smaller businesses lack IT staff and budgets to devote resources to following or participating in the development of industry standards. But they can take simple steps like updating passwords, firewalls, and ensuring they are configured to accept automatic security updates. Additionally, to help this population, the Council promotes its listings of validated products, and recently launched a program, the Qualified Integrator and Reseller program (QIR) to provide a pool of personnel able to help small businesses ensure high quality and secure installation of their payment systems.

The work of the Council covers the entire payment security environment with the goal of providing or facilitating access to all the tools necessary—standards, products, assessors, educational resources, and training—for stakeholders to successfully secure payment card data. We do this because we believe that no one technology is a panacea and effective security requires a multi-layered approach.

Public – private collaboration

The Council welcomes this hearing and the government's attention on this critical issue. The recent compromises underscore the importance constant vigilance in the face of threats to payment card data. We are hopeful that this hearing will help raise awareness of the importance of a multi- layered approach to payment card security.

There are very clear ways in which the government can help improve the payment data security environment. For example, by championing stronger law enforcement efforts worldwide, particularly due to the global nature of these threats, and by encouraging stiff penalties for crimes of this kind to act as a deterrent. There is much public discussion about simplifying data breach notification laws and promoting information sharing between public and private sector. These are all opportunities for the government to help tackle this challenge.

The Council is an active participant in government research in this area: we have provided resources, expertise and ideas to NIST, DHS, and other government entities, and we remain ready and willing to do so.

Almost 20 years ago, through its passage of the Technology Transfer and Advancement Act of 1995, Congress recognized that government should rely on the private sector to develop standards rather than to develop them itself. The substantial benefits of the unique, U.S. "bottom up" standards development process have been well recognized. They include the more rapid development and adoption of standards that are more responsive to market needs, representing an enormous savings in time to government and in cost to taxpayers.

The Council believes that the development of standards to protect payment card data is something the private sector, and PCI specifically, is uniquely qualified to do. It is unlikely any government agency could duplicate the expansive reach, expertise, and decisiveness of PCI. High profile events such as the recent breaches are a legitimate area of inquiry for the Congress, but should not serve as a justification to impose new government regulations. Any government standard in this area would likely be significantly less effective in addressing current threats, and less nimble in protecting consumers from future threats, than the constantly evolving PCI Standards.

Conclusion

In 2011, the Ponemon Institute, a non-partisan research center dedicated to privacy, data protection, and information security policy wrote, "The Payment Card Industry Data Security Standard (PCI DSS) continues to be one of the most important regulations for all organizations that hold, process or exchange cardholder information."

While we are pleased to have earned accolades such as this, we cannot rest on our laurels.

The recent breaches at retailers underscore the complex nature of payment card security. A complex problem cannot be solved by any single technology, standard, mandate, or regulation. It cannot be solved by a single sector of society—business, standards-setting bodies, policymakers, and law enforcement—must work together to protect the financial and privacy interests of consumers. Today as this committee focuses on recent damaging data breaches we know that there are criminals focusing on committing inventing the next threat.

There is no time to waste. The PCI Security Standards Council and business must commit to promoting stronger security protections while Congress leads efforts to combat global cyber-crimes that threaten us all. We thank the Committee for taking an important leadership role in seeking solutions to one of the largest security concerns of our time.

# # #

RETAIL INDUSTRY LEADERS ASSOCIATION
Educate. Innovate. Advocate.

1700 NORTH MOORE STREET
SUITE 2250
ARLINGTON. VA 22209
T (703) 841-2300 F (703) 841-1184
WWW.RILA.ORG

February 4, 2014

Senator Patrick Leahy
Chairman
Senate Committee on the Judiciary
United States Senate
224 Dirksen Senate Office Building
Washington, D.C. 20510

Senator Charles Grassley
Ranking Member
Senate Committee on the Judiciary
United States Senate
152 Dirksen Senate Office Building
Washington, D.C. 20510

Dear Chairman Leahy and Senator Grassley:

On behalf of the Retail Industry Leaders Association (RILA), I welcome the opportunity to offer
our comments on the record relevant to the Committee's hearing, "Privacy in the Digital Age:
Preventing Data Breaches and Combating Cybercrime." RILA is the trade association of the
world's largest and most innovative retail companies. RILA promotes consumer choice and
economic freedom through public policy and industry operational excellence. Its members
include more than 200 retailers, product manufacturers, and service suppliers, which together
account for more than $1.5 trillion in annual sales, millions of American jobs and operate more
than 100,000 stores, manufacturing facilities and distribution centers domestically and abroad.

Retailers take the threat of cyber attacks extremely seriously and work diligently every day to
stay ahead of the sophisticated criminals behind them. Retail companies individually and the
industry collectively, are taking aggressive steps to counter these threats. While enhanced
security measures help retailers thwart cyber-attacks nearly every day, unfortunately some
attacks are successful and the resulting incidents can affect millions of our American customers.
For retailers, such a breach can damage the relationship that we have with our customers.
However, more broadly, a breach can undermine consumers' faith in the electronic payments
system, as stolen information can be used to produce fraudulent cards for illicit use.

Given these facts, retailers take extraordinary steps to strengthen overall cybersecurity and prevent attacks. Retailers secure their systems with substantial investments in experts and technology. Retailers employ many tactics and tools to secure data, such as data encryption, tokenization and other redundant internal controls, including a separation of duties. While these enhanced security measures help to rebuff attacks, retailers are constantly working to expand existing cybersecurity efforts.

Collaboration within the industry and coordination with other stakeholders is essential. On January 27, RILA launched its Cybersecurity and Data Privacy Initiative which focuses on strengthening overall cybersecurity. As part of this initiative, RILA is forming the Retail Cybersecurity Leaders Council (RCLC) and calling for the development of both federal data breach notification legislation and federal cybersecurity legislation. Made up of senior retail executives responsible for cybersecurity, the RCLC will aim to improve industry-wide cybersecurity by providing a trusted forum for all stakeholders to share threat information and discuss effective security solutions.

In the weeks ahead, this Committee and others are likely to consider a range of legislative solutions to cybersecurity threats. RILA will engage with federal lawmakers and other stakeholders to develop sound and effective data breach notification and federal cybersecurity legislation that sets a national baseline to preempt the current patchwork of state laws and supports information sharing between the public- and private sectors.

While retailers understand and manage their internal systems and security, they have little or no influence over the actions taken by other players in the payments universe, actions with enormous implications on fraud. Instead, retailers must rely on others in the payments ecosystem to dictate critical security decisions, including card technology, retailer terminals, and when data can be encrypted during the transmission between retailers and the card networks. Retailers have long argued that the card technology in place today is antiquated and because of that criminals can use stolen consumer data to create counterfeit cards with stunning ease. For years, retailers have urged banks and card networks to adopt the enhanced fraud prevention technology in use around the world here in the United States. While their resistance to doing so has been great, retailers continue to press all other stakeholders in the payments system to make this a priority.

Also as part RILA's Initiative, RILA called for collaboration among retailers, banks and card networks to advance improved payments security. The RILA plan focused on four major steps that should be taken to improve the security of debit and credit cards. First, quickly establish a plan to retire the antiquated magnetic stripe technology in place today. Second, require cardholders to input a PIN on all card transactions. Banks require that cardholders enter a PIN number to withdraw money from an ATM, the same fraud protection should apply to retail transactions. Third, establish a roadmap to migrate to chip-based smart card technology with PIN security, also known as Chip and PIN. Finally, recognizing that card security must outpace criminal advancements, the members of the payments ecosystem must work together to identify new technologies and long-term, comprehensive solutions to the threats.

We have little doubt that all parties share the goals of protecting consumers and maintaining confidence in in our industry's cybersecurity. In order to accomplish these goals, the perpetual adversaries that make up the payments ecosystem must work together. That is why RILA is reaching out to representatives across the merchant community, as well as those representing the card networks and financial institutions of all sizes, in an effort to work together to identify near- and long-term solutions.

By working together with public-private sector stakeholders, our ability to develop innovative solutions and anticipate threats will grow, enhancing our collective security and giving our customers the service and peace of mind they deserve.

We look forward to working with the Committee and request that these comments be included in the record.

Sincerely,

William Hughes
Senior Vice President, Government Affairs
Retail Industry Leaders Association

Mrs. FEINSTEIN. Mr. President, I rise to introduce the Notification of Risk to Personal Data Act of 2003. This legislation will require that individuals are notified when their most sensitive personal information is stolen from a corporate or government database.

Specifically, the bill would require government or private entities to notify individuals if a data breach has compromised their Social Security number, driver's license number, credit card number, debit card number, or financial account numbers.

In most cases, if authorities know that someone is a victim of a crime, the victim is notified. But that isn't the case if an individual's most sensitive personal information is stolen from an electronic database.

Unfortunately, data breaches are becoming all too common. Consider the following incidents which have compromised the records of hundreds of thousands of Americans.

On April 5, 2002, a hacker broke into the electronic records of Steven P. Teale Data Center, the payroll facility for California State employees. The hacker compromises files containing the first initials, middle initials, and last names, Social Security numbers, and payroll deduction information of approximately 265,000 people. Despite the breathtaking potential harm of the crime, the breach was not publicly acknowledged and State employees were not made aware of their vulnerability to identify theft until May 24, 2002--17 days later.

On December 14, 2002, TriWest Health Care Alliance, a company that provides health care coverage for military personnel and their families, was burglarized at its Phoenix, AZ offices. Thieves broke into a management suite and stole laptop computers and computer hard drives containing the names, addressed, telephone numbers, birth dates and Social Security numbers of 562,000 military service members, dependents and retirees, as well as medical claims records for people on active duty in the Persian Gulf.

In February 2003, a hacker gained access to 10 million Visa, MasterCard, American Express Card and Discovery Card numbers from the databases of a credit processor, DPI Merchant services of Omaha, NE. Company officials maintained that the intruder did not obtain any personal information for these card numbers such as the account holder's name, address, telephone number or Social Security number. However, at least one bank canceled and replaced 8,800 cards when it found out about the security breach.

And in March of this year, a University of Texas student was charged with hacking into the university's computer system and stealing 55,000 Social Security numbers.

These are just some examples of the types of breaches that are occurring today. Except for California, which as a notification law going into effect in July, no State of Federal law requires companies or agencies to tell individuals of the misappropriation of their personal data.

I strongly believe Americans should be notified if a hacker gets access to their most personal data. This is both a matter of principle and a practical measure to curb identity theft.

Let me take a moment to describe the proposed legislation.

The Notification of Risk to Personal Data Act will set a national standard for notification of consumers when a data breach occurs.

Specifically, the legislation requires a business or government entity to notify an individual when there is a reasonable basis to conclude that a hacker or other criminal has obtained unencrypted personal data maintained by the entity.

Personal data is defined by the bill as an individual's Social Security number, State identification number, driver's license number, financial account number, or credit card number.

The legislation's notification scheme minimizes the burdens on companies or agencies that must report a data breach.

In general, notice would have to be provided to each person whose data was compromised in writing or through e-mail. But there are important exceptions.

First, companies that have developed their own reasonable notification policies are given a safe harbor under the bill and are exempted from its notification requirements.

Second, encrypted data is exempted.

Third, where it is too expensive or impractical, e.g., contact address information is incomplete, to notify every individual who is harmed, the bill allows entities to send out an alternative form of notice called ``substitute notice.'' Substitute notice includes posting notice on a website or notifying major media.

Substitute notice would be triggered if any of the following factors exist: 1. the agency or person demonstrates that the cost of providing direct notice would exceed $250,000; 2. the affected class of subject persons to be notified exceeds 500,000; or 3. the agency or person does not have sufficient contact information to notify people whose information is at risk.

The bill has a tough, but fair enforcement regime. Entities that fail to comply with the bill will be subject to fines by the Federal Trade Commission of $5,000 per violation or up to $25,000 per day while the violation persists. State Attorneys General can also file suit to enforce the statute.

Additionally, the bill would allow California's new law to remain in effect, but preempt conflicting State laws. It is my understanding that legislators in a number of States are developing bills modeled after the California law. Reportedly, some of these bills have requirements that are inconsistent with the California legislation. It is not fair to put companies in a situation that forces them to comply with database notification laws of 50 different States.

I strongly believe individuals have a right to be notified when their most sensitive information is compromised--because it is truly their information. Ask the ordinary person on the street if he or she would like to know if a criminal had illegally gained access to their personal information from a database--the answer will be a resounding yes.

Enabling consumers to be notified in a timely manner of security breaches involving their personal data will help combat the growth scourge of identity theft. According to the Identity Theft Resources Center, a typical identity theft victim takes six to 12 months to discover that a fraud has been perpetuated against them.

As Linda Foley, Executive Director of the Identity Theft Resources center puts it: ``Identity theft is a crime of opportunity and time is essential at every junction. Every minute that passes after the breach until detection and notification increases the damage done to the consumer victim, the commercial entities, and law enforcement's ability to track and catch the criminals. It takes less than a minute to fill out a credit application and to start an action that could permanently affect the victim's life. Multiply that times hundreds of minutes, hundreds of opportunities to use or sell the information stolen and you just begin to understand the enormity of the problem that the lack of notification can cause.''

If individuals are informed of the theft of their Social Security numbers or other sensitive information, they can take immediate preventative action.

They can place a fraud alert on their credit report to prevent crooks from obtaining credit cards in their name; they can monitor their credit reports to see if unauthorized activity has occurred; they can cancel any affected financial or consumer or utility accounts; they can change their phone numbers if necessary.

I look forward to working with my colleagues to pass this vitally needed legislation. This bill will give ordinary Americans more control and confidence about the safety of their personal information. Americans will have the security of knowing that should a breach occur, they will be notified and be able to take protective action.

I ask unanimous consent that the text of the bill be printed in the **RECORD**.